PMP Exam Prep Over 600 Practice Questions

Based on PMBOK Guide 6th Edition

Andrew Ramdayal, PMP, PgMP, CISSP-ISSMP

By Andrew Ramdayal, PMP, PgMP, CISSP-ISSMP

First Printing: May 2018
ISBN-13: 978-1719192316
ISBN-10: 1719192316

PMP, CAPM, PMI-ACP, PgMP, PMI-RMP, PMI-SP, PMBOK, Project Management Professional, Certified Associate in Project Management (CAPM), Project Management Professional (PMP), PMI Agile Certified Practitioner (PMI-ACP), Program Management Professional (PgMP), PMI Risk Management Professional (PMI-RMP), PMI Scheduling Professional (PMI-SP), A Guide to the Project Management Body of Knowledge (PMBOK Guide), The PMI R.E.P Logo are registered marks of the Project Management Institute, Inc.

Technical Institute of America has been reviewed and approved as a provider of project management training by the Project Management Institute (PMI). As a PMI Registered Education Provider (R.E.P), Technical Institute of America has agreed to abide by PMI established quality assurance criteria.

Technical Institute of America
545 8th Ave
New York, NY 10018
Phone: 212-564-2351
Fax: 800-490-7341
E-mail: info@tia.edu
Web: www.tia.edu

About the Author

Andrew Ramdayal, PMP, PgMP, PMI-ACP, CISSP-ISSMP has over 15 years of project management experience in IT. He holds over 50 professional certifications in IT and accounting from vendors such as Microsoft, Cisco, CompTIA, and PMI. He also holds a Master Degree in Management Information System with a minor in project management. Andrew has worked on many ERP, IT Security, and computer networking projects over his career.

Andrew has been teaching the PMP exam prep for over 10 years to thousands of student all over the world. His unique teaching methods have allowed his students not only to pass the exam but also to apply the concepts in real life. He is currently the CEO of the Technical Institute of America which provides training to thousands of students every year in IT and medical courses.

About Technical Institute of America

Technical Institute of America(TIA) is a nationally accredited school headquartered in New York City with locations in Arlington VA, and San Francisco, CA. TIA Is a PMI Registered Education Provider #3333. TIA provides online and in person classes in most IT certifications and short term medical courses.

Contents

chapter 1 7

    Project Management Framework Questions 8

    Project Management Framework Answers 12

Chapter 2 14

    Project Management Roles And Responsibilities Questions 15

    Project Roles And Responsibilities Answers 17

Chapter 3 18

    Project Management Processes Questions 19

    Project Management Processes Answers 22

Chapter 4 24

    Project Integration Management Questions 25

    Project Integration Management Answers 30

Chapter 5 32

    Project Scope Management Questions 33

    Project Scope Management Answers 38

Chapter 6 40

    Project Schedule Management Questions 41

    Project Schedule Management Answers 46

Chapter 7 49

    Project Cost Management Questions 50

    Project Cost Management Answers 54

Chapter 8 57

    Project Quality Management Questions 58

    Project Quality Management Answers 62

Chapter 9 64

    Project Resource Management Questions 65

      Project Resource Management Answers 69

Chapter 10 72

    Project Communications Management Questions 73

    Project Communications Management Answers 78

Chapter 11 80

    Project Risk Management Questions 81

    Project Risk Management Answers 85

Chapter 12 87

    Project Procurement Management Questions 88

Project Procurement Management Answers 93

Chapter 13 96

Project Stakeholder Management Questions 97

Project Stakeholder Management Answers 101

Chapter 14 103

Project Code Of Ethics And Professional Conduct Questions.. 104

Project Code Of Ethics And Professional Conduct Answers.. 108

Final Exam 110

Final Exam Questions 111

Final Exam Answers 137

CHAPTER 1

PROJECT MANAGEMENT FRAMEWORK

PROJECT MANAGEMENT FRAMEWORK QUESTIONS

1. What is the name of PMI's organization maturity model for project management that helps to determine the level of ability of an organization to deliver the desired strategic outcomes in a reliable, controllable, and predictable manner?

    A. ISO 9000

    B. OPM3

    C. Project Management Maturity Model (PMMM)

    D. Six Sigma

2. Success in portfolio management, which can be generally described as a group of projects or programs and other works to achieve a specific strategic business goal, is generally defined as:

    A. Aggregate performance of all components (projects, programs, and other related work).

    B. Control of changes to specific products and services.

    C. Compliance with schedule, budget, and specifications requirements.

    D. Realization of the business benefits and financial objectives.

3. Which one of the following is a strategy execution framework that keeps the entire organization focused on the overall strategy and provides guidance on how to prioritize, manage, execute, and measure projects, programs, portfolios, and other organizational work and practices to achieve a better result, improved performance, and a substantial advantage over the competitors?

    A. Organizational Project Management (OPM)

    B. Portfolio management

    C. Program management

    D. Process management

4. Which one of the following is the logical breakdown of what needs to be done to produce the project deliverables and is sometimes referred to as the performing organization's methodology for projects?

    A. Product life cycle

    B. Project life cycle

    C. Feedback loop

    D. Product development

5. The application of knowledge, skills, tools, and techniques to satisfy the project needs by establishing project objectives, identifying project requirements, managing stakeholders, and balancing project constraints (i.e., cost, time, quality, scope, risk, and others) is referred to as:

    A. Project management

    B. Project administration

    C. Project initiation

    D. Project coordination

6. All of the following are examples of Organizational Process Assets EXCEPT:

    A. Organizational policies, procedures, and guidelines for any area such as safety, ethics, risk, financial, change control, reporting, and others.

    B. Existing facilities and infrastructure.

    C. Templates for common project documents such as WBS, network diagram, SOW, and contract.

    D. Historical information and past lessons learned.

7. You are a team member working on a software application project. You realize that the project manager is choosing a project life cycle that has a predictive life cycle in which scope, schedule, and cost are determined in the early stage of the project prior to starting project work to produce the deliverables. This type of project life cycle is also known as:

    A. Change-driven project life cycle

    B. Adaptive project life cycle

    C. Preferred project life cycle

    D. Plan-driven project life cycle

8. All project phases conclude with a review of the deliverables and related work (phase exits or stage gates or kill points) for the purpose of:

    A. Determining if the project should continue and the next phase should be initiated.

    B. Detecting defects and correcting errors.

    C. Assessing project risks.

    D. Enforcing formal control procedure of the project.

9. A project life cycle is a representation of the generally sequential and sometimes overlapping project phases that a project typically goes through. All of the following statements about the project life cycle are true EXCEPT:

    A. Cost and staffing start low, increase toward the end, and drop rapidly near closing.

    B. Project risk is highest at the beginning of the project and reduces as the project approaches its end.

    C. Stakeholder influence is lowest at the start and increases as the project proceeds.

D. Cost of changes is low in the beginning but extremely high later in the project.

10. Which one of the following is generally considered to be the characteristic of operational works?
    A. It is a continuing endeavor that produces many identical or nearly identical products or provides repetition.
    B. It is temporary in nature and has a definite beginning and ending.
    C. It is completed when its goals and objectives have been met and signed off by the stakeholders.
    D. It is a unique undertaking.

11. You are overseeing a project to implement a new video game console. Since everything is not known upfront, you take the approach of defining and developing the product by incremental steps and continually reviewing and adjusting processes, assumptions, requirements, and decisions throughout the project life cycle as the project progresses. You are engaged in which of the following?
    A. Project selection
    B. Monitoring & Controlling
    C. Progressive elaboration
    D. Decomposition

12. You are managing a group of related or unrelated projects or programs and other works to achieve specific strategic business objectives and goals. You are a:
    A. Program owner
    B. Project manager
    C. Program manager
    D. Portfolio manager

13. You took over a software development project from another project manager who just left the company. You realize that the project is in a mess as there is a lack of management control and the previous project manager managed the project without much project organization. You decided to develop specific work plans for each of the 30 work packages and soon realize that the plan would help each phase, but would not control the integration of those phases into a cohesive whole. To your surprise, you also find out that there are no clearly defined project deliverables. You are in a desperate need to organize the project as soon as you can. What will be the BEST course of action?
    A. Capture lessons learned as you progress and update organizational process assets.
    B. Report the poor condition of the project to management.
    C. Adapt a life cycle approach to the project.
    D. Develop a detailed description of project deliverables.

14. You just completed a critical data center project for your organization. Currently the support team is conducting ongoing operations and maintenance to ensure that all routers, switches, firewalls, PCs, servers, and digital storages are operating as planned. A large portion of your project budget is allocated to maintenance and operations to run the data center smoothly. You will be sending out daily status updates and resolving issues but there is no need for planning or providing documentation. This ongoing operations and maintenance is extremely important to the products of your data center project and should be consider as:
    A. Not a part of your project
    B. An entirely separate project
    C. A separate phase in your project life cycle
    D. Activities in the closing process group

15. You have been assigned as project manager to implement a new and innovative smartphone application in a balanced matrix organizational structure. You experience difficulties in obtaining and assigning project resources in your project due to which one of the following factors?
    A. The power and authority are shared between you and the functional manager, and you do not have full authority over the project and its funding.
    B. Your role is like a coordinator or expeditor (communication coordinator or staff assistant).
    C. You have no real authority and power.
    D. The project budget is fully controlled by the functional manager.

16. Project Management Office (PMO), which is a centralized organizational unit to oversee and coordinate the management of projects and programs under its domain throughout the organization, has all of the following functions EXCEPT:
    A. Identify and develop the organization's methodology, administrative practices, guidelines, policies, procedures, and rules.
    B. Establish and maintain templates, policies, procedures, best practices, and standards for project management methodologies.
    C. Monitor compliance with organizational project management processes, policies, procedures, and other items.
    D. Be involved heavily during project initiation as a key decision maker and integral stakeholder to make recommendations, prioritize projects, terminate projects, or take other actions as required.

17. What is the name of PMI's organization maturity model for project management that helps to determine the level of ability of an organization to deliver the desired strategic outcomes in a reliable, controllable, and predictable manner?
    A. ISO 9000

B. OPM3

C. Project Management Maturity Model (PMMM)

D. Six Sigma

18. Which one of the following PMO structures mostly provides guidelines, policies, and templates and requires compliances and usually has a moderate level of control over projects and programs?

A. Supportive

B. Controlling

C. Directive

D. Constructive

19. Which one of the following is TRUE about power of the project managers in different organizational structures?

A. In a project-oriented organization, the project manager has no real authority and power.

B. A strong matrix maintains many characteristics of project-oriented organization, where much of the authority rests with the project manager.

C. In a weak matrix, the authority is shared between the functional manager and the project manager; the project manager does not have full authority over the project and its funding.

D. A balanced matrix maintains many characteristics of a functional matrix; the project manager role is like that of a coordinator or expeditor (communication coordinator or staff assistant) than that of a true project manager.

20. Which one of the following PMO structures mostly serves as a project repository, plays a consultative role, and usually has a low level of control over projects and programs?

A. Supportive

B. Controlling

C. Directive

D. Constructive

21. You are overseeing the implementation of the internal website of your organization to view the company's event calendar. Your role is to coordinate activities, resources, equipment, and information on the project, but you have limited authority in making project decisions and have to negotiate with the functional manager to get required resources for your project. Which kind of organization are you working in?

A. Balanced matrix

B. Composite structure

C. Weak matrix

D. Strong matrix

22. Which one of the following is NOT true about functional organizational structure?

A. Project work is considered to be priority work in all functional groups.

B. Similar resources are grouped by specialists.

C. The project manager has little or no authority and could even be part time.

D. Multiple projects compete for limited resources and priority.

23. All of the following are examples of Organizational Process Assets EXCEPT:

A. Organizational policies, procedures, and guidelines for any area such as safety, ethics, risk, financial, change control, reporting, and others.

B. Existing facilities and infrastructure.

C. Templates for common project documents such as WBS, network diagram, SOW, and contract.

D. Historical information and past lessons learned.

24. The level of power and authority of a project manager may fluctuate due to various factors. Typically, how much power and authority a project manager will have depends on which of the following?

A. The organizational structure

B. The negotiation skills of the project manager

C. Project management knowledge and technical competency of the project manager

D. The relationship of the project manager with senior management, especially with the sponsor

25. You are managing a group of related projects to accomplish a common objective. You are a:

A. Program owner

B. Project manager

C. Program manager

D. Portfolio manager

26. As a project manager in a balanced matrix organization, what type of authority you have?
    A. Low to moderate
    B. Little to none
    C. High to almost total
    D. Moderate to high

27. The management framework within which project decisions are made is called:
    A. Project Management Information System (PMIS)
    B. Configuration management system
    C. Project management plan
    D. Project governance

PROJECT MANAGEMENT FRAMEWORK ANSWERS

1. B: OPM3 is the PMI's organizational project management maturity model. This model helps to determine the level of ability of an organization to deliver the desired strategic outcomes in a reliable, controllable, and predictable manner.

2. A: Portfolio management encompasses identifying, prioritizing, authorizing, managing, and controlling the collection of projects, programs, other work, and sometimes other portfolios to achieve strategic business objectives. It is generally associated with the relationships between components in the portfolio, effective resource management to protect priority components, and the aggregate results of the portfolio as they relate to strategic performance. The components may not be related other than the fact that they are helping to achieve the common strategic goal.

3. A: Organizational Project Management (OPM) is a strategy execution framework that keeps the entire organization focused on the overall strategy. It provides guidance on how to prioritize, manage, execute, and measure projects, programs, portfolios, and other organizational work and practices to achieve a better result, improved performance, and a substantial advantage over the competitors. A portfolio can be generally described as a group of projects or programs and other works to achieve a specific strategic business goal. The programs may not be related other than the fact that they are helping to achieve the common strategic goal. A program is a group of related projects managed in a coordinated way to capitalize benefits and control what is not achievable by managing those projects individually. Program management is the centralized and coordinated management of a program to obtain the strategic objectives and benefits sought through the inception of the program. Project management is the application of knowledge, skills, tools, and techniques to satisfy project requirements.

4. B: The project life cycle is the logical breakdown of what needs to be done to produce the project deliverables, and sometimes it is referred to as the performing organization's methodology for projects. On the other hand, a product life cycle consists of generally sequential, non-overlapping product phases determined by the manufacturing and control needs of the organization. For instance, as predicted by Moore's law, each year a microprocessor company introduces new models of processors that are faster and more powerful than their predecessors. Microprocessors that are obsolete or do not sell well are quickly retired from production. This product life cycle begins in R and D, extends to manufacturing, and finally ends with phase out.

5. A: Project management is the application of knowledge, skills, tools, and techniques to satisfy project requirements.

6. B: Enterprise Environmental Factors are things that impact the project but are not part of the project itself. Existing facilities and infrastructure are Enterprise Environmental Factors.

7. D: Plan-driven projects have a predictive life cycle in which scope, schedule, and cost are determined in the early stage of the project prior to starting project work to produce the deliverables. This predictive life cycle is also referred to as waterfall or traditional life cycle. For example, most construction projects are typically managed using this sort of predictive approach. A change-driven project life cycle usually has a varying level of initial planning for scope, schedule, and cost. An adaptive life cycle is a change-driven life cycle, and it is also referred to as an agile life cycle. An adaptive life cycle, as the name suggests, broadly defines the fixed scope, schedule, and cost with the clear understanding that they will be refined and adjusted as the project progresses. Preferred project life cycle is a made-up term.

8. A: At the conclusion of a project phase, the project manager and team should assess the performance of the project and determine if acceptable conditions exist to support a decision to continue or terminate the project. If the decision is to move forward with the project, then the decision is also made about whether the next phase should be initiated or not. Risk levels will vary as the project progresses, and the end of a phase is generally considered to be a good point to reassess risk. Project control procedures should be enforced throughout the project life cycle.

9. C: Stakeholder influence is highest at the start and diminishes as the project proceeds.

10. A: Operational works are ongoing and support the day-to-day functions of an organization. Operational work differs from project work as operational work is any continuing endeavor that produces many identical or nearly identical products or provides repetitive services (e.g., frying burgers, manufacturing cars, and teaching algebra).

11. C: Progressive elaboration is defined as moving forward in increments and adding more detail as the project progresses.

12. D: A portfolio can be generally described as a group of projects or programs and other works to achieve a specific strategic business goal. The programs may not be related other than the fact that they are helping to achieve the common strategic goal. A portfolio manager is usually assigned to manage these groups of projects, programs, and other works. Portfolio management encompasses identifying, prioritizing, authorizing, managing, and controlling the collection of projects, programs, other work, and sometimes other portfolios to achieve strategic business objectives. For example, a construction business has several business units such as retail, single and multifamily residential, and others. Collectively, all the programs, projects, and work within all of these business units make up the portfolio for this construction business.

13. C: Adapting a life cycle approach to effectively run the project will ensure overall control and successful completion of the deliverables. You may want to report the situation to management, but it will not really solve the issue. Capturing lessons learned will certainly assist with the subsequent phases, but would not really help with controlling the project. Developing a detailed description of the project deliverables would not improve control.

14. A: Operations and maintenance are not considered to be temporary as they are ongoing. A project is always unique and temporary in nature. Thus, these activities should not be considered as a project or even part of a project.

15. A: In a balanced matrix organization, the project manager is assigned full time, and the authority of the project manager is usually at an equal level with the functional manager. This can result in conflict regarding resource assignments and priorities and in the general management of the project. The control of the budget is shared between the project manager and the functional manager.

16. A: The PMO identifies and develops the project management methodology, best practices, policies, procedures, and standards, but not the organizational methodology, administrative practices, guidelines, policies, procedures, and rules.

17. B: OPM3 is the PMI's organizational project management maturity model. This model helps to determine the level of ability of an organization to deliver the desired strategic outcomes in a reliable, controllable, and predictable manner.

18. B: The controlling PMO provides guidelines, policies, and templates and requires compliances. This type of PMO usually has a moderate level of control over projects and programs.

19. B: The authority of the project manager varies greatly depending on the organizational structure. In a project-oriented organization, the project manager has almost total authority. A strong matrix maintains many characteristics of project-oriented organization where much of the authority rests with the project manager. In a balanced matrix, the authority is shared between the functional manager and the project manager; the project manager does not have full authority over the project and its funding. A weak matrix maintains many characteristics of a functional organization; the project manager role is like that of a coordinator or expeditor (communication coordinator or staff assistant) than that of a true project manager. In a functional organization, the project manager has no real authority and power.

20. A: A Supportive PMO mostly serves as a project repository and plays a consultative role. This type of PMO usually has a low level of control over projects and programs.

21. C: You are working in a weak matrix organization. Your role is of a project expeditor or project coordinator where you mostly act as a staff assistant and communication coordinator with limited authority and have no control over the project's budget. You have to negotiate with the functional manager to get needed resources for the project.

22. A: In a functional structure, similar resources are grouped by technical expertise and are assigned to one supervisor. Team members give more importance to their functional responsibility to the detriment of the project.

23. B: Enterprise Environmental Factors are things that impact the project but are not part of the project itself. Existing facilities and infrastructure are Enterprise Environmental Factors.

24. A: The authority of the project manager varies greatly depending on the organizational structure. In a project-oriented organization, the project manager has almost total authority. A strong matrix maintains many characteristics of project-oriented organization where much of the authority rests with the project manager. In a balanced matrix, the authority is shared between the functional manager and the project manager, and the project manager does not have full authority over the project and its funding. A weak matrix maintains many characteristics of a functional organization; the project manager's role is like that of a coordinator or expeditor (communication coordinator or staff assistant) than that of a true project manager. In a functional organization, the project manager has no real authority and power. Relationship, negotiation skills, and technical ability may affect the level of authority in some organizations, but managerial structure is generally the major factor.

25. C: A program manager is someone who manages a program, which is a set of related projects that are done to accomplish a common goal.

26. A: A project manager has a low to moderate authority in a balanced matrix organization.

27. D: Project governance is the management framework within which project decisions are made. The role of project governance is to provide a decision-making framework that is logical, robust, and repeatable to govern an organization's capital investments. This framework provides the structure, processes, decision-making models, and tools to the project manager and team for managing the project. It also provides the team a comprehensive, coherent method of controlling the project and helps safeguarding project success by defining, documenting, and communicating reliable, repeatable project practices.

The PMIS consists of the data sources and tools & techniques used to gather, integrate, analyze, and disseminate the results of the combined outputs of the project management processes. It is an automated system that can serve as a repository for information and a tool to assist with communication and with tracking documents and deliverables. The PMIS also supports the project from beginning to end by optimizing the schedule and helping collect and distribute information. The Configuration Management System is the subset of the Project Management Information System (PMIS) that describes the different versions and characteristics of the product, service, or result of the project and ensures accuracy and completeness of the description. The Project Management Plan is a single-approved document that defines how the project is executed, monitored and controlled, and closed.

CHAPTER 2

PROJECT MANAGEMENT ROLES AND RESPONSIBILITIES

PROJECT MANAGEMENT ROLES AND RESPONSIBILITIES QUESTIONS

1. You are managing a group of related or unrelated projects or programs and other works to achieve specific strategic business objectives and goals. You are a:
    A. Program owner
    B. Project manager
    C. Program manager
    D. Portfolio manager

2. You are a member of a management team overseeing a critical construction project of constructing the tallest building in town. Your team, which is a subset of the project team, is responsible for project leadership and management activities. Which of the following statements is FALSE about your team?
    A. Your team is responsible for managing people, which has been defined as being able to produce key results.
    B. Your team is responsible for establishing mission and vision, aligning team members to the established direction, motivating individuals, and inspiring them.
    C. Your team is responsible for project funding.
    D. The management team should be aware of professional and ethical behaviors and ensure that team members are following them.

3. A project manager overseeing a data center deployment project just completed negotiation unsuccessfully for three additional resources and extra reserve money for her project. During the negotiation, two of the functional managers were very skeptical about the request for additional resources and were reluctant to assign their resources due to other priorities. In this case, the conflict will require the assistance of which of the following to reach a solution?
    A. Functional manager
    B. Contractor
    C. Project sponsor
    D. Key customer

4. A project manager is overseeing a complex custom CSM solution that has rigorous quality standards and tight schedule constraints. Since the project manager is working in a weak matrix environment, none of the resources are reporting to her functionally. She also does not have either the power or the budget to reward the team members to encourage and motivate them for their performance and contribution to the project. What kind of power should the project manager try to use in this type of situation?
    A. Formal
    B. Punishment
    C. Referent
    D. Expert

5. You were asked by management to identify the root cause behind a project not performing well in your organization. You find out that the project manager is hardly in contact with the team members and often places one of his team members in charge for days at a time. The project manager also allows the team members to act as per their preferences and only gets involved with them if requested. This style of management is generally considered to be:
    A. Delegating
    B. Democratic or participative
    C. Bureaucratic
    D. Laissez-Faire

6. You just got hired as a project manager in a software development project. What type of power can you use to gain the cooperation of others?
    A. Punishment
    B. Guilt-based
    C. Pressure-based
    D. Formal

7. You have 13 team members in your automation project. One of your team members is not performing as he is missing general job skills. Training of team members in general job skills is the responsibility of the:
    A. Project manager
    B. Functional manager
    C. Training director
    D. Sponsor

8. A project manager is expected to use all kinds of ethical, interpersonal, managerial, and conceptual skills to analyze various situation and interact appropriately. Steve is a project manager for a project that is not going well. The project has a CPI of .83 and SPI of .78. The team members are not motivated and avoiding responsibilities whenever they can. Steve is trying to maintain his cool and be composed no matter what level of presser he is under. Which of the following quality Steve mostly using in the situation?

A. Team building
B. Problem solving
C. Composure
D. Competence

9. Roger is very sensitive to ideas, customs, norms, believes, values, and social behavior of other cultures. What kind of personality does Roger have?

A. Courteous
B. Cultural
C. Emotional
D. Political

10. Amenda is transformational, consultative, participative, and innovative and doesn't mind taking risks but Michael is dictatorial, authoritative, and administrative and likes to control risks. Which of the following statement is true?

A. Amenda is a manager and Michael is a leader
B. Amenda is a leader and Michael is a manger
C. Both of them are leaders
D. Both of them are managers

PROJECT ROLES AND RESPONSIBILITIES ANSWERS

1. D: A portfolio can be generally described as a group of projects or programs and other works to achieve a specific strategic business goal. The programs may not be related other than the fact that they are helping to achieve the common strategic goal. A portfolio manager is usually assigned to manage these groups of projects, programs, and other works. Portfolio management encompasses identifying, prioritizing, authorizing, managing, and controlling the collection of projects, programs, other work, and sometimes other portfolios to achieve strategic business objectives. For example, a construction business has several business units such as retail, single and multifamily residential, and others. Collectively, all the programs, projects, and work within all of these business units make up the portfolio for this construction business.

2. C: The project sponsor usually assists with funding, not the project management team. The project management team is the subset of the project team responsible for project leadership and management activities. Project management is heavily dependent on managing people, which has been defined as being able to produce key results. On the other hand, leadership is all about establishing mission and vision, aligning team members to the established direction, motivating individuals, and inspiring them. The management team should be aware of professional and ethical behaviors and should ensure that team members are following them.

3. C: Customers and contractors should not be allowed to be involved in internal resource-related disputes in most cases. All efforts should be given to resolve the conflicts at the lowest levels or authority whenever possible. In some cases, conflict requires the involvement of the project sponsor or senior management, especially when there is a major concern regarding resource assignments.

4. D: Reward and Expert are the most effective forms of power, and Punishment/Penalty/Coercive should be used as the last resort only after all other forms have been exhausted. Since the project manager has no power or budget to reward the team members, she should use her expert power in this situation.

5. D: A manager with a "hands-off" attitude toward the project is considered "Laissez-Faire." With this style, management is not directly involved but manages and consults as required. This French term means "allow to act" or "leave alone."

6. D: Reward and Expert are the most effective forms of power. Since you just hired, people may not know that you are an expert. Formal power is the only logical answer as the reward or expert power is not the option here.

7. B: The project manager is responsible for making sure that the team is getting training on project specific skills and on the other hand, the functional manager is responsible for training in general job skills.

8. C: Steve has the composure quality as he can control his temper in kind of frustrating situations.

9. B: Roger has a cultural personality as he is respectful to all kind of cultures. A courteous person is polite and considerate who applies appropriate behaviors and good manners. An emotional person is good at recognizing emotions. A political person has the ability to understand the significance of organizational politics and demonstrates political intelligence.

10. B: A leader's styles are transformational, consultative, participative, and innovative whereas a manager's styles are dictatorial, authoritative, transactional, autocratic, consultative, democratic, and administrative. A leader takes risks but a manager likes to control risks.

CHAPTER 3

PROJECT MANAGEMENT PROCESSES

PROJECT MANAGEMENT PROCESSES QUESTIONS

1. Which statement is FALSE regarding the Initiating Process Group?
    A. Cost and staffing start low, increase toward the end, and drop rapidly near closing.
    B. Project risk is highest at the beginning of the project and reduces as the project approaches its end.
    C. Stakeholder influence is highest at the start and diminishes as the project proceeds.
    D. The project manager and team are always identified as part of the Initiating Process Group.

2. All of the following will occur during project initiating EXCEPT:
    A. Creation of a Project Scope Statement.
    B. Identification of internal and external stakeholders.
    C. Development and review of the business case and a feasibility study.
    D. Assignment of the project manager to lead a project.

3. Which of the following will occur only during the Planning Process Group?
    A. Identify Stakeholders
    B. Develop Schedule
    C. Acquire Resources
    D. Validate Scope

4. Which of the following process groups consists of the processes to complete the work defined in the Project Management Plan and ultimately satisfies the project specifications and objectives?
    A. Planning Process Group
    B. Executing Process Group
    C. Initiating Process group
    D. Closing Process Group

5. A Knowledge Area represents a complete set of activities, concepts, and terms that make up an area of specialization, project management field, or professional field. Each project management Knowledge Area is subdivided into which of the following?
    A. Best practices
    B. Policies
    C. Processes
    D. Guidelines

6. All of the following should be done during the Closing Process Group EXCEPT:
    A. Formal sign-off and formal acceptance are received from the customers.
    B. Customer acceptance criteria are determined.
    C. Final versions of the lessons learned are compiled and made available for future projects.
    D. Completed project deliverables are handed off to operations and maintenance.

7. In which process group does the team track, measure, inspect, monitor, verify, review, compare, and regulate the progress and performance of the project; ensure that the plan is working; identify any areas in which changes to the plan are required; and initiate the corresponding changes?
    A. Monitoring & Controlling
    B. Closing
    C. Initiating
    D. Executing

8. You are overseeing a project for your organization to implement a web-based application for accessing pay and tax information online. Currently, you are in the process of implementing approved changes, corrective actions, preventive actions, and defect repairs in the project. You are in which of the following process groups?
    A. Executing
    B. Monitoring & Controlling
    C. Planning
    D. Closing

9. Which one of the following statements is FALSE about the Executing Process Group?
    A. This process group usually takes the most time and resources.
    B. The processes in this process group measure and analyze the progress and performance of the project, ensure that the plan is working, identify any areas in which changes to the plan are required, and initiate the corresponding changes.
    C. Corrective actions, preventive actions, and defect repairs are implemented in this process group.
    D. This process group consists of processes to complete the work defined in the project management plan and ultimately satisfies the project specifications and objectives.

10. The sponsor has just signed the project charter and assigned you as a project manager to oversee a project to implement a simulator for a local golf club. What should you do FIRST as the project manager?
    A. Focus on identifying and classifying the stakeholders in the project.
    B. Start working on the Project Management Plan.
    C. Develop the project schedule.
    D. Create the WBS.

11. You have been assigned to manage a project to design a new type of vinyl-based resilient floor material. You came up with a few orders of magnitude estimates, high-level risks, constraints, and assumptions for the project. What project Management Process Group are you in?
    A. Monitoring & Controlling
    B. Closing
    C. Initiating
    D. Planning

12. Which one of the following process groups consists of iterative and ongoing processes to establish the total scope of effort, to define the objectives, and to identify the course of action required to attain those objectives?
    A. Planning
    B. Executing
    C. Initiating
    D. Monitoring & Controlling

13. Which of the following process groups serve as inputs to each other?
    A. Initiating, Planning
    B. Initiating, Executing
    C. Executing, Monitoring & Controlling
    D. Monitoring & Controlling, Closing

14. You are overseeing a construction project to construct a new fitness center at a local university. Currently, the team is working on collecting requirements and establishing estimates for the project. Which process group are you in?
    A. Initiating
    B. Executing
    C. Monitoring & Controlling
    D. Planning

15. Which one of the following is not an outcome when a project is initiated properly in the Initiating Process Group?
    A. Authorizing the project manager to manage the project
    B. Defining the scope of the project
    C. Identifying the key stakeholders
    D. Understanding the goal, objective, and business need of the project

16. Which one of the following is NOT a planning process?
    A. Create WBS
    B. Perform Qualitative Risk Analysis
    C. Estimate Costs
    D. Develop Team

17. Steve has been overseeing a project to implement a new wireless media streaming device for a local networking company. The team has completed all the technical work in the project. The senior management asked Steve to report on the remaining activities in the project. Which one of the following will Steve report as the remaining work?
    A. Completion of the lessons learned
    B. Validation of the Project Scope
    C. Completion of the Quality Management Plan
    D. Completion of Risk Response Planning

18. You just finished creating your project charter. Which of the following will NOT be included in the charter?
    A. Detailed work package descriptions
    B. High-level roadmap and milestones
    C. Assumptions and constraints
    D. Authority level of the project manager

19. While working in the Initiating Process Group, you are mainly focusing on creating a Project Charter and a Stakeholder Register. You will use all of the following as inputs EXCEPT:

A. Organizational values and work ethics
B. Project scope statement
C. Configuration management knowledgebase
D. Historical information and past lessons learned

20. Which one of the following is NOT a component of a change request?
A. Corrective actions
B. Preventive actions
C. Defect repairs
D. Issue Log

21. Your company, ITPro Consultancy, has assigned you as the project manager to upgrade the call center in your organization. The number of calls the customer support agents have to answer each month has increased drastically in the last five months, and the phone system is approaching the maximum load limit. While exploring the project status, you realize that the team just completed the Work Breakdown Structure (WBS) and WBS dictionary. The project team also started identifying risk items and developing a Risk Breakdown Structure (RBS). You are expecting to complete the project within the budget of $200,000 and in 7 months. What is the NEXT item the team should be working on?
A. Complete identifying all risk items and the Risk Breakdown Structure (RBS).
B. Participate in the development of the Project Scope Statement.
C. Focus on identifying and classifying the stakeholders in the project.
D. Create an activity list and identify activity attributes.

22. Which one of the following is the BEST approach you can take while planning for your project?
A. Develop the Quality Management Plan prior to determining the Process Improvement Plan and developing a quality checklist.
B. Create a Requirement Traceability Matrix before creating the Work Breakdown Structure (WBS).
C. Develop a Risk Register before you document the high level risks, assumptions, and constraints.
D. Inform stakeholders of the approved project charter and then start working on the Networking Diagram.

23. While managing a complex project, you realize that the processes of a certain Process Group occur simultaneously as the processes of all remaining 4 process groups. You are referring to:
A. Monitoring and controlling
B. Closing
C. Executing
D. Planning

24. Recently your stakeholder approved some of the deliverables that your team members just completed. These accepted deliverables will be used as inputs to which process group?
A. Initiating
B. Planning
C. Executing
D. Closing

25. Last week you submitted 5 new change requests to the Change Control Board (CCB). After exploring different options, the board approved 3 of the change requests. Approved change requests will be inputs to which process group?
A. Initiating
B. Planning
C. Executing
D. Closing

26. Senior management is concerned that the project will not be completed on time and within budget. They asked you to create a detailed project schedule as soon as possible. Management confirmed you that they would approve additional fund for the project if needed. Which of the following items you must have to create a detailed project schedule?
A. A detailed Risk Register with all identified risks and response strategies
B. A detailed Project Management Plan
C. A Project Cost Baseline
D. A Work Breakdown Structure (WBS)

27. Your team is very devoted to the project and can't wait to move on to the next phase of the project.
What is the most important factor to make sure prior to moving on to the next phase?
A. Making sure that you have sufficient fund for the next phase.
B. Verifying that the current phase satisfied its objective and stakeholders formally accepted its deliverables.
C. Making sure that you have all the resources you need for the next phase.
D. Confirming that there will be no negative stakeholders in the next phase.

PROJECT MANAGEMENT PROCESSES ANSWERS

1. D: The project manager is assigned during project initiating, but some of the team members will be acquired during Executing Process Group.

2. A: The project scope statement is an output of the Define Scope process and is part of the Planning Process Group.

3. B: Only Develop Schedule will occur during the Planning Process Group. Identify stakeholders occurs during initiating, Acquire Resources occurs during Executing, and validate Scope occurs during Monitoring & Controlling.

4. B: The Executing Process Group is intended to ensure that the work defined in the project plan is performed.

5. C: Each Project Management Knowledge Area is subdivided into specific processes, each of which is characterized by its inputs, tools & techniques, and outputs.

6. B: Customer acceptance criteria are determined during Initiating Process Group.

7. A: During the Monitoring & Controlling Process Group, project performance is measured and analyzed, and needed changes are identified and approved.

8. A: Usually a project will enter the Executing Process Group when the planning is completed or the project management plan has been updated due to change requests, including defect repairs and corrective and preventive actions. The Executing Process Group involves coordinating people and resources as well as integrating and performing the activities of the project in accordance with the project management plan. These approved change requests for corrective actions, preventive actions, and defect repairs are implemented in the Executing Process Group.

9. B: The processes in the Monitoring & Controlling Process Group track, measure, inspect, monitor, verify, review, compare, and regulate the progress and performance of the project; ensure that the plan is working; identify any areas in which changes to the plan are required; and initiate the corresponding changes.

10. A: The Project Charter is created and the project manager is assigned during the Initiating Process Group. Stakeholder identification is also started during initiating and carried on throughout the project life cycle. It is essential to classify stakeholders according to their level of interest, influence, importance, and expectation at the early stage of the project as much as possible. Prior to jumping on planning, creating the WBS, and developing the project schedule, the project manager should focus on identifying and classifying the internal and external stakeholders in the project.

11. C: High-level risks, constraints, and assumptions are identified in the Project Charter, which is created during project Initiating. Usually, orders of magnitude estimates are done during the Initiating Process Group when not much information is available about the project.

12. A: The Planning Process Group consists of iterative and ongoing processes to establish the total scope of effort to define the objectives and to identify the course of action required to attain those objectives.

13. C: The Executing Process Group and the Monitoring & Controlling Process Group serve as inputs to each other. The Planning Process Group and the Executing Process Group also feed each other.

14. D: Requirements are collected from the customers and other stakeholders, and estimates on time, cost, resources, and other things are made during the Planning Process Group.

15. B: Detailed Project Scope will be defined during the Planning Process Group. The success of subsequent processes and activities greatly depends on the way a project is initiated. If a project is initiated properly, it would have a clear business need and feasibility, a clear goal, objective reasons for selecting this project over other possibilities, a clear direction for the scope, a project manager assigned, and a list of stakeholders for the project. On the other hand, if a project is not initiated properly, it could result in limited or a total lack of authority for the project manager as well as ambiguous goals or uncertainties as to why the project was initiated.

16. D: Develop Team is a process in the Executing Process Group. All three remaining processes belong to the Planning Process Group.

17. A: The lessons learned are usually done once the work is completed in the project. The Quality Management Plan and the Risk Response Plan are created during the Planning Process Group. The Validate Scope process is done, not during closing, but in the Monitoring & Controlling Process Group.

18. A: High-level roadmap and milestones, assumptions and constraints, and authority level of the project manager should be included in the Project Charter. A Project Charter is created during Initiating Process Group, but a Project Scope Statement is created during Planning Process Group. The Scope Baseline will have the Project Scope Statement, WBS, and details on WBS work packages.

19. B: Organizational Process Assets such as configuration management knowledgebase, historical information, and past lessons learned as well as Enterprise Environmental Factors such as organizational values and work ethics are inputs in Initiating Process Group. Project Scope Statement is an output of the Planning Process Group.

20. D: A change request consists of corrective actions, preventive actions, and defect repairs. Corrective actions are taken to bring expected future performance of the project work in line with the project management plan. Preventive actions are taken to reduce the probability of risk items in the project. Defect repairs are taken to repair defects or entirely replace components that are faulty or dysfunctional. An issue is an obstacle that threatens project progress and can block the team from achieving its goals. An issue log is a written log to record issues that require solutions. It helps monitor who is responsible for resolving specific issues by a target date.

21. D: Refer to the "Figure 3-17: Process Groups Key Inputs and Outputs" and you should realize that during planning, creating an activity list and identifying activity attributes come next after creating the WBS and WBS dictionary. Identifying and classifying the stakeholders in the project is part of stakeholder analysis which is usually done during Initiating. Project scope must be defined and a Project Scope Statement should be created prior to the creation of the WBS and WBS dictionary. The team must complete an activity list, network diagram, and participate in the development of the schedule and budget before risk identification can effectively be completed.

22. B: Refer to the "Figure 3-17: Process Groups Key Inputs and Outputs" and you should realize that you need to develop a Requirement Traceability Matrix before the scope is defined and a WBS is created for the project, so this is the best option. The Process Improvement Plan and quality checklist are created as part of the Quality Management Plan, not after it. A Risk Register is created in the Planning Process Group, whereas the high-level risks, assumptions, and constraints are identified during initiating. Starting the network diagram immediately after informing the stakeholders of the approved Project Charter skips several important steps, such as defining the requirements, scope, and activities.

23. A: Monitoring and controlling is something we are continuously doing in a project. Don't get confused thinking that we monitor and control only after executing.

24. D: Refer to the "Figure 3-14: Monitoring & Controlling Process Group Processes" and "Figure 3-17: Process Groups Key Inputs and Outputs" and you should realize that accepted deliverables are outputs of the Validate Scope process in the Monitoring and Controlling Process Group. These accepted deliverables become inputs to the Closing Process Group. The output of the Closing Process Group is final product, service, or result transition.

25. C: You will be coming up with change requests both in the Executing and Monitoring and Controlling Process Groups. These change requests will be an input to the Perform Integrated Change Control process in the Monitoring and Controlling Process Group. Approved change requests from the Perform Integrated Change Control process are fed back into the Direct and Manage Project Work process for implementation in the Executing Process Group.

26. Refer to the "Figure 3-17: Process Groups Key Inputs and Outputs" and you should realize that the Project Schedule is created prior to the development of the Project Cost Baseline, Risk Register, and Project Management Plan. A Work Breakdown Structure (WBS) is needed to create a detailed Project Schedule.

27. A project phase must be formally closed by meeting its objective and by receiving the formal acceptance on its deliverables prior to moving on to the next phase.

CHAPTER 4

PROJECT INTEGRATION MANAGEMENT

PROJECT INTEGRATION MANAGEMENT QUESTIONS

1. You recently took over a project in the middle of executing from another project manager who left the organization. You became extremely worried to find out that a substantial amount of new change requests are coming from your key stakeholders, customers, and even from your manager. You are anxious that the changes will drastically increase the cost and time of the project, and you are not sure about how to process these incoming change requests. What should you refer to for any kind of help in this situation?
    A. The previous project manager who can provide guidance and relevant information
    B. The project charter to find out the key success criteria from the stakeholders
    C. The project requirements document to know more about the project requirements
    D. The Project Management Plan

2. John, the project manager, is in the process of Develop Project Charter to develop a document to formally authorize a project or a phase and identify the business objectives and needs, current understanding of the stakeholders' expectations, and the new product, service, or result that it is intended to satisfy. Which one of the following is NOT an input to this Develop Project Charter process?
    A. Enterprise Environmental Factors
    B. Business Documents – Business Case and Benefits Management Plan
    C. Agreements
    D. Project Management Plan

3. Which one of the following is FALSE about change management in a project?
    A. "Influencing the factors that affect change" means determining the source of changes and fixing the root causes.
    B. Whenever there is a change request, the project manager should evaluate the impact on project objectives such as scope, time, cost, quality, risk, resources, and other factors.
    C. The project manager should make all the effort to prevent unnecessary changes in the project.
    D. The project manager should make the change happen as soon as possible to meet and exceed customer expectations.

4. Your manager mentioned to you that the present value of a project is $350,000 and asked you to find out the future value that the project will have four years from now if the expected interest rate is 8 percent. What is the future value in this case?
    A. $350,000
    B. $400,000
    C. $476,000
    D. $257,352

5. Which one of the following statements is NOT true about the Project Management Plan?
    A. It is a single-approved document that defines how the project is executed, monitored and controlled, and closed.
    B. It is developed through a series of integrated processes.
    C. It is progressively elaborated by updates and controlled and approved through the Perform Integrated Change Control process.
    D. It provides project inputs, tools & techniques, and outputs to be used on the project for the purpose of managing the product of the project.

6. You are a technical specialist and domain expert working on an IT project to implement a new console video game. There is a change control process in place, and the project scope is already signed off by the sponsor and key stakeholders. While having a casual conversation with one of the stakeholders, you realize that a simple change in the design will add a great feature to the project. Since there is no visible impact, you made the change to the project without informing the project manager. What kind of reaction should you expect from the project manager?
    A. The project manager should simply ignore the change since it had no visible impact.
    B. You should be informed that your action was inconsistent with the change management plan, and this kind of unauthorized action should not be repeated again.
    C. The project manager should get the customer sign-off on the implemented change.
    D. You should be recognized for exceeding customer expectations without affecting the project cost or schedule.

7. You are approaching the end of your project and have been asked to release the resources so that they can be assigned to other projects. Before releasing the resources, you want to make sure that you have completed the necessary actions. Which of the following is the correct order of actions that you take during the closing process?
    A. Get formal acceptance, write lessons learned, release the team, and close the contract.
    B. Get formal acceptance, release the team, write lessons learned, and close the contract.
    C. Write lessons learned, release the team, get formal acceptance, and close the contract.
    D. Release the team, get formal acceptance, close the contract, and write lessons learned.

8. While overseeing the implementation of a new computer infrastructure at the local hospital, you notice that a substantial amount of change requests have originated from one single key stakeholder. The stakeholder is also insisting that all of his requests should be implemented as soon as possible. What will be your BEST course of action?
    A. Ask the sponsor to have a discussion with the key stakeholder and ask him not to request so many changes to the project.
    B. Call the stakeholder and request him not to send any more change requests.
    C. Have a meeting with the stakeholder to review the change process in the project and determine the causes of his changes.

D. Assign a team member to work solely with the stakeholder to understand his needs and expectations.

9. Which one of the following statements is FALSE about the Project Management Information System (PMIS)?
    A. It is incorporated as part of the Enterprise Environmental Factors (EEFs) to several processes since it is part of the environment in which the project is performed.
    B. It is an automated system that can serve as a repository for information and a tool to assist with communication and with tracking documents and deliverables.
    C. It consists of the data sources and the tools & techniques used to gather, integrate, analyze, and disseminate the results of the combined outputs of the project management processes.
    D. It defines how the project is executed, monitored and controlled, and closed.

10. Ashley is overseeing an IT project to implement a payroll system for a local doctor's office. The project has twelve team members and nine stakeholders, and it is supposed to be completed in six months. Ashley was unaware that a modification request to the product specifications by one of the stakeholders was immediately implemented by the project team. During the final testing, Ashley was surprised to find out that there was a major variance between the actual test results and the planned results. Which one of the following is a contribution to this kind of adverse consequence?
    A. Poor Quality Management Plan
    B. Lack of commitment to the change control process
    C. Poor definition of the test plan
    D. Lack of adherence to the communication plan

11. You have just been assigned as a project manager to implement a web-based accounting software for one of your clients. You have chosen a specific change-driven product development life cycle for the implementation of your project. As you are expecting many changes during the course of the project, you want to establish a robust configuration management system to describe the different versions and characteristics of the product, service, or result of the project and to ensure the accuracy and completeness of the description. Which of the following statements is FALSE about configuration management?
    A. It includes configuration identification, configuration status accounting, and configuration verification and audit.
    B. It focuses on establishing and maintaining consistency of a product's requirements.
    C. It compares the actual project performance against the project management plan and determines whether any corrective or preventive actions are required.
    D. Its purpose is to maintain integrity of the work product.

12. You just received a change request from the customer, which will require an additional $2,000 and will also delay the project by two weeks. The customer mentioned that they were OK with the delay and were willing to pay for the extra amount as the new change will drastically improve their business automation. As per your organizational policy, you are supposed to get the project office's approval for any change that will extend the project duration by more than a week. What should you do in this situation?
    A. Discuss the change with the project office.
    B. Do not allow the change since it would extend the project duration by more than one week.
    C. Allow the change and ask the team member to implement it since it will drastically help the customer and the customer is paying for the change anyway.
    D. Advise the customer to take the change request to the project office and explain to them the importance of the change and his/her willingness to pay for it.

13. The Project Management Information System (PMIS), such as any automated system that can be utilized during the Direct and Manage Project Work process, will include all of the following EXCEPT:
    A. A tool & technique to identify the internal and external stakeholders.
    B. An information collection and distribution system.
    C. A configuration management system.
    D. A scheduling software tool.

14. One of your colleagues recently took over a project and expressed her concern to you about the new changes that may be streaming in from various sources. What is the best piece of advice you can offer her regarding changes and where she should devote most of her attention?
    A. Implementing changes as accurately as possible
    B. Tracking and recording all changes as accurately as possible
    C. Preventing unnecessary changes in the project as much as possible
    D. Informing the sponsor about all changes

15. Which one of the following is a subset of the Project Management Information System (PMIS) that describes the different versions and characteristics of the product, service, or result of the project and ensures accuracy and completeness of the description?
    A. Quality Control
    B. Configuration Management
    C. Scope Change Control
    D. Product Change Control

16. A project is just initiated under a contract in your organization, and you were assigned as the project manager. You were expecting a Statement of Work (SOW), which will describe the business need, product scope, and other elements. In this case, from whom should you expect the SOW?
    A. The project sponsor
    B. The buyer
    C. The contractor
    D. The Project Management Office (PMO)

17. While managing a data center project, you used a Configuration Management System to describe the different versions and characteristics of the product, service, or result of the project and to ensure the accuracy and completeness of the description. All of the following are configuration management activities in the Integrated Change Control process EXCEPT:
    A. Configuration verification and audit
    B. Configuration identification
    C. Forecasting and variance analysis
    D. Configuration status accounting

18. You are a project manager at a dairy farm that offers several dairy products to its clients in different states, especially on the West Coast. You have sent a few of your team members to China to get specialized training on a spectacular dairy food processing equipment recently introduced in the market. The team members just completed the training, and this is one of the work results you have collected and recorded. This output describes which of the following in the Direct and Manage Project Work process?
    A. Deliverables
    B. Work Performance Data
    C. Change requests
    D. Project Management Plan update

19. All of the following statements are true regarding assumptions EXCEPT:
    A. Assumptions are factors used for planning purposes and may be communicated to a project team by several different stakeholders.
    B. Assumptions are generally considered to be true, real or certain, and nonfactual.
    C. Assumptions are absolute and nonnegotiable.
    D. Failure to validate assumptions may result in significant risk events.

20. You are one of the members of the project prioritization and selection committee in your organization. The selection team is debating between two projects, which are both considered to be very important. The organization has to make an initial investment of $250,000 with expected cash inflows of $75,000 in the first year and $25,000 per quarter thereafter for the first project. The second project has a payback period of thirty-five months. Based solely on this information, which project should the selection committee recommend?
    A. First project as it has a smaller payback period
    B. Second project as it has a smaller payback period
    C. None of them since both of them have the same payback period
    D. Either of the two projects since payback period is not important

21. You are the project manager for a cable service provider that is providing Internet, TV, and phone service throughout the United States. Your company recently introduced its service in Canada and made you the project manager for a critical project, which is two months in execution at this time. You are reporting on project elements such as deliverable status, schedule progress, resource utilization, costs incurred, and others. Which of the following outputs of the Direct and Manage Project Work does this describe?
    A. Deliverables
    B. Work Performance Data
    C. Change requests
    D. Project Management Plan update

22. While managing a large construction project, you are ready to assign resources to the project using a work authorization system. All of the following statements are true about a work authorization system EXCEPT:
    A. It is a formal, documented procedure to describe how to authorize and initiate work in the correct sequence at the appropriate time.
    B. It is a tool & technique of the Monitor and Control Project Work process.
    C. It is a component of the enterprise environmental factors, which are inputs in the Monitor and Control Project Work process.
    D. It is used throughout the project executing process.

23. You are working as a project manager at a consulting firm and recently received a Statement of Work (SOW) from the client. As per your expectation, the SOW should contain or reference which of the following elements?
    A. Business need, product scope description or what is to be done, and how the project supports the strategic plan
    B. Measurable project objectives, business need, product scope description or what is to be done, and how the project supports the strategic plan
    C. Project purpose, business need, product scope description or what is to be done, and how the project supports the strategic

plan
D. Business need, product scope description or what is to be done, and project purpose

24. You are the project manager for ITPro Consultancy. You have a project in mind that will be able to meet the strategic objective of your organization. While evaluating the project, your team found out that the project would cost $600,000. Since you are introducing a new potential product in the market, you are very hopeful that your expected inflows will be $30,000 per quarter for the first two years and then $90,000 per quarter thereafter. What is the payback period of this project?
    A. Thirty-six months
    B. Thirty-eight months
    C. Forty-eight months
    D. Fifty-two months

25. While managing a data recovery project, you are performing the following activities: comparing actual project performance against the project management plan, analyzing, tracking, monitoring project risks, assessing performance to determine whether any corrective or preventive actions are required, providing information to support status reporting, monitoring implementation of approved changes, providing forecasts to update current costs and schedule information, and other things. Which process are you in at this time?
    A. Manage Stakeholder Expectations
    B. Monitor and Control Risks
    C. Direct and Manage Project Work
    D. Monitor and Control Project Work

26. Your company can accept one of three possible projects. Project A has a Net Present Value (NPV) of $30,000, it will take five years to complete, and the associated cost will be $10,000. Project B has a NPV of $60,000, it will take three years to complete, and the cost will be $15,000. Project C has a NPV of $80,000, it will take four years to complete, and it will cost $40,000. Based on the information, which project would you pick?
    A. They all have the same value
    B. Project A
    C. Project B
    D. Project C

27. A project manager for a pharmaceutical project is reviewing the project contract and going through the narrative description of products and services to be supplied under the contract. He is meeting with subject matter experts, key stakeholders, and business analysts to evaluate whether or not the project is worth the required investment of $1 million. He also asked the team members to carry out a feasibility study on the project and report to him the findings as soon as possible. Which of the following documents would be created as an output in the process?
    A. Project Management Plan
    B. Project Statement of Work
    C. Project Charter
    D. Requirements Documentation

28. All of the following statements regarding Integration Management are true EXCEPT:
    A. The need for Integration Management is one of the major driving forces for communication in a project.
    B. Project integration is a key responsibility of the project team.
    C. The project manager's role as an integrator is to put all the pieces of a project into a cohesive whole.
    D. Project Integration Management is the set of combined processes implemented by the project manager to ensure all the elements of the project are effectively coordinated.

29. The Scope Management Plan, Schedule Management Plan, Schedule Baseline, Process Improvement Plan, Change Management Plan, and others are which one of the following to the project plan?
    A. Subsidiaries
    B. Appendixes
    C. Constraints
    D. Glossary

30. There are several potential projects in your organization. Unfortunately, the organization doesn't have the time, resources, or cash to work on all those projects. The senior management is particularly interested in two projects and ask you to identify the best one to work on based on the Net Present Value (NPV). While exploring those two projects, you discovered the following:
Project Alpha:
    Investment needed: $ 135,000
    Benefit: End of 1st year: $0, End of 2nd year: $75,000, End of 3rd year: 89,000
Project Beta:

Investment needed: $ 120,000

Benefit: End of 1st year: $55,000, End of 2nd year: 79,000

Assume an interest rate of 6%, which project should you recommend?

    A. Project Alpha

    B. Project Beta

    C. Neither of the projects should be recommended

    D. Both projects should be recommended

31. You are working on a construction project and successfully completed all the work. Your stakeholders were very pleased and recently communicated their final acceptance of the project. You are now meeting with your team to update the organizational process assets with a record of knowledge gained about the project to help future project managers with their projects. Once the lessons learned is completed, what should you do next?

    A. Release the team.

    B. Close the contract.

    C. Get formal acceptance.

    D. Write lessons learned.

32. Your cyber security implementation project has a Schedule Performance Index (SPI) of 1.2 and Cost Performance Index (CPI) of 1.3. Now that you are ahead of schedule and under budget, you can add work without delaying your project or exceeding the budget. You realized that throughout the project, your team made several mistakes and ignored few best methods for securing the network and preventing various types of attack. Your sponsor was very disappointed that a Denial of Service (DOS) attack was carried out against your organization recently. You tried to identify information on similar mistakes from previous projects but failed to identify any relevant Lessons Learned Register. You decided to develop a Lesson Learned Register that you need to update:

    A. At the completion of the entire project

    B. At the completion of each phase

    C. Bi weekly

    D. Throughout the project

33. You are in the Close Project or Phase process of your construction project. All of the following occur during this process EXCEPT:

    A. Confirm work completion to requirements

    B. Determine the Net Present Value of the project

    C. Gain formal acceptance of the product

    D. Hand off completed product

PROJECT INTEGRATION MANAGEMENT ANSWERS

1. D: Only the Project Management Plan contains the details about how to process, monitor, and control changes in a project.

2. D: The Project Management Plan is developed later in the Develop Project Management Plan process, not in the Develop Project Charter process.

3. D: The project manager should not implement any change request prior to evaluating the impact of the change and receiving approval from the Change Control Board.

4. C: We know $PV = FV / (1 + r)^n$, FV = future value, r = interest rate, n = number of time periods

We can say that $FV = PV * (1 + r)^n$
Thus, $FV = \$350,000 * (1 + .08)^4 = \$350,000 * (1.08)^4 = \$350,000 * 1.36 = \$476,000$

5. D: The Project Management Plan, developed through a series of integrated processes, is a single-approved document that defines how the project is executed, how it is monitored and controlled, and how it is closed. Generally, the project plan is considered to be a guide that is expected to change throughout the project life cycle, and any such change should be controlled and approved through the Perform Integrated Change Control process.

6. B: It may seem like there is no visible impact on time and cost for a minor change, but it can result in significant scope creep and may impact other project constraints such as risk, customer satisfaction, quality, and other things. The change control process should be followed by everyone on the project team. A team member should consult with the project manager prior to making a design change to evaluate the possible impact on all the different constraints.

7. A: You should not release the team until the lessons learned are documented and added to the organizational process assets, as you need the team's help with the lessons learned. Most contracts have payment terms that allow for some period of time before full payment is required; thus, the last thing you do on the project is close the contract.

8. C: The most appropriate action is to ensure that the stakeholder fully understands the project scope of work and the change control process. It is also very important to identify the root causes of his changes. You should have a meeting with the stakeholder first and get all the details prior to meeting with the sponsor about your concern.

9. D: The Project Management Plan, not the Project Management Information System defines how the project is executed, monitored and controlled, and closed. The Project Management Information System, which can be electronic or manual, is used to track project information and performance. Such information kept by these systems can include the tracking of time worked, project costs, and other factors that would be communicated to project stakeholders.

10. B: There is no indication that there is anything wrong with the quality plan, test plan, or communication plan. The change control process was not properly followed in this case. Failure to follow the agreed-upon change control processes may create adverse risk situations and jeopardize the entire project.

11. C: Comparing the actual project performance against the Project Management Plan and determine whether any corrective or preventive actions are required is done as a part of the Monitor and Control Project Work process. All the other statements are true regarding the configuration management process.

12. A: Any kind of organizational policy, process, or guideline must be followed, and the project manager should discuss the change request with the project office. The project manager simply should not approve or deny a change request as the Change Control Board (CCB) is responsible for approving or denying a change request after evaluating it. The customer should not do the project manager's job and take the change request to the project office.

13. A: Stakeholder identification is a continuous, complex, and manual process carried on by the project manager and the team members throughout the project. The Project Management Information System (PMIS) can be used for collecting and distributing information; describing the different versions and characteristics of the product, service, or result (Configuration Management System); and scheduling.

14. C: The project manager should be focusing on all of these options, but he/she should be very proactive and always try to prevent the unnecessary changes as much as possible.

15. B: Configuration management system is a subset of the Project Management Information System (PMIS) and is specifically associated with changes to features, functions, and physical characteristics of a product or deliverable.

16. B: Usually the buyers come up with the SOW in a project that is initiated by a contract.

17. C: Configuration management activities in the Integrated Change Control process are configuration identification, configuration status accounting, and configuration verification and audit.

18. A: This output describes a deliverable. Note that deliverables can be intangibles, such as the completion of a training program.

19. C: Assumptions are not based on factual information, and failure to validate may result in significant risk events. Assumptions

are documented mostly during the project initiating and planning processes. These assumptions are not absolute and can be negotiable.

20. A: The first project will have the cash inflows of $75,000 in the first twelve months, and for the rest of the investment ($250,000 – $ 75,000 = $175,000) it will take seven quarters to recapture it; thus, for the first project, the total payback period is 12 + 21 (each quarter has three months; thus, seven quarters have 7 * 3 = 21 months) = 33 months. The first project has a smaller payback period than that of the second project; thus, we should select the first project.

21. B: Work Performance Data describes how far along a deliverable is and how it is progressing against the plan. It can include several work performance data of interest, such as deliverable status, schedule progress, resource utilization, costs incurred, and quality standards.

22. B: A Work Authorization System is not a tool & technique of the project monitoring & controlling process. It is a subset of the Project Management Information System (PMIS) and is considered a component of the Enterprise Environmental Factors, which are inputs in the Monitor and Control Project Work process. It is a formal, documented procedure to describe how to authorize and initiate work in the correct sequence at the appropriate time and is used throughout the executing process group.

23. A: The project SOW should contain the business need, product scope, and strategic plan.

24. A: The cash inflow is $30,000 per quarter, so in the first year the project will get back $120,000 in four quarters. In the first two years, the project will have a return of $240,000. The remaining investment will be $600,000 – $ 240,000 = $360,000. It will take four quarters or twelve months to have it back at a rate of $90,000 per quarter in the third year. The total amount of time it will take to get the entire investment back will be 24 months + 12 months = 36 months, or three years.

25. D: All these activities are performed in the Monitor and Control Project Work process.

26. D: The number of years and cost are not relevant as they are accounted for in the calculation of Net Present Value (NPV). You simply select the project with the highest NPV; in this case, it is Project C that has a NPV of $80,000.

27. C: The project manager is in the Develop Project Charter process in Project Integration Management. The output of this process is a Project Charter, which is used to formally initiate a project. In this case, the project manager is using a Statement of Work (SOW) to understand the product requirements and descriptions. The project will be initiated under the contract, and the SOW was given to the project manager by the client.

28. B: Project integration is a key responsibility of the project manager.

29. A: The subsidiary plans are usually included to support the overall project management plan and are developed for the purpose of providing more detailed information, guidelines, and control processes for specifically defined project elements or planning components. These are the outputs of some of the other planning processes associated with scope, time, cost, quality, human resources, communications, risk, procurement, and stakeholder management. Additional plans such as change management, process improvement, and configuration management plans, can also be added to the project management plan.

30. A:

PV of $75,000 received at the end of 2nd year: $PV = \frac{FV}{(1+r)^n} = \frac{\$75,000}{(1+.06)^2} = \frac{\$75,000}{(1.06)^2} = \frac{\$75,000}{1.123} = \$66,785$

PV of $89,000 received at the end of 3rd year: $PV = \frac{\$89,000}{(1+.06)^3} = \frac{\$89,000}{(1.06)^3} = \frac{\$89,000}{1.191} = \$74,727$

Therefore, the NPV of project Alpha = ($66,785 + $74,727) – $135,000 = $6512

Project Beta:

PV of $55,000 received at the end of 1st year: $PV = \frac{\$55,000}{(1+.06)^1} = \frac{\$55,000}{1.06} = \$51,886$

PV of $79,000 received at the end of 2nd year: $PV = \frac{\$79,000}{(1+.06)^2} = \frac{\$79,000}{(1.06)^2} = \frac{\$79,000}{1.123} = \$70,347$

Therefore, the NPV of project Beta = ($51,886 + $70,347) – $120,000 = $2233

Since project Alpha has a higher NPV than project Beta, you should recommend project Alpha.

31. A: You should release the team once the lessons learned are documented and added to the organizational process assets. Most contracts have payment terms that allow for some period of time before full payment is required; thus, the last thing you do on the project is close the contract. When closing the project, the order should be get formal acceptance, write lessons learned, release the team, and close the contract.

32. D: A live document such as Lesson Learned Register should be regularly updated throughout the project for the benefit of the entire organization. It should be an excellent source of information on mistakes and areas for improvements for current and future similar projects.

33. B: Determining the Net Present Value (NPV) is done during the Develop Project Charter process in the initiating phase, not during the Closing Project or Phase process.

CHAPTER 5

PROJECT SCOPE MANAGEMENT

PROJECT SCOPE MANAGEMENT QUESTIONS

1. You have been assigned as the project manager for a web-based application project to automate the sales and marketing processes for one of your clients. You have decided to utilize a Data Gathering Technique to identify the project and product requirements during the Collect Requirements process. All of the following are valid group creativity techniques EXCEPT:
   A. Focus Groups
   B. Brainstorming
   C. Questionnaires and Surveys
   D. Tornado Diagram

2. The Project Scope Statement that describes project deliverables and the work required to create them in detail, enables the project team to perform more detailed planning, guides the project team's work during execution, and provides the baseline for evaluating changes includes all of the following EXCEPT:
   A. Detailed Work Breakdown Structure (WBS)
   B. Project constraints
   C. Project deliverables
   D. Product acceptance criteria

3. Which one of the following are the unapproved and undocumented changes and what occurs when changes to the scope are not detected early enough or are not managed?
   A. Scope baseline
   B. Residual risks
   C. Scope creeps
   D. Variances

4. You are the project manager for a cashier system project to produce cashier applications and software for the retail industry. You have recently discovered that one of your key competitors is also working on a similar project, but their new applications will include a computer-aided program and a web-based interface that your project does not offer. You have implemented a change request to update your project in order to include these exciting missing features. This is an example of which of the following?
   A. A change due to an error and omission in the business case
   B. A change due to a legal requirement and constraint
   C. A change due to an error or omission in the planning phase
   D. A change due to an external event

5. While trying to obtain the formal acceptance of the completed project scope and associated deliverables, with whom should the project manager validate the product?
   A. The sponsor, key stakeholders, and customers
   B. The customers
   C. The quality control team members
   D. The change control board members

6. The Scope Baseline, which consists of the Project Scope Statement, the WBS, and the WBS dictionary, is used as an input in all of the following processes EXCEPT:
   A. Determine Budget process
   B. Plan Procurement Management process
   C. Define Activities process
   D. Develop Team

7. Determining if the project scope has been completed by describing project deliverables and the work required to create them in detail, enabling the project team to perform more detailed planning, guiding the project team's work during execution, providing the baseline for evaluating changes, and other factors relies mostly upon the use of:
   A. Statement of work
   B. Project plan
   C. Project charter
   D. Project Scope Statement

8. You are working as a project manager for an Enterprise Resource Planning (ERP) application to automate the accounting and financial processes for one of your key customers. Due to a mismatch with the customer's requirement, you have been forced to redesign one of the major components. This is a significant setback since a substantial amount of code that has already been developed will have to be recoded to match the updated design. This rework has caused huge expenses, and you noticed a sign of extremely low morale among team members. Which of the following is TRUE in this situation?
   A. The team discovered this issue as a result of the Identify Risks process.
   B. The team did a poor job while creating the WBS.
   C. This problem was a result of poor scope definition.
   D. The team carried on a rigorous Control Quality process and discovered the issue.

9. While overseeing a construction project, you discovered that one of the team members, on her own initiative, added extra windows to increase air circulation and light in the basement. The original plan did not include the cost of these extra windows, but the team member thought they were absolutely required due to poor air circulation and low light in the basement. This is an example of which of the following?
   A. Value-added change
   B. Self-motivated team member
   C. Team member exceeding expectations
   D. Inefficient change control

10. After a major milestone release, some of the key stakeholders are not happy and complain that their requirements are not met. The project manager should have involved them in which of the following processes to ensure their approval for the release?
   A. Project Management Plan Development
   B. Identifying Constraints
   C. Validate Scope
   D. Schedule Management

11. Which one of the following mostly includes the product acceptance criteria that outline requirements a project must meet before stakeholders accept the final product or service?
   A. Quality Management Plan
   B. Project Scope Statement
   C. Scope Management Plan
   D. Requirements Management Plan

12. ITPro Consultancy, LLC has been offering cable TV, Internet, and phone services to its East Coast customers for almost five years now. Recently, they have initiated a project to introduce their service to the West Coast and have assigned a project manager. The project manager left the company, and you took over the project, as per the instruction of the CEO, when the project is almost ready to enter in execution. While reviewing the existing documents, you discovered that the team had done a great job in developing the requirements document and the Project Scope Statement, but there was no WBS. What should you do FIRST in this situation?
   A. Immediately inform management and provide them with relevant oversight.
   B. Politely request to be excused from the project.
   C. You should not enter execution until the WBS is created for the project.
   D. You should refer to the WBS dictionary for the required detail needed to continue to execution.

13. While discussing the scope in your project with the stakeholders and team members, you realized that all of the following statements are TRUE about scope EXCEPT:
   A. Product scope describes the features and functions that characterize a product, service, or result.
   B. Project Scope Management includes the processes concerned with "all the work" and "only the work" required to successfully deliver to the stakeholders' expectations, manage changes, minimize surprises, and gain acceptance of the product in order to complete the project.
   C. Project scope describes work needed to deliver a product, service, or result with the specified features and functions.
   D. The project team should go above and beyond the defined scope and impress the customers by implementing extra features that will be beneficial for them.

14. Which one of the following is NOT true about the Define Scope process?
   A. It is the process of developing a comprehensive, detailed description of the project and product.
   B. Data Analysis is used as a tool & technique in this process.
   C. The requirements document is the key output in this process.
   D. A detailed Project Scope Statement that is created in this process is critical to project success and builds upon the additional analysis of requirements, major deliverables, assumptions, constraints, and other factors that are documented earlier in the project.

15. You have been assigned as the project manager for a web-based application project to automate the recruiting process for one of your clients. You have decided to utilize a Voting Technique to generate, classify, prioritize, and drive decisions forward. All of the following are valid Voting techniques EXCEPT:
   A. The decision is based on the most influential block in a group even if a majority is not achieved.
   B. The decision is based on a single course of action decided by everyone in the group.
   C. The decision is based on the support from more than 50 percent of the members of the group.
   D. The decision is based on the largest block in a group even if a majority is not achieved.

16. Product scope describes the features, functions, and physical characteristics that characterize a product, service, or result. Completion of the product scope is measured against which one of the following?
   A. Scope statement
   B. Project requirements
   C. Project objectives

D. Product requirements

17. As per the project manager's instruction, the team has decomposed project deliverables and project work into smaller, more manageable components to develop a WBS and WBS dictionary. The team finalized the WBS by establishing control or cost accounts and unique identifiers for the lower-level components of the WBS called work packages. Normally presented in the chart form, this WBS provides a structure for hierarchical summation of:
   A. Cost and schedule information
   B. Cost and requirements information
   C. Cost, resource, and schedule information
   D. Schedule and requirements information

18. A project manager managing a data center project had the opportunity to attend several meetings about the project prior to the creation of the project charter. In one of the meetings, the sponsor specifically denied funding for two very specific items. Two months into the project, a couple of stakeholders requested the project manager add work for one of the items that was strongly denied by the sponsor. What will be the best thing the project manager can do in this situation?
   A. Add the work if it does not have much impact on the schedule.
   B. Inform the stakeholders that the work cannot be added.
   C. Evaluate the impact of adding the work on time, cost, quality, risk, human resource, and other elements.
   D. Immediately inform the sponsor about the request that was denied by him.

19. Verified deliverables are inputs in which of the following scope management processes?
   A. Define Scope
   B. Create WBS
   C. Validate Scope
   D. Control Scope

20. All of the following are true regarding the Control Scope process EXCEPT:
   A. It assures that underlying causes of all requested changes and recommended corrective actions are understood and processed through the Integrated Change Control process.
   B. One of the key focuses in the process may be dispute resolution related to project scope.
   C. It monitors the status of the project and product scope, maintains control over the project by preventing overwhelming scope change requests, and manages changes to the scope baseline.
   D. It verifies the correctness of work results.

21. Your project is approaching completion, and you were able to release some of the team members from the team to be assigned to other projects. Your team has successfully resolved all the issues in the issue log except for one, which will be fixed in the next version of the application as per the agreement with the client. You are ahead of schedule but $3,500 over budget due to an unexpected price increase for one of the major pieces of equipment. Your team also successfully performed quality control inspections and met quality requirements for all of the items except one. You called a meeting and requested the client for product verification, and surprisingly the client mentioned that they wanted to make a major change to the scope. In this situation, the project manager should:
   A. Immediately inform management about this surprising new change.
   B. Have an urgent meeting with the team members to explore the feasibility of making the change.
   C. Inform that it is too late now to make a major change.
   D. Request the client for a description of the change.

22. Your company, ITPro Consultancy, has assigned you as the project manager to upgrade the call center in your organization. The number of calls the customer support agents have to answer each month has increased drastically in the last five months, and the phone system is approaching the maximum load limit. Your team has worked on the requirements document and the Project Scope Statement, and you are now ready to create the WBS with the help of your team members. All of the following are true regarding the WBS EXCEPT:
   A. The WBS represents all the work required to be completed in the project.
   B. Each level of the WBS represents a verifiable product or results.
   C. Activities in the WBS should be arranged in the proper sequence they will be performed.
   D. The WBS should be decomposed to a level called the work package level where cost and schedule can easily be calculated.

23. The sponsor has recently assigned you as a project manager to design and develop a custom video conferencing tool. As per the sponsor, the project must be completed in four months and should integrate with the existing infrastructure and applications in the organization. This is an example of which of the following?
   A. Constraints
   B. Assumptions
   C. Expert judgment
   D. High-level planning

24. All of the following are TRUE about the Validate Scope process EXCEPT:
    A. Customer acceptance of the project deliverables is a key output of this process.
    B. It is an input to the Develop Project Management Plan process and an output of the Control Quality process.
    C. It should be performed at the end of each phase of the project.
    D. This process is closely related to the Control Quality process.

25. A project manager is in the Control Scope process of monitoring the status of the project and product scope, maintaining control over the project by preventing overwhelming scope change requests, and managing changes to the scope baseline. Which one of the following is NOT true about this process?
    A. The Control Scope process must be integrated with other control processes.
    B. It should be performed prior to scope planning.
    C. Variance analysis is used as a tool & technique in this process.
    D. Work Performance Information and Change Requests are the key deliverables in this process.

26. Your project to build a new substation to supply power to a newly developed industrial park is not going too well. You are overwhelmed with numerous issues in the project and got really frustrated when the city conducted an inspection and reported a building code violation. You were asked by management to ensure full compliance to the mandatory city and construction industry standards. At this time, you are also approaching the final deadline of the project in two weeks. You have identified a couple of changes that will drastically enhance performance and make your clients very happy. While trying to sort all these messes out, you received a call from the senior engineer informing you that he would be leaving the company soon. Which is the MOST critical issue you should address first?
    A. Notify the customers about the possible delay in the project.
    B. Initiate the change control process to implement new changes.
    C. Find a replacement for the senior engineer.
    D. Ensure compliance with the city and construction industry standards.

27. Sarah, a project manager, is in the Define Scope process of developing a comprehensive, detailed description of the project and product. Which of the following is NOT a tool & technique used in this Define Scope process?
    A. Interpersonal and Team Skills
    B. Product Analysis
    C. Decision Making
    D. Inspection

28. You have been selected as the project manager for a major data center upgrade at your company headquarters. The sponsor has handed you a Project Charter and wished you best of luck. What should you do next as the first step?
    A. Instruct the team to work on a Project Scope Statement.
    B. Instruct the team to work on the WBS.
    C. Review the charter and make sure that all key stakeholders have inputs into the scope.
    D. Start working on planning the project.

29. Walkthroughs, reviews, product reviews, and audits are examples of which one of the following methods of examining work or a product to determine whether it conforms to documented standards or not?
    A. Observation
    B. Verification
    C. Inspection
    D. Decision Making Techniques

30. A project manager is in the Collect Requirements process of collecting and documenting quantifiable needs and expectations of the sponsor, customer, and other stakeholders. Which of the following is NOT true regarding this process?
    A. It describes project deliverables and the work required to create them in detail as well as deliverables description, product acceptance criteria, requirements assumptions and constraints, and exclusions from requirements.
    B. Requirements Documentation and Requirements Traceability Matrix are the key outputs in this process.
    C. Various Data Gathering Techniques and Decision Making techniques are used as tools & techniques in this process.
    D. The Scope Management Plan and Requirements Management Plan are inputs in this process.

31. The team members are analyzing the objectives and description of the product stated by the customer or sponsor and turning them into tangible deliverables and finally creating the Project Scope Statement. Which of the following BEST describes what the team members are doing?
    A. Performing the product analysis
    B. Performing the plan quality management
    C. Conducting a multi-criteria decision analysis
    D. Determining the product description

32. Your project to build a new substation to supply power to a newly developed industrial park is not going too well. The Net Present Value (NPV) of the project is $560,000 and the payback period is 3 years. After six-and-a-half months of work, the project is on schedule and budget, but requirements have been changing throughout the project. You became extremely worried to find out

that a substantial amount of new change requests are coming from your key stakeholders, customers, and even from your manager. You are anxious that these changes will drastically increase the cost and time of the project. Which of the following will MOST likely happen in your project?

- A. You may need to add additional resources.
- B. You may need to cut cost.
- C. You may need to terminate the project.
- D. You may not be able to measure completion of the product of the project.

PROJECT SCOPE MANAGEMENT ANSWERS

1. D: A Tornado diagram is not a component of the Group Creativity technique. It is mostly used during the Perform Quantitative Risk Analysis process to display the sensitivity analysis data in order to determine which risks have the most potential impact on a project. This diagram can be used to determine sensitivity in cost, time, and quality objectives and will be helpful to determine a detailed response plan for the elements with greater impacts.

2. A: The detailed Work Breakdown Structure (WBS) is developed after the Project Scope Statement has been defined and accepted. The scope baseline consists of the Project Scope Statement, WBS, and WBS dictionary.

3. C: Scope creeps are the unapproved and undocumented changes, and they occur when changes to the scope are not detected early enough or managed. All these minor changes slowly add up and may have drastic impact on budget, schedule, and quality.

4. D: This is a change due to an external event mainly to remain competitive. The features that the competitors are offering were not included in the scope of the project; thus, they were never discussed during the initiation or planning phases. Due to the risk of losing a potential market, the project manager decided to include them in the project. Also, there was no legal requirement or constraint to include the missing features in this case.

5. A: The project manager should get the approval from the sponsor, key stakeholders, and the customers.

6. D: Except for the Develop Team process, scope baseline is used as an input in all of the listed processes.

7. D: The statement of work generally precedes a contract and provides a narrative description of work to be completed. The project plan is derived from the Project Scope Statement. Once a project is selected or a contract is signed to perform a project, a project charter is created to formally authorize a project or a phase but is not a detailed plan. The scope statement answers the questions of what, why, who, where, and how and in combination with the work breakdown structure provides a detailed description of what must be accomplished.

8. C: This problem was a direct result of scope misunderstanding due to poor scope definition. Obviously, the team did not utilize all the tools & techniques to collect requirements from the customers and also did not spend quality time defining and developing a detailed description of the project and product.

9. D: This is an example of inefficient change control as the team should be focused on "all the work" and "only the work" needed to complete the project, not extra. The key objective should be to complete the project with the agreed- upon deliverables in time, with quality, and within budget. This kind of "gold plating" increases risk and uncertainties and introduces problems into the project and should be monitored and controlled by the project manager.

10. C: Validate Scope is the process of formal acceptance of completed project scope and deliverables by stakeholders through a signature on paper or via an e-mail that specifically states project approval. Prior scope validation would have avoided the dissatisfaction of stakeholders after the milestone release.

11. B: The Project Scope Statement documents the characteristics and boundaries of the project and its associated products, results, and services in addition to the acceptance criteria.

12. C: You should inform management and provide relevant oversight, but doing so will not resolve the issue immediately. You can refuse to manage a project in case there is a conflict of interest or an ethical concern but not in this kind of situation. A WBS dictionary is the detail of the work packages, so a WBS should be created first. You should always have a WBS since it is the foundational block to the initiating, planning, executing, monitoring & controlling, and closing phases. Creating the WBS should not be a lengthy process that will require a long time; thus, you should take the time to create it prior to entering the execution.

13. D: The project team should be concerned with "all the work" and "only the work" required to successfully complete the project and try to avoid extra work or gold plating in every way possible.

14. C: The requirements document is the output in the Collect Requirements process, not in the Define Scope process.

15. A: The decision may be based on the largest block, not the most influential block in a group even if a majority is not achieved.

16. D: Completion of the product scope is measured against the product requirements to determine successful fulfillment. The project requirements, project objectives, and the Project Scope Statement are associated with project scope.

17. C: A Work Breakdown Structure (WBS) is the foundational block to the initiating, planning, executing, monitoring & controlling, and closing phases. Normally presented in chart form, it is a deliverable-oriented hierarchical decomposition of the work to be executed by the project team to accomplish the project objectives and create the required deliverables. It provides a structure for hierarchal summation of cost, schedule, and resource information.

18. B: The most appropriate thing to do in this kind of situation is to find out the root cause of the problem, but the option is not presented here. Based on the information provided, there is no reason to find out the details and try to convince the sponsor to add the work (C & D). The project manager should inform the sponsor, but the best course of action will be to inform the stakeholders that the work could not be added. Even though there is no impact on the schedule, there may be impact on other areas. A project

manager should not implement a change request without performing an impact analysis and must get the approval for the change from the Change Control Board.

19. C: Verified deliverables are the deliverables that have been completed as per the documented scope and checked for defects by the project team members in the Control Quality process. These deliverables are inputs in the Validate Scope process and are given to the customers and stakeholders for their acceptance.

20. D: Verifying the correctness of work is associated with the Control Quality process.

21. D: Note that in this kind of situation you should always try to gather as much information as possible if the time allows. You simply should not say no without knowing the details of the change and its possible impact on the project (C). The client only mentioned that they wanted a change but did not provide you with any description of it. You may inform management (A) and also have a meeting with the team if their inputs are needed (B) but not before understanding what the change is all about.

22. C: Note that we do not usually include the activities in the WBS, especially for the large projects, even though we decompose the WBS work packages to get our activities during the Define Activities process in time management. Once the activities are defined, sequencing is done in the Sequence Activities process. Note that WBS has no particular sequence to it.

23. A: Constraints specify the limitations and restrictions, such as constraints on time, budget, scope, quality, schedule, resources, and technology that a project faces. By specifying a time limit and technology compliance, the sponsor is limiting the options for the project.

24. B: The output of the Validate Scope process is the customer acceptance of the project deliverables. This process is performed during the monitoring & controlling process group. To get approval of the phase deliverables, it is done at the end of each project phase in addition to other points to get approval for the interim deliverables. Both the Control Quality and Validate Scope processes can be performed simultaneously, but Control Quality is usually performed prior to Validate Scope. Control Quality verifies correctness of the work, whereas Validate Scope confirms completeness. Control Quality is focused on measuring specific project results against quality specifications and standards, whereas Validate Scope is mainly focused on obtaining acceptance of the product from the sponsor, customers, and other stakeholders. It is not an input to the Develop Project Management Plan or an output of the Control Quality process.

25. B: Scope planning should be performed prior to the Control Scope process. A change in one control process impacts the others; thus, the Control Scope process is integrated with other control processes.

26. D: A project manager is responsible for prioritizing the most critical issue to concentrate on. The situation here does not really specify whether the senior engineer is playing a vital role in the project or not. "Gold Plating," or giving customers extra, is not actually required in the project. The project manager should evaluate the current situation and then determine if the project will require additional time or not to complete. The most critical item for the project manager is to ensure full compliance with the city and construction industry standards.

27. D: Inspection is used as a tool & technique in the Validate Scope process, not in the Define Scope process.

28. C: You should review the Project Charter and make sure that you have inputs from all key stakeholders in order to avoid confusion and unnecessary change requests in the future. You should then concentrate on creating the Project Scope Statement, the WBS, and the project plan.

29. C: Inspection includes activities such as measuring, examining, and verifying to determine whether work and deliverables meet requirements and product acceptance criteria. Inspections are sometimes called walkthroughs, reviews, product reviews, and audits.

30. A: The Project Scope Statement, not the Requirements Documentation, describes project deliverables and the work required to create them in detail as well as the deliverables description, product acceptance criteria, requirements assumptions and constraints, and exclusions from requirements.

31. A: The team members are gaining a better understanding of the product of the project to create the Project Scope Statement by performing the product analysis. The team must have a product description before they can perform product analysis. The level of quality desired is analyzed in the plan quality management, not in product analysis. The multi-criteria decision analysis is a technique to evaluate and rank ideas. This technique uses a decision matrix based on factors such as uncertainty, expected risk levels, cost and benefit estimates, and time estimates to quantify requirements.

32. D: Nothing in this question is suggesting that you may need to cut cost, add resources, or terminate the project. Not having complete requirements will make it difficult to measure as requirements are used to measure the completion of the product of the project.

CHAPTER 6

PROJECT SCHEDULE MANAGEMENT

PROJECT SCHEDULE MANAGEMENT QUESTIONS

1. One of your team members working on the project informed you that a work package will most likely require ten weeks to complete. In the best-case scenario, if everything goes well and there are no surprises, it will take eight weeks. Since he is involved in more than two projects and has several pending deliverables, this specific work package may take eighteen weeks to complete. Based on this information, what is the range of the work package?
   A. Eleven weeks to twelve weeks
   B. Eight weeks to ten weeks
   C. 9.34 weeks to 12.66 weeks
   D. Ten weeks to eighteen weeks

2. Your project sponsor is extremely disappointed with the project as it is over budget by $15,000 and also behind schedule by several weeks. The sponsor has asked you to take care of the situation immediately and do whatever it takes. While exploring different options to shorten the project duration, you decide to put some of the noncritical activities on hold so that some of the resources working on these activities can be assigned to the activities with the most schedule risk. You also asked for a couple of additional external resources to be added to the project. The sponsor agrees to pay the additional cost since time is now a critical factor. This is an example of which of the following?
   A. Crashing
   B. Fast-tracking
   C. Critical chain method
   D. Resource leveling

3. A project manager is in the Sequence Activities process of identifying and documenting relationships among defined activities and arranging them in the order they must be performed. While in this process, the project manager decided to utilize a software tool to create a Precedence Diagramming Method (PDM) network diagram. This network diagram creates a schematic display of the sequential and logical relationships, dependencies, and the order in which activities in a project must be performed. The project manager also added the duration of each activity in the network diagram to calculate the critical path. Which one of the following is FALSE about the critical path?
   A. It is the longest duration path through a network diagram.
   B. It determines the shortest time to complete the project.
   C. The activities on the critical path represent the highest schedule risk in the project.
   D. The activities on the critical path represent critical functionality.

4. While reviewing your project resource histogram, you notice several peaks and valleys, as resources are not evenly distributed in your project. In order to evenly utilize resources as much as possible, you decide to move some activities from the week when you are using a lot of resources to the week when you are hardly using any. Which technique are you using in this case?
   A. Resource leveling
   B. Overtime
   C. Schedule compression
   D. Schedule control

5. Which one of the following takes the progressive elaboration approach and plans the work in the near term in detail and future work in a higher level?
   A. Scope definition
   B. Rolling wave planning
   C. Decomposition
   D. SWOT analysis

6. Your team just finished the design activities for a software development project. You have ordered a server and a couple of PCs to set up the development environment and are waiting for the vendor to deliver to you so that the team can start the development work. The vendor informs you that it will take twelve days for the equipment delivery, set up, and configuration. The twelve days waiting time can be defined as:
   A. Mandatory dependency
   B. Lag
   C. Lead
   D. Internal dependency

7. Which one of the following estimating techniques uses mathematical models based on historical records from other projects and can produce higher levels of accuracy?
   A. One-point estimating
   B. Analogous estimating
   C. Parametric estimating
   D. Three-points estimating

8. One of your team members is always late completing his deliverables. In order to help him out with proper planning for his activities, you like to explore different options with him. You asked the team member to send you information about the total float

and free float for all of his activities if there is any. How does free float differ from total float?
- A. Total float and free float are the same thing.
- B. Free float affects only the early start of the successor activities.
- C. Total float is the accumulated amount of free float.
- D. Subtracting the total float from the critical path duration will give the free float.

9. You are managing a project that has the following activities:
- – Activity A can start immediately and has an estimated duration of eight weeks.
- – Activity B can also start immediately and has an estimated duration of seven weeks.
- – Activity C can start after Activity A is completed and has an estimated duration of one week.
- – Activity D can start after Activity B is completed and has an estimated duration of six weeks.
- – Activity E can start after both Activities C and D are completed and has an estimated duration of seven weeks.
- – Activity F can start after Activity D is completed and has an estimated duration of two weeks.

Your sponsor is very disappointed that the project is taking longer than he expected and asked you to shorten the project duration by at least two weeks. You decided to shorten Activity A first as it is not a very critical activity in the project and has the longest duration. What will be the impact of your decision?
- A. It will not shorten the duration of the project.
- B. It will shorten the duration of the project.
- C. It will create a new critical path.
- D. The project duration will be eighteen weeks now.

10. A project manager is managing a web-based application project to automate the accounting processes of his organization. The project has an estimated budget of $120,000 and a duration of nine months. While reviewing the project, the project manager notices that activities were scheduled in sequential order but coding work was initiated twelve days earlier than planned. What type of relationship represents the start of the coding work to the completion of the design work?
- A. Finish-to-start relationship with a twelve-day lag
- B. Finish-to-start relationship with a twelve-day lead
- C. Start-to-finish with a twelve-day lag
- D. Start-to-finish with a twelve-day lead

11. While working with your team members on activity sequencing, a team member identifies that even though a series of activities are planned to be completed in a specific sequence, they can be performed in parallel. What type of activity sequencing method may be utilized in this situation?
- A. Critical path
- B. Resource leveling method
- C. Monte Carlo simulation
- D. Precedence Diagramming Method (PDM)

12. You are the project manager overseeing the implementation of a new computer infrastructure at the local hospital. Your sponsor has informed you that all the existing applications must work in the new infrastructure, and the project should be completed in three months. These are examples of:
- A. A lag
- B. A lead
- C. An estimation
- D. A constraint

13. One of your team members is always late completing his deliverables. You decided to keep an eye on this team member's activities to avoid any delay in the project. While reviewing one of the activities of this team member, you found out that the activity has an early start of day 5, an early finish of day 12, a late start of day 15, and a late finish of day 22. The team member tells you that he needs an additional four days to complete the activity due to various reasons he can think of. Which one of the following statements is TRUE?
- A. This activity will delay the project.
- B. This activity will most probably not delay the project.
- C. The activity has a lag.
- D. The successor activity will be delayed.

14. Which one of the following analysis methods usually uses Monte Carlo simulation to simulate the outcome of a project by making use of three-point estimates (Optimistic, Pessimistic, Most Likely) for each activity, a huge number of simulated scheduling possibilities, or a few selected scenarios that are most likely, and the network diagram?
- A. Precedence Diagramming Method (PDM)
- B. What-if scenario analysis
- C. Critical chain method
- D. Resource leveling

15. A project manager managing a recruitment automation application project just completed developing the schedule and

requested stakeholders and the client for their approval. The sponsor has expressed her frustration about the unexpected long duration of the project and has demanded the schedule be compressed as much as possible. While exploring different options, you find out that you cannot really change the network diagram due to various constraints, but the sponsor has agreed to pay for additional personnel resources if needed. What will be your BEST option in this situation?

A. Apply the critical chain method
B. Fast-track the project and also apply the resource leveling method
C. Crash the project
D. Crash and fast-track the project

16. Your project sponsor is extremely disappointed with the project as it is over budget by $20,000 and also behind schedule by several weeks. The sponsor has asked you to take care of the situation immediately. While exploring different options to shorten the project duration, you decide, with management's approval, to perform several activities in parallel rather than in sequential order as originally planned. You know your option will possibly result in rework, increase risks, and require more communication, but you decide to go for it any way. This is an example of which of the following?

A. Critical chain method
B. Crashing
C. Resource leveling
D. Fast-tracking

17. You have recently been assigned as a program manager to implement an ERP solution in your organization. Initially, the team will only work on five key modules in the first phase of the project. The second phase of the project has not been approved yet. You have estimated that three of the modules will take ten days each, and the remaining two will be completed in fifteen days each. It is not possible to work on these modules in parallel. What would be the approximate duration for the first phase of your project?

A. Fifty-five to sixty-five days
B. Fifty days
C. Ten days
D. Ninety days

18. You are in the Control Schedule process of monitoring the status of the project by comparing the result to the plan, updating project progress, and managing changes to the project schedule baseline. You are mainly focused on the current status and changes to the project schedule, influential factors that create schedule changes, and management of actual changes as they occur. Which of the following is NOT a tool or technique in this Schedule Management process?

A. Schedule compression
B. Critical Path Method
C. Resource optimization
D. Schedule forecasts

19. Steve has just been assigned as a project manager for a newly approved software development project. The sponsor is interested in knowing a high-level estimation on the total duration of the project and asks Steve to send him the information by the end of the day. What kind of estimate should Steve use in this kind of situation?

A. An analogous estimate
B. A heuristic estimate
C. A three-point estimate
D. A bottom-up estimate

20. You are in the Estimate Activity Durations process to estimate durations for the activities of the project. These estimates usually originated from project team members most familiar with the activity and then progressively elaborated. Which one of the following is TRUE about this process?

A. This process must be performed after the Develop Schedule process.
B. Padding is a common practice and the project manager should not be too worried about it.
C. The duration estimates are outputs in this process.
D. It is not important that all estimates in this process should use a common work unit/period.

21. You just completed developing the schedule for your project and got the approval from stakeholders and the sponsor. One of the team members assigned to work on a critical component informs you that she needs additional time to complete her activities as several relevant pieces were missed during planning. Her updated estimate would have no impact on the critical path; thus, the project duration would be the same. The best approach the project manager may take in this situation will be:

A. Find a replacement for the resource who can complete the task within the allocated time.
B. Inform the resource that it is too late for any kind of change in the project schedule.
C. Inform her that it is OK as you have sufficient schedule reserve to handle this kind of situation.
D. Update the project schedule and other relevant plans to reflect the new estimate.

22. You are overseeing a data center project for one of your clients. The team members have finished creating the Work Breakdown Structure (WBS) and Work Breakdown Structure Dictionary. The team members also submitted their activity duration estimates to you. What should you focus on NEXT?

A. Sequence the activities using the precedence diagramming method.
B. Create the activity list.
C. Determine high-level project assumptions and constraints.
D. Develop the project schedule.

23. You are overseeing a data center project for one of your clients. The team members have finished creating the Work Breakdown Structure (WBS) and Work Breakdown Structure Dictionary. The team members also completed activity sequencing and submitted their activity duration estimates to you. Recently, you developed the project schedule. What should you focus on NEXT?
A. Finalize the schedule
B. Control the schedule
C. Compress the schedule
D. Gain approval

24. Your IT project is progressing well and is on schedule when a vendor sends you an e-mail stating that the equipment delivery will be delayed by a week due to severe snow storm on the East Coast. Which of the documents would best capture the impact of the delay on the project schedule?
A. Risk Register
B. Issue Log
C. Network Diagram
D. Work Breakdown Structure

25. Your IT project has ten team members, and recently you have hired three more database developers. You are using a time-phased graphical display of activity start dates, end dates, and durations for tracking progress and reporting to the team. Which chart are you using?
A. Milestone Chart
B. Work breakdown Structure
C. Network Diagram
D. Gantt Chart

26. You are overseeing a project to implement a web-based traffic monitoring system. You have requested three programmers, three database developers, and two testers; senior management only approved five team members for your project. Which one of the following may you use to produce a resource-limited schedule by letting the schedule slip and cost increase in order to deal with a limited amount of resources, resource availability, and other resource constraints?
A. Resource Leveling
B. Fast-Tracking
C. Crashing
D. Critical Path Method

27. Steve is the project manager for a construction project to convert an old nursing home into a new multistory office complex. The architectural design and site surveys are completed, and Steve is now waiting for the clearance and permit from the city to start the construction. This is an example of which kind of dependency?
A. Mandatory dependency
B. Internal dependency
C. External dependency
D. Discretionary dependency

28. Your team has been working with the WBS for a while and has completed the decomposition of the work packages. After a week, the team finalized the estimates of all activities and completed the network diagram. Which of the following activities will be the next to concentrate on for the project manager?
A. Develop a preliminary schedule and get the approval from the team members
B. Finalize the Project Scope Statement
C. Use the precedence diagramming method for sequencing the activities
D. Develop the risk management plan and add it to the total Project Management Plan document

29. Which of the following is FALSE about analogous estimating?
A. It measures the project parameters such as budget, duration, size, complexity, and duration based on the parameters of a previous similar project and historical information.
B. It is usually done during the early phase of the project when not much information is available.
C. It uses a bottom-up approach.
D. It usually is the overall project estimate given to the project manager from management or the sponsor.

30. You recently took over a project from another project manager. While reviewing the network diagram, you find that there are four critical paths and three near-critical paths. What can you conclude about the project?
A. The project will likely be completed on time and within budget.
B. The project is at high risk.
C. The project will require more people and additional budget.

D.   The project should be terminated.

31. You are overseeing a data center project for one of your clients. The team members have finished creating the Work Breakdown Structure (WBS) and Work Breakdown Structure Dictionary. The team members also submitted their activity duration estimates to you. Recently, you came up with the project estimate by adding estimates for all activities from the team members. What did you do wrong in this case?

A. The estimates should be coming from senior management
B. The project estimate should be the same as the required completion date from the customer
C. You didn't use a Network Diagram
D. You should come up with the estimates for all activities by yourself

32. Your project sponsor is extremely disappointed with the project as it is over budget by $20,000 and also behind schedule by several weeks. The sponsor has asked you to take care of the situation immediately. While desperately exploring different options to shorten the project duration, you realize that you have no access to additional resources. Your team took care almost all of the risk items and currently you have only discretionary dependencies. As a project manager, what will be your best course of action?

A.   Remove a big activity from the project
B.   Remove resources from an activity
C.   Add additional resources to complete remaining activities faster
D.   Fast track the project

PROJECT SCHEDULE MANAGEMENT ANSWERS

1. C: PERT allows the estimator to include three estimates: optimistic, pessimistic, and most likely, given by the equation:
Expected Activity Duration (EAD) – Beta distribution = (O + M + P) / 6

= (8 + 4*10 + 18) / 6 = 11 weeks
STD Dev = (P – O) / 6 = (18 – 8) / 6 = 1.66
Range = EAD – / + Std Dev
Thus, the range is 11 – / + 1.66 = 9.34 to 12.66

2. A: The best option here is to add additional resources to the project activities on the critical path to complete them quickly. Fast-tracking is the technique of doing critical path activities in parallel when they were originally planned in series. Resource leveling is used to produce a resource-limited schedule by letting the schedule slip and cost increase in order to deal with a limited amount of resources, resource availability, and other resource constraints. The critical chain method is another way to develop an approved, realistic, and resource-limited formal schedule. It provides a way to view and manage uncertainty when building the project schedule.

3. D: The activities on the critical path do not necessarily represent the critical functionalities in the project. The critical path is the longest duration path in the network diagram, and this duration is the shortest time needed to complete the project. The activities on the critical path have no buffer, and any delay in the critical path activities will delay the project; thus, the critical path activities represent the highest schedule risk.

4. A: Resource leveling is used to produce a resource-limited schedule by letting the schedule slip and cost increase in order to deal with a limited amount of resources, resource availability, and other resource constraints. It can be used when shared or critically required resources are only available at certain times, are in limited quantities, or when resources have been over allocated. We may have several peaks and valleys in our resource histogram. In order to level the resources, evenly utilize them as much as possible, or to keep resource usage at a constant level, we can move some of our activities from the week when we are using a lot of resources to the week when we are hardly using any.

5. B: The rolling wave planning takes the progressive elaboration approach and plans the work in the near term in detail and future work in a higher level. During the early strategic planning phase, work packages may be decomposed into less-defined milestone levels since all details are not available, and later they are decomposed into detailed activities. This kind of planning is usually used in IT and research projects but is very unlikely in construction projects where any unknowns are extremely expensive and destructive.

6. B: A lag is an inserted waiting time between activities.

7. C: This estimate uses mathematical models based on historical records from other projects. It utilizes the statistical relationship that exists between a series of historical data and a particular delineated list of other variables. Depending upon the quality of the underlying data, this estimate can produce higher levels of accuracy and can be used in conjunction with other estimates to provide estimates for the entire project or for specific segments of the project. Measures such as time per line of code, time per installation, and time per linear meter are considered in this type of estimate.

8. B: Total float is the amount of time an activity can be delayed without affecting the project completion date. Free float is the amount of time an activity can be delayed without affecting the early start of its successor.

9. A: Shortening Activity A will have no impact on the project duration as it is not on the critical path. We have three paths here:
Start, A, C, E, End = 16 wks
Start, B, D, F, End = 15 wks
Start, B, D, E, End = 20 wks
We should not always look for the activity with the longest duration to cut as it will not shorten the duration of the project if the activity is not on the critical path. Shortening Activity A will not shorten the project duration as it is not on the critical path, and neither will a new critical path be created. To shorten the project duration, we should always try to shorten the duration of the activities on the critical path.
Here the critical path is Start, B, D, E, End, which has a duration of twenty weeks. We can explore the option to shorten the duration of Activities B, D or E, but it is better to go for the first activity and shorten the duration of Activity B.

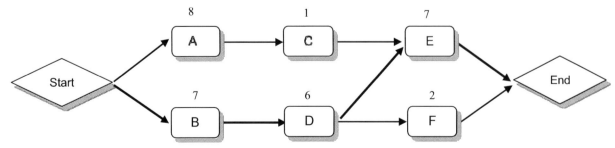

10. B: A lead is an acceleration of the successor activity, or in other words, a successor activity getting a jump start. A lead may be added to start an activity before the predecessor activity is completed. There is a finish-to-start relationship between the design and coding, meaning that design work should be completed prior to starting coding. But in this case, coding work had a jump start as it was initiated twelve days before the design was completed. This can be shown as a finish-to-start relationship with twelve days lead.

11. D: The precedence diagramming method creates a schematic display of the sequential and logical relationships of the project activities. Usually, it shows dependencies and the order in which activities in a project must be performed. Critical path is not a diagramming method.

12. D: These are examples of a constraint or limitation that limits options and eliminates alternatives in the project.

13. B: There is not much information to determine if the activity has a lag or not. The float/buffer of this activity is Late Finish – Early Finish = 10 days. The activity is not on the critical path because it has a float or buffer of ten days. Even if the team member takes four additional days to complete the activity, it probably will have no impact on the project schedule or on the successor activity.

14. B: What-if Scenario Analysis usually uses Monte Carlo simulation to simulate the outcome of a project by making use of three-point estimates (optimistic, pessimistic, most likely) for each activity, a huge number of simulated scheduling possibilities, or a few selected scenarios that are most likely, and the network diagram. The outcome of this analysis may be used to evaluate the project schedule under adverse conditions and to develop the preventive and contingency action plan to reduce the impact and probability of the unexpected situations.

15. C: Fast-tracking is the technique of doing critical path activities in parallel when they were originally planned in series. Fast-tracking will not be an option in this case since you cannot change the network diagram, or in other words, you cannot perform activities in parallel that were originally planned to be completed in sequence. The best option here is to add additional resources to the project activities on the critical path to complete them quickly. Resource leveling is used to produce a resource-limited schedule by letting the schedule slip and cost increase in order to deal with a limited amount of resources, resource availability, and other resource constraints. The critical chain method is another way to develop an approved, realistic, resource-limited, and formal schedule. It provides a way to view and manage uncertainty when building the project schedule.

16. D: Fast-tracking is the technique of doing critical path activities in parallel when they were originally planned in series.

17. A: The duration of three modules is 10 * 3 = 30 days, and the remaining two modules is 2 * 15 = 30 days. The first phase of the project will take 30 + 30 = 60 days, or approximately between fifty-five and sixty-five days.

18. D: The schedule forecasts are outputs of the Control Schedule process, not tools & techniques.

19. A: An analogous estimate is usually done during the early phase of the project when not much information is available about the project. It is less accurate even though it is less costly and less time consuming. In a bottom-up approach, one estimate per activity is received from the team members; it requires significant time to develop. A heuristic estimate is based on rule of thumb. A PERT estimate, also known as a weighted average estimate, is usually associated with specific project activities and requires significant time to develop as well.

20. C: The duration estimates are outputs in the Estimate Activity Durations process. This process should be performed before the Develop Schedule process. Adding additional time or padding the estimate is a common practice in this process, so the project manager should make sure that the estimates from the team members are realistic. It is important that all estimates in this process should use a common work unit/period.

21. D: The best course of action will be to update the project schedule and other relevant plans to reflect the new estimate.

22. A: Your team has created the WBS, WBS Dictionary, and activity list and has submitted the activity durations. The next step should be to sequence the activities by creating a network diagram using the precedence diagramming method. Determining high-level project assumptions and constraints is done as part of project initiation and is completed much earlier. The Develop Schedule process follows the Sequence Activities process. Note that sequencing activities can be done before or after the activity duration estimation is done.

23. C: The Control Schedule process is the next process after the Develop Schedule process, but all the activities of the Develop Schedule process are not completed yet. Once the schedule is developed, it should be compressed, finalized, and approved by the stakeholders. Then you should start controlling the schedule.

24. C: The project network diagram represents activities and their logical relationships, dependencies, and sequence; thus, the network diagram will best capture the impact of the delay on the project schedule. The work breakdown structure is a deliverable-oriented hierarchical decomposition of the work to be executed by the project team to accomplish the project objectives and create the required deliverables, but it does not focus on the duration of the project activities. The risk register would show an increase in project risk but would not help to determine the impact of a delay on the project schedule. An issue log will also capture the root cause, person assigned, due date, and other factors but will not give out much information about the impact of the delay on the project schedule.

25. D: A Gantt chart or bar chart is a time-phased graphical display of activity start dates, end dates, and durations. It is useful for

tracking progress and reporting to the team and can be easily modified to show the percentage of completed work. As the project progresses, bars are shaded to show which activities are now completed. The work breakdown structure is a deliverable-oriented hierarchical decomposition of the work to be executed by the project team to accomplish the project objectives and create the required deliverables, but it does not focus on the duration of the project activities. A milestone chart is similar to a bar chart but only shows major events. It is a good tool for reporting to management and customers. This type of chart is reserved for brief, high-level presentations as too much detail may be undesirable and distracting to senior management. A network diagram is a schematic display of the sequential and logical relationships of the project activities. It shows dependencies and the order in which activities in a project must be performed.

26. A: Resource leveling is used to produce a resource-limited schedule by letting the schedule slip and cost increase in order to deal with a limited amount of resources, resource availability, and other resource constraints. It can be used when shared or critically required resources are only available at certain times, are in limited quantities, or when resources have been over allocated. Fast-tracking is the technique of doing critical path activities in parallel when they were originally planned in series. Crashing is the technique of adding additional resources to a project activity to complete it more quickly. The critical path is the longest path through a network diagram and determines the shortest time to complete the project as well as any scheduling flexibility. It is not the project schedule, but it indicates the time period within which an activity could be scheduled considering activity duration, logical relationships, dependencies, leads, lags, assumptions, and constraints.

27. C: External dependencies are driven by circumstances or authority outside the project and must be considered during the process of sequencing the activities. Internal dependencies are based on the needs of the project and are mostly under the control of the project team. Mandatory dependencies are mandatory and unavoidable dependencies that are inherent in the nature of the work or are contractually required. They are like laws of nature and are also called "hard logic." Discretionary dependencies are also called "preferred logic" or "soft logic" as they are the preference of the project planner and the team members. These dependencies may be determined by best practices or by local methodology and may vary from project to project.

28. A: The project manager should now focus on developing the preliminary schedule and get the approval from the team members. Finalizing the Project Scope Statement should have been completed prior to completing the WBS. The team members have completed the network diagram, which suggests that the activities sequencing is also completed. Since the project schedule is an input to risk management, developing the risk management plan should be done once the schedule is completed.

29. C: Analogous estimates take a top-down approach, and the overall project estimate is usually given to the project manager from the management or the sponsor. It is usually done during the early phase of the project when not much information is available. It is less accurate even though it is less costly and less time consuming. In a bottom-up approach, one estimate per activity is received from the team members.

30. B: The project is definitely at high risk because activities on critical path and near critical path can be delayed anytime causing the entire project to be delayed. Having more than one critical path and several near-critical paths does not necessarily mean that more resources and additional budget will be required to complete the project. There is no valid reason to terminate the project just because it is at high risk of schedule delay.

31. C: As a project manager, you should not be coming up with individual activity estimate. The team members will be working on the activities and should come up with the estimates for their activities. Estimates should also not be coming from senior management or customers but they may let you know their expected completion date for the project. You will be able to identify that some activities may take place concurrently by refrying to your Network Diagram. If you just add up all the activity estimates without considering the sequence and concurrent activities, your estimate will not be correct.

32. D: Removing an activity may save you time but your customer will be very unhappy if you do so. Removing resources will not really save you any time. You can't add additional resources as you have no access to it. Since most of the risk items are closed and you have discretionary or preferential dependencies, you should be fast-tracking or working on some of the activities concurrently.

CHAPTER 7

PROJECT
COST
MANAGEMENT

PROJECT COST MANAGEMENT QUESTIONS

1. For an IT project your EV = $130,500, PV = $125,500, and AC = $129,000. Which one of the following statements is TRUE?
   - A. The project is behind schedule and over budget.
   - B. The project is ahead of schedule and under budget.
   - C. The project is behind schedule and under budget.
   - D. The project is ahead of schedule and over budget.

2. You recently took over a project from another project manager who left the organization. You find out that the project has a BAC = $45,000, PV = $30,000, cumulative AC = $25,000, and cumulative EV = $24,000. You decided to perform a forecasting analysis and calculated the values for EAC, ETC, TCPI, and VAC. Which of the following is NOT true?
   - A. You will need $21,875 more to complete this project.
   - B. The project will cost $46,875.
   - C. The project performance is not good as TCPI is 1.05.
   - D. The project will be under budget by $1,875.

3. You are in the Determine Budget process of developing a budget or cost baseline and project funding requirements. All of the following are inputs in this process EXCEPT:
   - A. Work performance data
   - B. Cost Management Plan
   - C. Activity cost estimates
   - D. Project schedule

4. To develop an online accounting application for your software development project, you are working on figuring out the total funding requirements and periodic funding requirements of the project. Which of the following will help you the MOST in this case?
   - A. Project budget and contingency reserves
   - B. Funding limit reconciliation
   - C. Cost baseline and management reserves
   - D. Management reserves and contingency reserves

5. You are in the Determine Budget process of developing a budget or cost baseline and project funding requirements. All of the following are tools & techniques in this process EXCEPT:
   - A. Cost aggregation
   - B. Reserve analysis
   - C. Funding limit reconciliation
   - D. Performance review

6. You are the project manager of a construction project that will take six months to complete and will cost $75,000/month. At the end of the third month, you were asked to find out the cumulative SPI for the project and report it to management. While reviewing the project status, you found that you have spent $80,000 in the first month, $72,000 in the second month, and $75,000 in the third month. You also found that the project was 15 percent complete at the end of first month, 35 percent complete at the end of second month, and 45 percent complete at the end of third month. If you planned to complete 50 percent of the work by this time, what is the cumulative SPI at the end of month three?
   - A. 0.5
   - B. 0.9
   - C. 0.34
   - D. 1.1

7. A project manager working on a construction project planned to install new carpets in all four rooms of the house. She measured the square footage of all the rooms and then multiplied that figure by a set cost factor to estimate the cost for installing the carpet. This is an example of:
   - A. Bottom-up estimating
   - B. Analogous estimating
   - C. Parametric estimating
   - D. Three-point estimating

8. With the help of your team members, you just finished the development of an approximation of the costs of all resources, such as labor, materials, equipment, services, facilities, and other special items associated with each schedule activity. What should you do NEXT?
   - A. Control costs
   - B. Resource leveling
   - C. Bottom-up estimating
   - D. Determine budget

9. Steve, a project manager, is trying to figure out the performance that must be achieved in order to meet the financial and schedule goals in his project. He is using a measurement that will give him the status on the remaining work with respect to the funds

remaining. Which of the following measures is Steve using?
- A. Cost aggregation
- B. Variance analysis
- C. Trend analysis
- D. To-Complete Performance Index (TCPI)

10. You are overseeing a mobile application development project. While reviewing an earned value report, you observe that the SPI is 1.2 and the CPI is 0.9. Which statement can you make about the project?
- A. On track according to schedule and budget baselines.
- B. Behind the schedule and over budget.
- C. Ahead of the schedule and over budget.
- D. On schedule and under budget.

11. Your project has a budget of $900,000 and is running well. In the latest earned value report, the team reported that the CPI = 1.1, the SPI = 0.9, and the PV = $600,000. You want to know, from this point on, how much more the project will cost but could not find it in the report. What will be the estimate to complete, or ETC, be in this case?
- A. $300,000
- B. $327,272
- C. $818,181
- D. $490,909

12. You recently finalized your project cost estimate and cost baseline. The difference between the project cost estimate and the cost baseline can be BEST described as:
- A. The control account estimates
- B. The work package estimates
- C. The management reserves
- D. The contingency reserves

13. You asked one of your team members about the schedule variance (SV) for one of her key deliverables. She mentioned that she is behind schedule but there would not be any cost variance. Which of the following is NOT true in this case?
- A. EV and PV were the same
- B. EV and AC were the same
- C. EV is less than PV
- D. CPI is 1

14. There were eight potential projects in your organization, and your senior management wanted to select the best project that would meet and exceed the organizational strategic goals and objectives. As your organization has limited resources and time constraints, it developed business cases for these projects and compared the benefits to select the best project. Out of eight projects, management has selected two projects and later on decided to go for Project X, which would yield $250,000 in benefits instead of Project Y, which would yield $200,000. What is the opportunity cost for selecting Project X over Project Y?
- A. $250,000
- B. $200,000
- C. – $250,000
- D. – $200,000

15. You are overseeing a project to implement an accounting application for a dentist's office. In one of the performance meetings, you came up with the following measurement: AC = 500, PV = 600, and EV = 650. What is going on with this project?
- A. Both CV and SV are positive numbers; thus, you are under budget and ahead of schedule.
- B. You do not have enough information to calculate SPI and CPI.
- C. The CV is a negative number, which means you have spent more than planned.
- D. The SV is a negative number, which means the project is behind schedule.

16. The project manager and the team members have just finished working on the WBS and have almost finalized the project schedule. The project manager is also planning to start working on the project budget. Which document will be used for planning, estimating, budgeting, and controlling costs so that the project can be completed within the approved budget?
- A. Earned value management
- B. Cost baseline
- C. Cost Management Plan
- D. Funding limit reconciliation

17. The Earned Value Management (EVM) will NOT be very beneficial in which situation?
- A. To measure a project's progress against the project scope, cost, and schedule baselines.

B. To forecast future performance and the project's completion date and final cost.

C. To provide schedule and budget variances during the project.

D. To develop the project cost baseline.

18. A project manager is working on a project designed to create an internal website for ITPro Consultancy, LLC that will allow them to schedule the conference room online. While reviewing the status of the project, the project manager found out the EV, AC, and PV (listed in the table below). What are the cumulative SPI and CPI for Week 5?

Week	PV	EV	AC
Week 1	$20,000	$20,000	$17,500
Week 2	$25,000	$24,000	$19,000
Week 3	$40,000	$36,000	$27,000
Week 4	$70,000	$64,000	$32,000
Week 5	$87,000	$80,000	$45,000

A. 0.925 and 1.59

B. 1.59 and .925

C. 0.919 and 1.77

D. 1.77 and 0.919

19. You are preparing a Cost Management Plan for the data center project you are managing for ITPro Consultancy, LLC. All of the following is true regarding this plan EXCEPT:

A. Activity cost estimates will be rounded to a prescribed precision; for example, $100, $1,000, and so on.

B. Units of measurement such as hours, days, weeks, or a lump sum amount will be used to estimate resources.

C. The primary concern is determining the amount of resources needed to complete the project activities.

D. The WBS provides a framework for the Cost Management Plan, and a control account (CA) in the WBS is used to monitor and control the project cost.

20. You estimated your project cost to be $80,000 with a timeline of eight months. After four months in the project, you found out that 40 percent of the project is completed; the actual cost is $25,000. What does the SPI tell you in this case?

A. There is not enough information to calculate the SPI.

B. The project is behind schedule.

C. The project is ahead of schedule.

D. The project is progressing as per the plan.

21. You estimated your project cost to be $80,000 with a timeline of eight months. As of today, you found out that 40 percent of the project is completed; the actual cost is $30,000. What does the CPI tell you in this case?

A. There is not enough information to calculate the CPI.

B. The project is over budget.

C. The project is under budget.

D. The project is costing as per the plan.

22. You just completed your Cost Management Plan and defined how the project cost will be planned, managed, expended, and controlled throughout the project life cycle. You also looked into your variance threshold, which is usually expressed as percentage deviations from the cost baseline that the sponsor or stakeholders are willing to allow before any action is required. This threshold is called:

A. Approved threshold

B. Variance limit

C. Control threshold

D. Control limit

23. Which one of the following is FALSE about TCPI?

A. TCPI calculates the performance that must be achieved in order to meet financial or schedule goals.

B. TCPI usually determines the status on the remaining work with respect to the funds remaining.

C. If the cumulative CPI falls below the baseline plan, all future work must be performed at the TCPI to achieve the planned BAC.

D. If the cumulative CPI falls below the baseline plan, all future work must be performed below the TCPI to achieve the planned BAC.

24. All of the following statements are true about cost baseline EXCEPT:

A. It is a time-phased budget used to monitor, measure, and control cost performance during the project.

B. It is usually displayed in the form of an S-curve.

C. It assigns cost estimates for expected future period operating costs.

D. It aggregates the estimated costs of project activities to work packages, then to control accounts, and finally to the project.

25. While working on your project budget, you also calculated the contingency reserve. This contingency reserve is the estimated cost to be determined, managed, and controlled at your discretion to deal with which of the following?

A. To compensate inadequacies in your original cost planning.

B. To address the cost impact of the risks remaining during the Plan Risk Responses process.

C. To handle anticipated and certain events in your project.

D. To handle unanticipated events or surprises in your project.

26. Lori is the project manager for a software development firm and has been assigned to create an accounting automation application for a dentist's office. While reviewing the cost estimate with Lori, the sponsor expressed her frustration with the higher cost and asked to reduce the estimate by at least ten percent. The sponsor is not too worried about the project duration estimate and suggested that Lori seek her help with the schedule if needed. What is the best course of action for Lori in this kind of situation?

A. Replace a couple of expensive resources with lower-cost resources.

B. Continue with the project and constantly find an opportunity to save money for a total savings of 10 percent.

C. Have an urgent meeting with the team members and ask them to be innovative and squeeze their estimate.

D. Inform the sponsor of the activities to be cut.

27. Selina is a project manager involved in the Estimate Costs process in the early phase of her project when a limited amount of detail was available to her. The range of her estimate was $75,000 to $200,000, and the actual cost came to be around $150,000. What would you call such an estimate?

A. A variable estimate

B. A definitive estimate

C. A rough order of magnitude estimate

D. A budget estimate

28. You have fifteen components to work on in a software development project. As per your estimation, the first six components would cost $1,500 each, and the remaining nine would cost $1,400 each. Your schedule projected that you would be done with 40 percent of the components today. While collecting the status updates from the team members, you found out that the first five components were completed at a cost of $8,000. What is the SPI?

A. 1.20

B. 0.132

C. 0.833

A. Cannot be determined

29. You are working on a project to convert an old nursing home to a new office complex. While reviewing the progress of your project, you found out that your EV = $26,000 and AC = $27,000. One of your site supervisors calls to inform you that there are several damages in the foundation that were not discovered earlier, and it will result in a significant cost overrun. What will you do FIRST?

A. Make sure that the contingency reserves you have will be sufficient enough to cover the cost overrun.

B. Call the sponsor immediately and inform her that additional funds will be needed.

C. Ask the supervisor to figure out why these damages were not discovered earlier.

D. Evaluate the cause and size of this cost overrun.

30. You are managing a software application project budgeted for $90,000 to develop an online PMP exam simulator. The team has completed design work, received approval from technical review team, and initiated coding work. You think that the current variances are atypical, and that similar variances will not occur in the future. You found that AC = $30,000 and EV = $35,000. What is your Estimate at Completion (EAC)?

A. $85,000

B. $77,586

C. $90,000

D. $60,000

PROJECT COST MANAGEMENT ANSWERS

1. B: The EV is greater than the PV, which indicates the project is ahead of schedule. The AC is smaller than the EV, which indicates the project is under budget.

2. D: We are given the following values: BAC = $45,000
PV = $30,000
Cumulative AC = 25,000 Cumulative EV = 24,000
We know

$EAC = BAC/CPI^c$
$ETC = EAC - AC$
$VAC = BAC - EAC$ and
$TCPI = (BAC - EV) / (BAC - AC)$
$CPI^c = EV^c/AC^c$
Thus $CPI^c = \$24,000/\$25,000 = 0.96$

So $EAC = BAC/CPI^c = \$45,000/0.96 = \$46,875$
$ETC = EAC - AC = \$46,875 - \$25,000 = \$21,875$
$TCPI = (BAC - EV) / (BAC - AC) = (45,000 - 24,000) / (45,000 - 25,000) = 21,000 / 20,000 = 1.05$
$VAC = BAC - EAC = \$45,000 - \$46,875 = -\$1,875$

The project will cost $46,875 since the EAC is $46,875. The ETC is $21,875, so you will need $21,875 to complete the project. The VAC is –$1,875; thus, the project will be over budget by $1,875. The project performance is not good as TCPI is 1.05. All of the statements are true except D. The project is over budget by $ 1,875, not under budget.

3. A: Work performance data is not an input in the Develop Budget process but an input in the Control Costs process.

4. C: Total fund or cost budget = cost baseline + management reserves Cost baseline = project cost + contingency reserves
The cost baseline is the project cost plus the contingency reserves, and the cost budget, or how much money the company should have available for the project, is the cost baseline plus the management reserves. The project manager determines, manages, and controls the contingency reserves, which will address the cost impact of the risks remaining during the Plan Risk Responses process. On the other hand, management reserves are funds to cover unforeseen risks or changes to the project. In this case, the cost baseline and the management reserves will be most helpful to calculate the total funding and periodic funding requirements. Funding limit reconciliation is the technique of reconciling the expenditure of funds with the funding limits set for the project. As per the variance between the expenditure of funds and planned limit, the activities can be rescheduled to level out the rate of expenditures.

5. D: Performance review is not a tool & technique in the Develop Budget process but a tool & technique in the Control Costs process.

6. B: We have BAC = 6 * $75,000 = $450,000
At the end of month three, we were supposed to finish 50 percent of the work.
Thus, PV = BAC * Planned % Complete or PV = $450,000 * 50 percent = $225,000
Also, project work is 45 percent completed at the end of three months.
Thus, EV = BAC * Actual % Complete or EV = $450,000 * 45 percent = $202,500
Both the PV and EV are cumulative values in three months.
We know $SPI^c = EV^c/PV^c$ or $SPI^c = \$202,500/\$225,000 = 0.9$

7. C: This estimate uses mathematical models based on historical records from other projects. It utilizes the statistical relationship that exists between a series of historical data and a particular delineated list of other variables. Depending upon the quality of the underlying data, this estimate can produce higher levels of accuracy and can be used in conjunction with other estimates to provide estimates for the entire project or specific segments of a project. Measures such as time per line of code, time per installation, and time per linear meter are considered in this type of estimate.

8. D: You just completed the Estimate Costs process and should be focusing on the Determine Budget process.

9. D: To-Complete Performance Index (TCPI) calculates the performance that must be achieved in order to meet financial or schedule goals.
If targeting the current plan, $TCPI = (BAC - EV) / (BAC - AC)$
If targeting the current EAC, $TCPI = (BAC - EV) / (EAC - AC)$
Here AC = Actual Cost, EV = Earned Value, EAC = Estimate at Completion, and BAC = Budget at Completion. Here (BAC – EV) is the remaining work and (BAC – AC) or (EAC – AC) is the remaining fund.

10. C: A SPI of 1.2 means that the project is ahead of schedule, and a CPI of 0.9 or less than one means that the project is over budget.

11. B: We know ETC = EAC – AC, so we need to find out the values for Estimate at Completion (EAC) and Actual Cost (AC).

We are given the following values: BAC = \$900,000
CPI = 1.1
SPI = 0.9
PV = \$600,000
We also know that EAC = BAC/CPI; thus EAC = \$900,000/1.1 = \$818,181 Now we have SPI = 0.9 or EV/PV = 0.9; thus EV = 0.9 * PV
So EV = 0.9 * 600,000 = \$540,000
We also know that CPI = 1.1 or EV/AC = 1.1; thus, EV = 1.1 * AC So AC = EV/1.1 or AC = 540,000/1.1 = \$490,909
So ETC = EAC – AC or ETC = \$818,181 – \$490,909 = \$327,272

12. D: The cost baseline is the project cost plus the contingency reserves; thus, the difference between the project cost estimate and the cost baseline can be best described as contingency reserves.

13. A: We know SV = EV – PV. Since SV has a negative value, EV must be less than PV.
Also, CV = EV – AC. Since there will be no cost variance, EV and AC have the same value. CPI is also EV/AC = 1.

14. B: The opportunity cost is the value of the project that was not selected or the opportunity that was missed out on. In this case, the opportunity cost for Project X is the value of the Project Y, or \$200,000.

15. A: We know SV = EV – PV and CV = EV – AC So SV = 650 – 600 = 50 and CV = 650 – 500 = 150
A positive CV indicates that the project is under budget, and a positive SV indicates that the project is ahead of schedule.

16. C: The project Cost Management Plan is a component of the overall project management plan, and it defines how the project cost will be planned, managed, expended, and controlled throughout the project life cycle.

17. D: Earned value analysis provides a means to determine cost and schedule variances, not to develop the project cost baseline.

18. A: We know that $SPI^c = EV^c/PV^c$ and $CPI^c = EV^c/AC^c$
At the end of Week 5, the cumulative EV = \$20,000 + \$24,000 + \$36,000 + \$64,000 + \$80,000 = \$224,000
Cumulative PV = \$20,000 + \$25,000 + \$40,000 + \$70,000 + \$87,000 = \$242,000
Cumulative AC = \$17,500 + \$19,000 + \$27,000 + \$32,000 + \$45,000 = \$140,500
$SPI^c = EV^c/PV^c$
= 224,000/242,000
= 0.925
$CPI^c = EV^c/AC^c$
= 224,000/140,500
= 1.59

19. C: The primary concern for Project Cost Management is to determine the cost of resources, not the amount to complete the project activities.

20. B: Here we have BAC = \$80,000
We know that EV = BAC * Actual % Complete
So EV = BAC * 40 percent completion = \$80,000 x 40 percent = \$32,000 Also PV = BAC * (Time Passed/Total Scheduled Time)
And PV = \$80,000 * (4 months/8 months) = \$40,000 So SPI = EV/PV = 32,000/40,000 = 0.8
SPI is less than one, which suggests that the project is behind schedule.

21. C: Here we have BAC= \$80,000 and AC = \$30,000 We know that EV = BAC * Actual % Complete
So, EV = BAC * 40 percent completion
= \$80,000 * 40 percent = \$32,000
So, CPI = EV/AC = 32,000/30,000 = 1.066
CPI is more than one, which suggests that the project is under budget.

22. C: Control thresholds are usually expressed as percentage deviations from the cost baseline that the sponsor or stakeholders are willing to allow before any action is required.

23. D: TCPI calculates the performance that must be achieved in order to meet financial or schedule goals and determines the status on the remaining work with respect to the funds remaining. If the cumulative CPI falls below the baseline plan, all future work must be performed at the TCPI to achieve the planned BAC.

24. C: Expected future period operation costs are considered to be ongoing costs and should not be part of the project costs.

25. B: The project manager determines, manages, and controls the contingency reserves, which will address the cost impact of the risks remaining (residual risks or known unknown risks).

26. D: The project manager is expected to come up with a realistic estimate that does not include padding. The project manager also should not simply reduce the estimate whenever asked by the sponsor or clients. If the project manager must reduce the estimate, she needs to explore other options such as cutting scope, reducing quality, or replacing expensive resources with lower-cost

resources. In this case, Lori should inform the sponsor the activities to be cut in order to reduce the estimate by ten percent.

27. C: A rough order of magnitude (–25 percent to 75 percent) is an approximate estimate made without detailed data. This type of estimate is used during the formative stages for initial evaluation of a project's feasibility. In this example, $75,000 and $200,000 are –25 percent to +75 percent of $150,000.

28. C: The budget for the first six components is 6 * $1,500 = $9,000, and the budget for the remaining nine components is 9 * $1,400 = $12,600. So, BAC = $9,000 + $ 12,600 = $21,600
We know PV = BAC * Planned % Complete
So, PV = 21,600 * 40 percent = $8,640
We have a total of fifteen components and so far, completed five components.
EV = BAC * (Work Completed/Total Work Required)
So, EV = $21,600 * 5/15 = $7,200
So, SPI = EV/PV = 7200/8640 = 0.833

29. D: The first step should be to get as much information as possible about the damages in the foundation by evaluating the cause and size of the damage and the amount needed for the fix. You can take other actions as appropriate once you have all the details.

30. A: If current variances are considered as atypical and you anticipate that similar variances will not occur in the future, the correct EAC formula is EAC = AC + (BAC – EV).
In this case, BAC = $90,000
EAC = $30,000 + ($90,000 – $35,000) = $85,000

CHAPTER 8

PROJECT QUALITY MANAGEMENT

PROJECT QUALITY MANAGEMENT QUESTIONS

1. You have been asked to identify the primary reasons for the substantial amount of customer complaints your company is experiencing every day. Which of the following tools will most effectively assist you in further identifying the reasons for the failures?
   A. Cause and effect diagram
   B. Run chart
   C. Statistical sampling
   D. Design of experiments

2. While trying to isolate the root cause of a critical problem in the production process, your team has detected two variables—temperature and humidity—as the conceivable contributors to the problem. There is a concern that these two variables are complicating the problem by affecting each other. Which of the following tools or techniques will assist to see if there is any interdependency between them?
   A. Cause and effect diagram
   B. Influence diagram
   C. Scatter diagram
   D. Pareto chart

3. Control Quality is the process of monitoring specific project results to determine if they comply with applicable quality standards and identifying ways to eradicate causes of unsatisfactory results. All of the following are tools & techniques used in the Control Quality process EXCEPT:
   A. Inspection
   B. Flow chart
   C. Quality metrics
   D. Statistical sampling

4. While using a control chart to monitor processes and to assure that they remain within acceptable limits or "in control," you noticed that seven data points are grouped together in a series on one side of the mean. All of the following are false EXCEPT:
   A. This type of situation needs to be investigated and a cause should be found.
   B. This trend is normal and expected within process.
   C. This is a random cause of variation and can be ignored.
   D. The process is stable and in control as none of the data points are outside control limits.

5. The project to build a ship that you are supervising is not progressing well. You were notified by the quality lead that the system design team has to redesign the ship due to poor quality and significant shortcomings in the design. Also during a walkthrough inspection, you have discovered that a considerable amount of scrap material has been generated by a team of newly hired engineers. The scrap material and rework are examples of:
   A. External failure
   B. Cost of conformance
   C. Prevention costs
   D. Internal failure

6. Your team is using a particular method of measuring quality and approving only a tiny portion of the outputs as per an unyielding pass/fail standard. Which of the following techniques is your team using?
   A. Product analysis
   B. Process analysis
   C. Attribute sampling
   D. Statistical sampling

7. A project manager is working on a project to install a generator in a local power company. She is anxious that her project practices are not robust enough and asked for your expert opinion. You advised her to compare her actual or planned practices to those of other projects both in and beyond the performing organization to identify a basis for performance measurement, improvement ideas, and best practices. Which of the following tools & techniques have you asked her to utilize?
   A. Design of experiments
   B. Cost-benefit analysis
   C. Statistical sampling
   D. Benchmarking

8. You are the project manager of a project to implement a golf simulator for a local golf club. Quality is the first thing in your mind, and you hired a Subject Matter Expert (SME) to ascertain if the project activities comply with organizational and project policies and procedures. The SME is particularly interested in identifying ineffective and inefficient activities or processes used in the project as well as gaps and deficiencies in your processes. You have initiated which of the following?
   A. Design of experiments
   B. Develop quality control measurements
   C. Quality audit
   D. Prevention functions

9. You discovered a pattern of flaws in several projects you are working on as a senior project manager. You have the impression that some kind of deficiency in the process your organization is using may be contributing to these repetitive defects. You conducted a cause and effect analysis and formulated a few recommendations for process change to avoid this recurring problem in future projects. You are in which of the following processes?
   A. Perform Qualitative Risk Analysis
   B. Plan Quality
   C. Manage Quality
   D. Control Quality

10. A plastic molding workshop wants to reduce injection molding rejects and performs a set of experiments that change injection pressure, mix, temperature, and setting times. Analysis of the results shows a combination of temperature and setting times as the most significant factors. Which of the following techniques is being used?
    A. Statistical sampling
    B. Brainstorming
    C. Nominal group technique
    D. Design of experiments

11. You are the project manager supervising a project to develop a new wireless media streaming device. The client asked you to have vigorous quality as it is one of their major concerns. You are in the Plan Quality Management process of identifying all the pertinent quality requirements, specifications, and standards for the project and product and specifying how those specifications will be met. You will be using all of the following as inputs of the Plan Quality Management process EXCEPT:
    A. Scope baseline
    B. Stakeholder register
    C. Quality metrics
    D. Schedule baseline

12. Costs associated with inspection, laboratory measurements and analysis, machinery maintenance and calibration, field testing, and procedure checking are examples of which of the following?
    A. Opportunity costs
    B. Sunk costs
    C. Prevention costs
    D. Appraisal costs

13. Plan-Do-Check-Act is a cycle of activities designed to drive continuous improvement. This theory was popularized by which of the following quality theorists?
    A. W. Edwards Deming
    B. Ishikawa
    C. Joseph Juran
    D. Philip Crosby

14. You are a project manager for one of a top wood furniture producers in the world. You are currently overseeing a project to create and manufacture a large amount of custom furniture for several major local retailers. Your organization has decided to practice just-in-time management and asked you to explore the practice. You found out that all of the following are FALSE about just-in-time EXCEPT:
    A. The project team will have no control over the inventory.
    B. It will allow less range of deviation than other inventory solutions.
    C. It will decrease the inventory investment.
    D. The organization will have lower quality of parts.

15. Monitoring specific project results to determine if they comply with relevant quality standards and identifying ways to eliminate causes of inadequate results is:
    A. Quality assurance
    B. Quality planning
    C. Quality control
    D. Quality management

16. Conformance to specifications—or making sure a project produces what it was created to produce—prevention over inspection, and zero defects are key items emphasized by:
    A. W. Edwards Deming
    B. Phil Crosby
    C. Joseph Juran
    D. None of the above

17. You are planning to hire a third-party auditor to perform a scheduled or random structured review to determine whether your quality management activities comply with organizational and project processes, policies, and procedures. All of the following will

be done in this quality audit EXCEPT:
- A. Identify ineffective and inefficient activities or processes used on the project.
- B. Identify required improvements, gaps, and shortcomings in the processes.
- C. Create quality metrics.
- D. Recommend changes and corrective actions to Integrated Change Control.

18. You are overseeing a software application project to implement a custom accounting and financial system for medium to large-sized corporations. The quality assurance team submitted a defect report that has relevant information on the description, severity, root causes, possible resolutions, owner, due date, and reporter of the defects. You intend to know which causes of defects are most serious so that you can prioritize the potential causes of the problems. Which of the following tools should you use to isolate the critical few causes of defects from the uncritical many?
- A. Control chart
- B. Pareto chart
- C. Scatter diagram
- D. Fishbone diagram

19. A project manager was recently recognized for delivering a high-quality product with no noticeable defects. Some of the stakeholders were skeptical about limited features offered by the product. This kind of product that has a high- level of quality but does not include many of the features of comparable products is referred to as:
- A. Low quality
- B. Low grade
- C. Inaccurate
- D. Sketchy

20. Plan Quality Management is the process of identifying all the relevant quality requirements, specifications, and standards for the project and product and detailing how the specifications will be met and should be performed:
- A. During the initial phase of the project.
- B. Prior to the approval of the Project Charter.
- C. After the work breakdown structure has been developed.
- D. In parallel with the other planning processes.

21. A project manager working on implementing WIMAX connectivity in a rural area has to deploy several network devices and set up POPs to house those devices. She performed a cost-benefit analysis and was apprehensive about the high cost of nonconformance, or cost that will incur if proper quality is not implemented in her project. In quality management, which one of the following is NOT an attribute of the cost of nonconformance?
- A. Processing customer complaints
- B. Machinery maintenance and calibration
- C. Bad word-of-mouth advertising
- D. Field repair work

22. As a project manager, you are trying to decide the trade-offs between quality and grade in your project. Which one of the following is correct with respect to a product developed or a service performed?
- A. There is no difference between quality and grade.
- B. Neither low grade nor low quality is acceptable.
- C. Low quality is acceptable, but low grade is not.
- D. Low quality is not acceptable, but low grade is.

23. A project manager is in the Plan Quality Management process of identifying all the applicable quality requirements, specifications, and standards for the project and product and detailing how the specifications will be met. All of the following are true about the Plan Quality Management process EXCEPT:
- A. It should begin in the early planning phase in parallel with other planning processes.
- B. It should balance the needs of quality with scope, cost, time, risk, and customer satisfaction.
- C. It ensures that processes and procedures are giving us the intended results and we are meeting quality objectives.
- D. Inputs of this process are Scope Baseline, Stakeholder Register, Risk Register, Enterprise Environmental Factors, and Organizational Process Assets.

24. A project manager for a business automation project is working with the quality assurance department to improve stakeholders' confidence that quality management activities will comply with organizational and project processes, policies, and procedures. Which of the following MUST the project manager and quality department have prior to initiating this Manage Quality process?
- A. Quality control measurements
- B. Change requests
- C. Verified deliverables
- D. Quality Reports

25. Proprietary quality management methodologies are used as tools & techniques in which of the following quality processes?

A. Plan Quality Management
B. Manage Quality
C. Control Quality
D. Perform Quality Management

26. You are using standard deviation to set the level of quality that your company has decided to achieve and also to set upper and lower control limits to determine if a process is in control. Standard deviation is a measure of how:
   A. Accurate the sample data is.
   B. Close the estimate is from the lowest estimate.
   C. Far the measurement is from the mean.
   D. Far apart the upper and lower control limits are.

27. While developing the quality metrics, you have defined the product attributes and ascertained how quality will be measured in your project. You have spent a substantial amount of time defining key attributes that are crucial to you and your stakeholders. Which of the following is NOT an example of a product attribute?
   A. Number of defects
   B. Desirability
   C. Availability
   D. Defect frequency

28. A project manager supervising a project to develop an auto crash video simulator for a local auto maker recently created a project budget, formalized a communications management plan after identifying all major stakeholders and their information needs, and was about to contemplate on completing the work packages. As per the instruction of senior management, the project manager has to move to a higher-priority project, leaving the simulator project to another project manager. What should the new project manager do NEXT?
   A. Enter in the executing process group.
   B. Initiate the Identify Risks process.
   C. Facilitate completion of work packages.
   D. Identify quality standards.

29. Which one of the following statements is TRUE about verified deliverables? Verified deliverables are:
   A. Outputs of the Control Quality process and inputs to the Validate Scope process.
   B. Inputs to the Control Quality process and outputs of the Validate Scope process.
   C. Tools and techniques of the Control Quality and Validate Scope processes.
   D. Outputs of the Control Quality and Validate Scope processes.

30. There are 33 work packages in your cyber security implementation project. The project is supposed to safeguard all your clients' critical and sensitive information using different cryptographic and hashing techniques. While reviewing the packages, you realized that 2 of the packages have not met the quality metrics. After further research, your team concludes that it is not possible to meet the metric at this time. You met with the team and other relevant stakeholders to analyze the situation and determine the impact. Which of the following process are you involved in?
   A. Plan Quality Management
   B. Manage Quality
   C. Control Quality
   D. Perform Integrated Change Control

31. Your team has just completed implementing a Data Loss Prevention Application to stop internal employees from stealing valuable top secret information for one of your valuable customers. You realized that the developers added some features that were not asked for to add value and impress the customer. The customer sent out a note to your manager expressing satisfaction with the project. Which one of the following is the most accurate statement about this project?
   A. It is a successful project for meeting and exceeding the customers' expectation
   B. There is a good possibility that the customer will give you more business in future
   C. The project is a success as it gave the team the opportunity to learned new features
   D. The project is unsuccessful as it was gold plated

32. As an experienced construction project manager, you realize that almost all construction projects vary from the original design, scope and definition due to technological advancement, statutory changes or enforcement, change in conditions, geological anomalies, non-availability of specified materials, or simply because of the continued development of the design after the contract has been awarded. In your project, the design requires thickness tolerances of +3/8 to -1/4 inch for slabs less than 12 inches and +1/2 to -3/8 inch for slabs more than 12 inches thick. In which document will the project manager document this if needed?
   A. Quality Report
   B. Quality Policy
   C. Quality Management Plan
   D. Risk Register

PROJECT QUALITY MANAGEMENT ANSWERS

1. A: A cause and effect diagram or fishbone diagram is a root cause analysis tool. A run chart is a line graph that displays process performance over time. Upward and downward trends, cycles, and large aberrations may be spotted and investigated further using a run chart. Statistical sampling involves choosing part of a population of interest for inspection instead of measuring the entire population. Design of Experiments (DOE) is a statistical method, usually applied to the product of a project, and provides a "'what-if'" analysis of alternatives to identify which factors might improve quality.

2. C: The scatter diagram is used to determine the correlation between two variables.

3. C: Quality metrics are an output of the Plan Quality Management process and an input to both the Manage Quality and Control Quality processes.

4. A: The rule of seven refers to nonrandom data points grouped together in a series that total seven on one side of the mean. This type of situation needs to be investigated and a cause should be found, because even though none of the points are out of the control limit, they are not random and the process may be out of control.

5. D: Internal failure results in defects, repairs, scrap, and rework, vendor follow-up on defective goods, and quality control follow-ups. External failure is associated with quality issues experienced by the customer such as processing customer complaints, loss of future sales, bad word-of-mouth advertising, field repair work, and returned goods from customer. Cost of conformance refers to the costs incurred to ensure compliance. Prevention costs are included in the cost of conformance.

6. C. Attribute sampling is a method of measuring quality that consists of observing the presence (or absence) of some characteristics (attributes) in each of the units under consideration to determine whether to accept a lot, reject it, or inspect another lot.

7. D: Benchmarking is comparing actual or planned practices to those of other projects, both in and beyond the performing organization, to provide a basis for performance measurement, to generate improvement ideas, and to identify best practices. Design of Experiments (DOE) is a statistical method usually applied to the product of a project and provides a "'what-if'" analysis of alternatives to identify which factors might improve quality. Statistical sampling involves choosing part of a population of interest for inspection instead of measuring the entire population. Cost-benefit analysis is a comparison of the cost of quality to the expected benefit. The benefit of quality must outweigh the cost of achieving it. The primary benefit of quality is increased stakeholders' satisfaction and less rework, which means higher productivity and lower cost.

8. C: A quality audit during the Manage Quality process is performed to determine if project activities comply with organizational policies and procedures.

9. C: You are in the Manage Quality process. This is the process to determine if the project activities comply with organizational and project policies, standards, processes, and procedures. This process is primarily concerned with overall process improvement and does not deal with inspecting the product for quality or measuring defects. The primary focus is on steadily improving the processes and activities undertaken to achieve quality.

10. D: Design of Experiments (DOE) is a statistical method usually applied to the product of a project. This method provides a "'what-if'" analysis of alternatives to identify which factors might improve quality. It provides statistical analysis for changing key product or process elements all at once to optimize the process. Statistical sampling is performed after products have been produced. Brainstorming and nominal group techniques are tools & techniques associated with defining requirements or identifying problems.

11. C: Quality metric is an operational definition that specifies how quality will be measured. It is an output of the Plan Quality Management process, not an input.

12. D: Appraisal costs are associated with the cost of conformance and include inspection, laboratory measurements and analysis, machinery maintenance and calibration, field testing, and procedure checking.

13. A. Plan-Do-Check-Act is a cycle of iterative activities designed to drive continuous improvement. Initially implemented in manufacturing, it has broad applicability in business. First developed by Walter Shewhart, it was popularized by Edwards Deming. This theory advocates that business processes should be scrutinized and measured to detect sources of variations that cause products to deviate from customer requirements. The recommendation is to place the business processes in an unremitting feedback loop so that managers can isolate and change the parts of the process that need improvement. The four phases in the Plan-Do-Check-Act cycle involve the following:
   - Plan: Design or revise business process components to improve results.
   - Do: Implement the plan and measure its performance.
   - Check: Assess the measurements and report the results to decision makers.
   - Act: Decide on changes needed to improve the process.

14. C: Just-in-Time (JIT) is an inventory management method whereby materials, goods, and labor are scheduled to arrive or to be replenished exactly when needed in the production process; this brings inventory down to zero or to a near-zero level. It decreases costs by keeping only enough inventory on hand to meet immediate production needs.

15. C: Quality control is utilized to monitor and record results during execution of quality activities.

16. B: Phil Crosby popularized the concept of the cost of poor quality, advocated prevention over inspection and "zero defects,"

and defined quality as conformance to specification (project produces what it was created to produce).

17. C: A quality audit is done in the Manage Quality process, and quality metrics, which are the outputs in the Plan Quality Management process, are used as inputs in the Manage Quality process.

18. B: A Pareto chart illustrates which causes of error are most serious. It is displayed as a histogram and shows frequency of error according to cause. The concept is based on the 80/20 rule: "80 percent of the problems come from 20 percent of the causes;" thus, it is important to pay close attention to the 20 percent of critical causes in order to resolve 80 percent of the problems. A Pareto chart:
   - Helps focus attention on the most critical issues
   - Prioritizes potential causes of the problems
   - Is used to determine priorities for quality improvement activities
   - Separates the critical few from the uncritical many

19. B: Products that are produced at an acceptable level of quality and meet the desired requirements of the customer but have limited functionality and features compared to similar products are referred to as low grade.

20. D: Quality management is integrated with many other project planning processes, especially cost and time management.

21. B: Machinery maintenance and calibration is an appraisal function that is included in the cost of conformance. All other costs listed are costs of nonconformance.

22. D: A product that is produced at a high-level of quality but does not include many of the features of comparable products is referred to as low grade. A low grade product with limited features may be acceptable, but a low quality product or service is unacceptable.

23. C: Manage Quality, not Plan Quality Management process ensures that processes and procedures are giving us the intended results and we are meeting quality objectives.

24. A: Quality control measurements are relevant quality level and compliance measurements. These measurements are inputs to the Manage Quality process. Change requests are outputs for both the Manage Quality and Control Quality processes, and verified deliverables are outputs for the Control Quality process. Quality Reports are the result of the Manage Quality process.

25. A: Proprietary quality management methodologies such as Six Sigma, Lean Six Sigma, Quality Function Deployment, and CMMI® are used as tools & techniques in the Plan Quality Management process.

26. C: Standard deviation is a measurement of range around the mean.

27. B: Attributes are those items associated with the actual physical product or deliverable. Failure rate, defect frequency, reliability, cost control, number of defects, availability, test coverage, and on-time performance are product attributes, but desirability is not.

28. D: The previous project manager did not complete the planning; thus, planning should be completed first followed by executing. Identifying risks and quality standards are both done in the planning process group, but quality standards are identified prior to risk identification in the project.

29. A: Verified deliverables are Outputs of the Control Quality process and inputs to the Validate Scope process.

30. C: Measuring specific project results against quality standards and required metrics is part of the Control Quality process. In this situation, there is a high probability that a change request will be submitted to Perform Integrated Change Control process.

31. Gold plating is the practice of making changes to a project that are beyond the original agreed-upon scope. Gold plating is time consuming and expensive in most cases. Gold plating is generally seen as a poor practice. Despite best intentions, the added work is often risky. Gold plating may take longer than anticipated, pushing a project past its due date. The additional changes can even have a negative effect on the existing functionality. Advanced quality thinking doesn't recommend gold plating as a best practice. The project manager should make sure that team members are not providing extra features, extra functionalities, or higher quality than expected in the project.

32. The Quality Management Plan documents quality objectives, expected quality level, quality standards, metrics, and other quality related items. The defined level of required thickness tolerances would be documented in the Quality Management plan.

CHAPTER 9

PROJECT RESOURCE MANAGEMENT

PROJECT RESOURCE MANAGEMENT QUESTIONS

1. You are in the Plan Resource Management process of identifying and documenting project roles, responsibilities, required skills, competencies, reporting structure, and other items. The structure that you are using is arranged according to an organization's existing departments, units, or teams with their respective work packages. Which of the following are you using?
   A. Resource Breakdown Structure (RBS)
   B. Responsibility Assignment Matrix (RAM)
   C. Position descriptions
   D. Organizational Breakdown Structure (OBS)

2. Project success is heavily dependent on the leadership and management style of the project manager. Even though we do not usually distinguish between leading and managing, it is generally believed that there is a difference between these two. Which of the following is typically considered to be a responsibility associated with managing?
   A. Consistently producing key results expected by stakeholders
   B. Establishing direction, mission, and vision
   C. Aligning team members to the established direction
   D. Motivating and inspiring

3. You made sure that one of the junior team members in your team received the required training to perform his activities. While assessing the team member, you were concerned to find out that the team member was still lacking the competency and required further improvement. What will be the BEST course of action?
   A. Replace the team member with an experienced resource.
   B. Have an urgent discussion with the team member and inform him that he will be out of the project if there is no immediate improvement.
   C. Have a discussion with the functional manager about the lack of competency of the team member.
   D. Identify the team member's current lacking and provide more focused training.

4. A project manager is overseeing a complex custom CSM solution that has rigorous quality standards and tight schedule constraints. The project manager just found out that one of the key deliverables in the project was not completed because the team member responsible for it was assigned to another higher-priority project by her functional manager. Who will be the person for the project manager to address the issue with in this kind of situation?
   A. The sponsor
   B. The president of the company
   C. The customers
   D. The team

5. A project manager recently got her PMP certification and joined a professional project management group. The group members meet on a regular basis to discuss new opportunities, trends, and issues in project management. The satisfaction that the project manager gains from the association with this group is MOST closely aligned with:
   A. Victor Vroom's Expectancy theory
   B. The third level of Maslow's Hierarchy of Needs
   C. Herzberg's Motivator-Hygiene theory
   D. Theory X

6. You are currently managing the team through observing, using issue logs, keeping in touch, providing feedback, completing performance appraisals, resolving issues and conflicts, and through other methods. You are in which of the following Resource Management processes?
   A. Plan Resource Management
   B. Acquire Resources
   C. Develop Team
   D. Manage Team

7. You are the project manager overseeing a project to build a navigation system for an auto company. You are in the Develop Team process, and your key focus is to enhance the project performance by building a sense of team and improving the competencies, team interaction, and overall team environment. You will be using all of the following tools & techniques in the process EXCEPT:
   A. Pre-Assignment
   B. Interpersonal and Team Skills
   C. Colocation
   D. Recognition and rewards

8. You are overseeing the implementation of a library management system for a local library. While in the execution phase, the functional manager informs you that his team needs to work on a higher-priority project and he will be pulling out two critical resources from your project. What should you do FIRST as a project manager?
   A. Evaluate the impact by referring to the resource histogram.

B. Reassign activities of these two members to the other team members.

C. Immediately inform higher management.

D. Request the functional manager to assign two new resources first before pulling out the existing members.

9. A project manager is in the Develop Team process focusing on enhancing project performance by building a sense of team and improving competencies, team interaction, and overall team environment. While referring to Tuckman's model, she notices that the greatest level of conflict in the five different stages of team building is most likely to appear in which of the following stages:

A. Forming

B. Adjourning

C. Storming

D. Exploring

10. While in the Manage Team process, the project management team met with the team members and provided feedback on team members' performance and how effectively they were performing their tasks. A 360-degree feedback was used to provide feedback from all directions, including from peers, from superiors and subordinates, and sometimes from vendors and external contractors. This tool & technique is referred to as:

A. Team Performance Assessments

B. Project Performance Appraisals

C. Observations and conversations

D. Team-building activities

11. You just completed working on your staffing management plan and identified how human resources should be defined, staffed, managed, and eventually released from your project. Which portion of the Resource Management Plan will help you the most to determine when to release resources from your project?

A. Training needs and certification requirements

B. Recognition and rewards

C. Compliance considerations

D. Resource histogram

12. While in the Manage Team process, the project management team met with the team members and provided feedback on team members' performance and how effectively they were performing their tasks. A 360-degree feedback was used to receive feedback from all directions, including from peers, from superiors and subordinates, and sometimes from vendors and external contractors. Which of the following is the most important factor when utilizing 360-degree feedback?

A. All team players such as peers, superiors, subordinates, and vendors should participate in the evaluation.

B. Participants should remain anonymous.

C. Results of the evaluation should not be disclosed.

D. Only team members should evaluate other team members.

13. Which motivational theory below is concerned with increasing employee loyalty and support for the organization by emphasizing the well-being of employees both at work and outside of work and encouraging steady employment?

A. Expectancy theory

B. Theory Z

C. Theory Y

D. Theory X

14. A project team member's abilities or competencies, communication capabilities, relevant knowledge, skills, experience, cost (for adding the team member), attitude or ability to work with others, availability, and other factors such as time zone and geographical location are some examples of selection criteria that can be used to rate and score that team member. Which one of the following looks at all of these selection criteria while acquiring a team member for the project?

A. Decision Making (Multi-Criteria Decision Analysis)

B. Monte Carlo analysis

C. Team Performance Assessment

D. Project Performance Appraisal

15. You are in the Plan Resource Management process to create an overall Resource Management Plan by identifying the availability of resources and those resources' skill levels. Which of the following is NOT a tool & technique is this process?

A. Expert Judgment

B. Data Representation

C. Organizational theory

D. Colocation

16. You are in the Plan Resource Management process of identifying and documenting project roles, responsibilities, required skills, competencies, reporting structure, and other items. Which of the following Hierarchical-Type chart can help you track project cost as it ties to the organization's accounting system?

A. Resource Breakdown Structure (RBS)

B. Organizational Breakdown Structure (OBS)

C. Responsibility Assignment Matrix (RAM)
D. Position descriptions

17. A project manager is in the Develop Team process, focusing on enhancing project performance by building a sense of team and improving the competencies, team interaction, and overall team environment. While referring to Tuckman's model, she notices that the team members begin to start trusting and working together as they adjust work habits and behaviors to work as a team. What stage of team development is the project manager referring to?
    A. Forming
    B. Adjourning
    C. Storming
    D. Norming

18. You are considering the idea of putting all team members in the same physical location for the first time. All of the following is true about colocation EXCEPT:
    A. The goal is to enhance team members' ability to perform as a team.
    B. It is also called a war room.
    C. It is meant to identify concerns and issues and to come up with mutually agreed-upon solutions.
    D. The goal is to identify the individual(s) or team responsible for project issues and inform them about it.

19. You are in the Plan Resource Management process of identifying and documenting project roles, responsibilities, required skills, competencies, reporting structure, and other items. Which one of the following will you NOT use as a tool & technique in this process?
    A. Hierarchical-type Charts
    B. Recognition and Rewards
    C. A responsibility Assignment Matrix
    D. Organizational Theory

20. You were informed by management that an external audit team will be auditing your project to make sure that the project complies with standard organizational project management policies and procedures. During the audit, the key auditor wants to review the training plan for the team members as well as their certification requirements. You should refer the auditor to which of the following?
    A. Resource Management Plan
    B. RACI Chart
    C. Training and Certification Management Plan
    D. Resource Breakdown Structure

21. While overseeing a data center project, you notice that one of the team members is extremely dedicated to the project and a consistent overachiever. In order to appreciate her spectacular work and great contribution, you made her the 'team member of the month' three times in a row. What kind of impact will this have on the project team?
    A. This will initiate a healthy competition among the team members.
    B. This will drastically improve team cohesiveness.
    C. This will negatively impact team morale.
    D. Team members hardly care about recognition and rewards; thus, there will be no impact.

22. You are a project manager who believes steady employment leads to high employee satisfaction and morale, increased loyalty to the organization, and increased productivity. Which theory do you subscribe to?
    A. McGregor Theory X and Theory Y
    B. Fred E. Fiedler's Contingency theory
    C. Dr. Willam Ouchi's Theory Z
    D. Victor Vroom's Expectancy theory

23. Mary, a project manager, is in the Develop Team process, focusing on enhancing project performance by building a sense of team and improving the competencies, team interaction, and overall team environment. While referring to Tuckman's model, she notices that the team is in a stage where her role is mostly overseeing and delegating. The team is in which stage of team development?
    A. Forming
    B. Adjourning
    C. Storming
    D. Performing

24. A project manager overseeing a construction project notices that her team members are having constant conflicts over issues. The situation was causing her a lot of concern, and she decides to identify the key causes of the conflicts. While exploring the causes,

she finds that the most common causes of conflicts among team members are project priorities, resources, and:

    A. Personality
    B. Schedule
    C. Technical options
    D. Administration procedures

25. You are overseeing a video conferencing application project and just completed negotiation for three additional resources from different functional areas and extra reserve money for your project. During the negotiation, two of the functional managers were very skeptical about the request for additional resources and were reluctant to assign their resources to your project. At last, a solution was reached in which you were allowed to obtain the resources you requested, but you had to agree to give up some other resources at an earlier date than you had originally planned. What type of conflict resolution technique was used in this situation?

    A. Smoothing
    B. Compromising
    C. Forcing
    D. Collaborating

26. Your data center project is in a mess, and the entire team is under enormous pressure from management to complete the project on time. At team meetings, team members are continuously pointing fingers at each other and blaming others for the delay in their deliverables. You had an urgent meeting with the sponsor to discuss the situation, and he expressed his interest to attend the meeting to evaluate the situation himself. What will be the BEST course of action for you in this type of situation?

    A. Request the sponsor to provide help if possible but not to attend the meeting.
    B. Inform the team members that the sponsor will be attending the meeting.
    C. Remove the team member from the team who is most vocal and who is causing the most issues.
    D. Create new ground rules for the meetings and introduce them to the team members.

27. Your project has 13 team members, 6 stakeholders, and 2 sponsors. You used a Responsibility Assignment Matrix (RAM) to maps specific resources to the work packages from the Work Breakdown Structure (WBS). Your Project Management Office (PMO) asked you to use a Resource Histogram as well. You don't really understand the benefit of using a Resource Histogram and asked PMO to explain the reason of using it. The PMO explained that one of the following items would be shown in the Resource Histogram but not in the Responsibility Assignment Matrix.

    A. Who reports to whom
    B. Who will do the work
    C. Number of resources used in each time period
    D. Interrelationships

28. You received numerous complaints about an individual from several other team members. This specific team member was not attending meetings or responding to her emails. You tried to smooth the situation and cooled down the other team members as much as you could and even took some her responsibilities. At last, she called you and explained that she was going through a bad divorce which impacted her work. You were really concerned about her and rescheduled some of the activities to allow her more time to cope with the disastrous personal situation. This is a good example of:

    A. Contingency theory
    B. Theory Z
    C. Problem-solving
    D. Emotional Intelligence

29. You team is getting ready to start the testing phase of your Enterprise Resource Planning (ERP) project. The duration of the project is 2 years and a total of six modules will be implemented to automate most of the business processes in your organization. The IT support team just set up a testing environment with a high-end server and spent a big budget on the DBMS licenses. Another project manager also requested to use the testing environment for her project around the same time your team wants to use it. Your organization can only afford to have one such high cost testing environment and leasing is not at all feasible at this time. What should be your last course of action in this situation?

    A. Make changes to your project plan to make best use of this situation
    B. Ask the sponsor to get involve
    C. Have a discussion with the other project manager on a win-win situation
    D. Negotiate with the procurement department to lease a testing environment

30. Your project is on track and has all the support from sponsors and senior management. You like to motivate and encourage your employees so that they will contribute more to the project. You spent a considerable amount of money from your project budget on shifting the team to an expensive office space with a nice view and also added the term "senior" to their job titles. What is true about this situation?

    A. You are paying a lot of attention to motivating agents
    B. You have a good understanding of the Herzberg's theory
    C. You took the correct step by giving more attention to the hygiene factors
    D. You don't really understand Herzberg's theory

PROJECT RESOURCE MANAGEMENT ANSWERS

1. D: An Organizational Breakdown Structure (OBS) is similar to a company's standard organizational chart that looks like a Work Breakdown structure (WBS) but only includes the positions and relationships in a top-down, graphic format. It is arranged according to an organization's existing departments, units, or teams with their respective work packages. Any operations department such as manufacturing or engineering, can identify all of its project responsibilities by looking at its portion of the OBS. A Resource Breakdown structure (RBS) also looks like a typical organizational chart, but this one is organized by types of resources. An RBS can help track project cost as it ties to the organization's accounting system. A RAM cross-references team members with the activities or work packages they are to accomplish. One example of a Responsibility Assignment Matrix (RAM) is a Responsible, Accountable, Consult, and Inform (RACI) Chart, which can be used to ensure clear divisions of roles and responsibilities. A text-oriented position description, or role-responsibility-authority form, is particularly important in recruiting. It is used to describe a team member's position title, responsibilities, authority, competencies, and qualifications in detail.

2. A: Project management is heavily dependent on managing people, which has been defined as being able to produce key results. On the other hand, leadership is all about establishing mission and vision, aligning team members to the established direction, and motivating and inspiring individuals.

3. D: The role of the project manager is to make sure that team members, specially the junior members with limited experience, get the required training and assistance to perform their activities.

4. A: It is one of the key roles of the sponsor to prevent unnecessary changes in the project in addition to providing funding for the project.

5. B: The third level of Maslow's Hierarchy of Needs is the need for social connections or belonging, such as love, affection, approval, friends, and association. The Expectancy theory, first proposed by Victor Vroom, demonstrates that employees who believe their efforts will lead to effective performance and who expect to be rewarded for their accomplishments remain productive as rewards meet their expectations. Herzberg's Motivator-Hygiene theory suggests that hygiene factors can destroy motivation but improving them under most circumstances will not improve motivation. Motivating people is best done by rewarding people and letting them grow. Theory X managers believe that average workers are incapable, avoid responsibility, have an inherent dislike of work, and are only interested in their own selfish goals. The workers must be forced to do productive work as they dislike their work and are not devoted and motivated.

6. D: Manage Team is the process of managing the team through observing, using issue logs, keeping in touch, providing feedback, completing performance appraisals, resolving issues and conflicts, and other factors.

7. A: Pre-Assignment is used as a tool & technique in the Acquire Resources process, not in the Develop Team process. Under most circumstances a role is defined first, and then the resource is assigned to perform the role and fulfill the responsibilities. However, some of the team members will be selected in advance and considered as pre-assigned to fill roles before the Resource Management Plan has been created or the project has been formally initiated.
Resources can be pre-assigned as a part of a competitive proposal, as per some staff assignment defined in the Project Charter, or for dependency on the experience and expertise of particular individuals.

8. A: In this sort of situation, a project manager should always evaluate the impact of the changes and gather as much information as possible prior to taking any further steps.

9. C: Storming follows the Forming stage, and it is where the team begins to address project work, technical decisions, areas of disagreement, and project management approaches. The team typically goes through some conflicts and difficulties in this stage more than any other.

10. B: For the Project Performance Appraisals, the project management team meets with the team members and provides feedback on team members' performance and how effectively they are performing their tasks. A 360-degree feedback is used to receive feedback from all directions, including from peers, from superiors and subordinates, and sometimes from vendors and external contractors. Here the focus is the individual, and in team performance assessments the focus is on the team performance, not on the individual. The goal of team performance assessments is to identify the specific training, coaching, mentoring, assistance, or changes required to improve the team's performance and effectiveness. The project management team makes formal or informal assessments of the project team's effectiveness while team development efforts such as training, team building, and colocation are implemented. A team's performance is measured against the agreed-upon success criteria, schedule, and budget target.

11. D: A resource histogram is a graphical display that shows the amount of time that a resource is scheduled to work over a series of time periods.

12. B: A 360-degree evaluation is an effective tool to evaluate team members' performance and effectiveness and to identify areas of improvement. Effort should be given to include all the team players in the evaluation process, but it is not mandatory. Team members not only evaluate other team members, but they should evaluate the project manager as well. Individual comments should not be disclosed, but the general feedback results should be shared with each team member in a private session. In order to have complete and

honest feedback, it is vital that the participants remain anonymous.

13. B: Theory Z was introduced by Dr. Willam Ouchi. This theory is concerned with increasing employee loyalty to his/her organization. This theory emphasizes the well-being of the employees both at work and outside of work, it encourages steady employment, it leads to high employee satisfaction and morale, and overall it results in increased productivity and support for the organization. Theory X managers believe that average workers are incapable, avoid responsibility, have an inherent dislike of work, and are only interested in their own selfish goals. The workers must be forced to do productive work as they dislike their work and are not devoted and motivated. Theory Y managers believe that workers are creative and committed to project objectives and goals. They are willing to work without supervision, need very little external motivation, can direct their own efforts, and want to achieve. The Expectancy theory, first proposed by Victor Vroom, demonstrates that employees who believe their efforts will lead to effective performance and who expect to be rewarded for their accomplishments remain productive as rewards meet their expectations.

14. A: Potential team members are often rated and scored by various selection criteria during the Acquire Resources process. These selection criteria are weighted according to their relevant importance and are developed using the multi-criteria decision analysis tool. A project team member's ability or competencies, communication capabilities, relevant knowledge, skills, experience, cost (for adding the team member), attitude or ability to work with others, availability, and other factors such as time zone and geographical location are some examples of selection criteria that can be used to rate and score team members.

15. D: Colocation is a tool & technique used in the Develop Team process, not in the Plan Resource Management process.

16. A: A Resource Breakdown Structure (RBS) looks like a typical organizational chart, but it is organized by types of resources. An RBS can help track project cost as it ties to the organization's accounting system. An Organizational Breakdown Structure (OBS) is similar to a company's standard organizational chart that looks like a WBS but only includes the positions and relationships in a top-down, graphic format. It is arranged according to an organization's existing departments, units, or teams with their respective work packages. Any operations department such as manufacturing or engineering, can identify all of its project responsibilities by looking at its portion of the OBS. A Responsibility Assignment Matrix (RAM) cross-references team members with the activities or work packages they are to accomplish. One example of a RAM is a Responsible, Accountable, Consult, and Inform (RACI) chart, which can be used to ensure clear divisions of roles and responsibilities. A text-oriented position description, or role-responsibility-authority form, is particularly important in recruiting. It is used to describe a team member's position title, responsibilities, authority, competencies, and qualifications in detail.

17. D: The team members are in the Norming stage as they are adjusting work habits and behaviors to work as a team. They begin to start trusting and working together.

18. D: The objective of collocation, or the war room, is to build a better relationship among the team members, enhance their ability to perform as a team, identify concerns and issues in the project, and figure out solutions for those issues. The idea is not to point fingers at other team members or get involved in any kind of argument.

19. B: Recognition and Rewards are used as a tool & technique in the Develop Team process, not in the Plan Resource Management process. Hierarchical-type charts, a Responsibility Assignment Matrix (which is a matrix-type organizational chart), and Organizational Theory all are used as tools & techniques in the Plan Resource Management process.

20. A: The Resource Management Plan identifies the training needs and certification requirements of the team members. One example of a responsibility assignment matrix is a RACI (Responsible, Accountable, Consult, and Inform) chart, which can be used to ensure clear divisions of roles and responsibilities. Training and Certification Management Plan is a fake term. A Resource Breakdown Structure (RBS) looks like a typical organizational chart, but this one is organized by types of resources. An RBS can help track project cost as it ties to the organization's accounting system.

21. C: A project manager can kill the team morale by consistently rewarding the same individual repeatedly as it can be perceived that the project manager is playing favorites. If the team members believe that the rewards are win-lose and that only certain team members will be rewarded, it may demoralize them. In this kind of situation, the project manager can consider team awards, which is a win-win as all the team members are recognized for their contributions.

22. C: Theory Z was introduced by Dr. Willam Ouchi. This theory is concerned with increasing employee loyalty to his/her organization. This theory emphasizes the well-being of employees both at work and outside of work, it encourages steady employment, it leads to high employee satisfaction and morale, and overall it results in increased productivity.

23. D: As per Tuckman's model, in the Performing stage, the team functions as a well-organized unit. They are interdependent and work through issues smoothly and effectively. The role of the project manager is mainly overseeing and delegating.

24. B: There are several sources of conflict, including schedule priorities, scarce resources, personal work style, cost, and other elements, but it's important to note that personality differences are not the root cause of conflict; in fact, it's rarely the case. The three main causes of project conflicts are schedule, project priorities, and resources, as approximately 50 percent of all conflicts come from these three sources.

25. B: Compromising is bargaining to some level of mutual (dis)satisfaction to both parties. Parties are asked to lose something to gain something. Smoothing is emphasizing areas of agreement and downplaying differences of opinion. Forcing is exerting one opinion over another. Collaborating focuses on working to combine multiple differing perspectives into one shared perspective and results in a

win-win situation for allparties.

26. D: The most effective solution in this type of situation will be to create ground rules and introduce them to the team members. Ground rules identify acceptable and not acceptable behaviors on the project and try to minimize the negative impacts of bad behaviors. Some of the ground rules that will be applicable in this situation include the following:
- Methods of how conflict should beresolved
- Ways to treat sensitive data in theproject
- Methods of notifying the project manager about difficulties, issues, and concerns
- Acceptable ways to interrupt someone talking at ameeting
- Methods to stop talking over a team memberinappropriately
- Rules for joining meetings and consequences of being late

27. C: The Responsibility Assignment Matrix (RAM) shows who will do the work and a Resource Histogram shows the number of resources used in each time period that a RAM doesn't show.

28. D: Emotional Intelligence is the capacity to be aware of, control, and express one's emotions, and to handle interpersonal relationships judiciously and empathetically utilizing observation, interpersonal skills, and communication. By making team members feel important and valued, you tried to bring out the best in the team members. In this case, you showed empathy and also worked out a plan for the team member to fulfill her job responsibilities.

29. B: As a project manager, you should always deal with a situation and try out different options prior to asking help from the sponsor. You should also be considerate to the needs of the entire organization, not only your ones.

30. D: You are trying to make a great working condition better by renting a new office space and upgrading the team members' titles. Herzberg classified needs under two much larger categories of motivators (opportunity for advancements and achievement, variety of work, sense of responsibility, recognition, and professional growth) and hygiene (compensation, personal life, working conditions, supervisors, security, status, and relationships with peers, subordinates, and supervisors). Destroying hygiene factors can destroy motivation but improving them under most circumstances will not improve motivation. Hygiene factors are not sufficient to motivate people, and motivating agents provide the best positive reinforcement. Motivating people is best done by rewarding people and letting themgrow.

CHAPTER 10

PROJECT COMMUNICATIONS MANAGEMENT

PROJECT COMMUNICATIONS MANAGEMENT QUESTIONS

1. In your network infrastructure project XYZ, you have determined the type, format, value, and information needs of the stakeholders through communication requirements analysis. Project resources should be expended only on communicating information that:
   - A. Originates from the sponsor or the project management office.
   - B. Has been generated by the project team members only.
   - C. Is relevant to the most influential and powerful stakeholders.
   - D. Contributes to project success or where a lack of communication can lead to a failure.

2. A project manager is in the process of ensuring that the information needs of the project stakeholders are met by monitoring and controlling communication throughout the project life cycle. The project manager is involved in which process?
   - A. Direct and Manage Project Work
   - B. Monitor and Control Project Work
   - C. Monitor Communications
   - D. Manage Communications

3. As a project manager, Henry is cognizant of the importance of effective communication, and he always makes sure that he has the proper physical mannerisms such as facial expressions, hand gestures, and body language, while conveying a message. He is also particularly observant to the pitch and the tone of his voice, and he tries to receive comments and feedback from the receiver while communicating. What percentage of Henry's message is sent through nonverbal communication?
   - A. Approximately 10 to 20 percent
   - B. No more than 30 percent
   - C. No more than 45 percent
   - D. More than 50 percent

4. You are in the Plan Communications Management process to identify the information and communication needs of the people involved in your project by determining what needs to be communicated, when, to whom, with what method, in which format, and how frequently. Which of the following is MOST closely linked to this process?
   - A. Communication Requirements Analysis
   - B. Information Management System
   - C. Interpersonal skills
   - D. Project reporting

5. A project manager is leading a team of fifteen team members. One of the team members is not dedicated to the project and is having a performance issue. What form of communication can the Project Manager use to address this kind of situation?
   - A. Informal written
   - B. Informal verbal
   - C. Formal written
   - D. Formal verbal

6. You recently successfully completed a data center project that has been in production for more than a month. All the stakeholders have formally approved the project, and no issues have been reported since it has been in production. While reviewing one of the deliverables of your project with a Project Manager who is preparing for a similar project, you discover a problem in your project that may cause a minor safety issue in the future. What should you do under this circumstance?
   - A. Communicate with your management about your finding both verbally and in writing.
   - B. There is no need to bring this minor safety issue to the attention of the customers since no complaints have been filed.
   - C. Call the customers immediately and inform them about the safety issue.
   - D. Since it is a minor safety concern, it can be fixed without letting the customers know about it.

7. As a project manager, you know you will be spending 90 percent of your time communicating with all the players involved in your project. You need to make sure that you have the proper physical mannerisms such as facial expressions, hand gestures, and body language, while conveying a message. You also need to be particularly observant to the pitch and the tone of your voice, and you should try to receive comments and feedback from the receiver while communicating. Your communication skills will be utilized MOST during which of the following processes?
   - A. Communication Change Control
   - B. Manage Communications
   - C. Report Performances
   - D. Plan Communications Management

8. You are successfully managing a software project to automate the business processes for one of your clients. A key stakeholder articulates her concern to you about the lack of relevant information on her team's deliverables in the project status reports that you have been sending out. She is worried that her team has no visibility in this project and has requested you to look into the matter as soon as possible. What should you do FIRST in this situation?
   - A. Revisit the information distribution process in your project.
   - B. Have an urgent meeting with the stakeholders to understand what her team is working on.
   - C. Ask the stakeholder to send the status of her team so that you can incorporate them in your report.

D. Revisit your Communications Management Plan.

9. A project manager overseeing an ERP implementation project planned to distribute large volumes of information about the project to a large audience. He decided to post the information in an online knowledge repository for access at the discretion of the stakeholders. This type of communication method is known as:
    A. Interactive communication
    B. Push communication
    C. Pull communication
    D. Expert judgment

10. As a project manager, you are required to report project performance to all your stakeholders on a regular basis. Which one of the following can utilize Earned Value Management (EVM) in its preparation for management?
    A. Status reports
    B. Trend reports
    C. Progress reports
    D. All of the above

11. Which communication method is used essentially for prominent documents that go into project records?
    A. Informal verbal
    B. Informal written
    C. Formal verbal
    D. Formal written

12. In your project you are facing many multifaceted problems that need to be discussed and resolved. You have explored different communication methods to use in solving complex problems. Extensive use of which of the following methods will most likely assist in solving complex problems in your project?
    A. Nonverbal
    B. Verbal
    C. Written
    D. Paralingual

13. A project manager supervising a video conferencing implementation project has several internal and external stakeholders whom she needs to send project progress, status, and forecast reports to on a regular basis. The Project Manager is making sure she is sending information to specific recipients who need to know it. Even though she ensures that the information is distributed, she is not concerned with whether it reached or was understood by the intended audience. This type of communication method is known as:
    A. Interactive communication
    B. Push communication
    C. Expert judgment
    D. Pull communication

14. A project manager is in the process of making relevant information available to project stakeholders in a timely manner as planned. The project manager is involved in which of the following processes?
    A. Plan Communications Management process
    B. Manage Communications process
    C. Monitor Communications process
    D. Distribute Information process

15. The sender-receiver model is a basic model of communication that demonstrates how information is sent from the sender and how it is received by the receiver. This model is designed to assist project managers and team members in improving their communication skills. This communication model highlights which one of the following?
    A. Horizontal communication
    B. Noise and feedback loops
    C. Downward communication
    D. Verbal and nonverbal communication

16. A Project Manager is in the Manage Communications process of collecting and distributing performance information and is especially focused on reporting against the performance baseline. Which one of the following is an output in this process?
    A. Performance reporting
    B. Information Management System
    C. Communication methods
    D. Project communications

17. Your project currently has ten more people assigned to the team besides you. As your project is getting delayed, management

wants you to add four additional team members to your project at the end of the month. How many more communication channels will you have once the additional team members are added?

A. 55
B. 50
C. 105
D. 160

18. You have been asked to provide information about your project's current performance in terms of the relationships between scope, schedule, and budget. The most appropriate type of report that will accomplish this is:

A. Progress report
B. Earned Value Management report
C. Trend report
D. Status report

19. Which one of the following is not a noteworthy factor in the determination of the method that may be used to transfer information to, from, and among project stakeholders?

A. Availability of technology: Appropriate systems may already be in place, or you may need to procure a new system or technology.
B. Urgency of the need for information: There may be a need to have frequently updated information available at a moment's notice, or regularly issued written reports may be sufficient.
C. Stakeholder identification: It will provide a list of stakeholders affected by the project and who have interest in the project.
D. Duration of the project: Technology will not likely change prior to the project's completion or it may need to be upgraded at some point.

20. You are leading a project status meeting with key stakeholders and customers, but it is not going too well. Participants are discussing various topics at random, talking at the same time and interrupting each other, a few of the attendees are not participating in the discussion at all, and two of the customers are busy over the phone. To avoid this kind of situation and have an effective meeting, what meeting rules should you apply?

A. You should have a real purpose of the meeting and invite the right people.
B. You should always schedule your meeting in advance so that people have plenty of time to be prepared for the meeting.
C. You should create and publish an agenda with specific topics to discuss and establish ground rules.
D. You should control who is allowed to speak and who is not and ask everyone to demonstrate courtesy and consideration to each other.

21. You have several internal and external stakeholders involved in your construction project. As a project manager, you need to identify the information type, format, value, and needs for all these stakeholders. Which of the following tools & techniques is used to identify this type of information?

A. Stakeholder Engagement Plan
B. Communications Requirements Analysis
C. Trend Analysis
D. Value Analysis

22. You have been managing a multi-year construction project for one of your most important clients. You requested your lead business analyst to develop a report that will capture project results for the last four years and illustrate whether project performance is improving or deteriorating. You are interested in which of the following reports?

A. Trend report
B. Variance report
C. Forecasting report
D. Progress report

23. You have fifteen identified internal and external stakeholders in the network infrastructure project you are supervising. You are sending out progress and status reports to all your stakeholders on a regular basis as per your communications management plan. One of the stakeholders needs a very specific progress report on her team's deliverables and sends you an urgent e-mail requesting you to send the report as soon as possible. Your bandwidth is almost fully occupied in various project-related activities, but you have to find some spare time to fulfill this unexpected request from the stakeholder. What will be your BEST course of action?

A. Consider it as part of the Manage Communications process and send out the requested report.
B. Consider it as gold plating and ignore the request from the customer.

C. Inform the stakeholder that you are unable to send out ad hoc reports as it is not included in the project Communications Management Plan.

D. Complain to the sponsor about this unreasonable request from the stakeholder.

24. You are the project manager of a very important software development project in your organization. As you are closely monitoring and managing your project, you are happy that the project is progressing as per your plan. You reviewed the status of all the deliverables with your team members prior to having a project status update meeting with the stakeholders. Your team has developed a prototype, or a working model of the proposed end product, and it will be presented to the stakeholders for interaction and feedback. This will be an iterative process, and the prototype may be modified numerous times to incorporate the feedback until the requirements have been finalized for the product. Which one of the following will you do in your status meeting?

A. Do not mention anything about the prototype.

B. Demo the prototype to the stakeholders and obtain their formal approval.

C. Report on the progress of the prototype and point out that it's a completed task.

D. Review the technical documentation of the prototype and obtain the formal approval.

25. While planning communication for the network infrastructure project to which you have been assigned as project manager, you know you have to pay particular attention to your body's mannerisms, facial expressions, and the tone and pitch of your voice to communicate effectively. All of the following are FALSE about communication EXCEPT:

A. Acknowledge means the receiver has received and agreed with the message.

B. Encode means to translate ideas or thoughts so that others can understand them.

C. Noise has nothing to do with sending and receiving messages.

D. Verbal communication is more important than nonverbal communication.

26. While working on your communications plan, you have considered several communication technologies to transfer information among project stakeholders. Communication technology will take into account the following factors that can affect the project EXCEPT which one?

A. Urgency of the need for information: Are regularly issued written reports enough for the project, or is frequently updated information needed at a moment's notice?

B. Expected project staffing: Are the proposed communication systems compatible with the experience and expertise of the project participants, or is extensive training and learning required?

C. Duration of the project: Is the available technology likely to change before the project is over?

D. Reason for the distribution of information: What are the reasons for distributing information?

27. A project manager overseeing a construction project has several stakeholders involved in the project. During project implementation, the project manager is required to submit several reports that will communicate information about the project. The report that describes where the project now stands regarding performance measurement baselines in cost, schedule, scope, and quality is called:

A. Status report

B. Quality report

C. Progress report

D. Forecast report

28. You are managing a software development project and have worked on a Stakeholder Register and a Communications Management Plan. Now you are about to execute your Communications Management Plan. Which one of the following is TRUE regarding Manage Communications?

A. Manage Communications will end when the product has been accepted.

B. Communication methods such as individual and group meetings, video and audio conferences, computer chats, and other remote communication methods are used to manage communications.

C. Manage Communications is a monitoring & controlling process.

D. Manage Communications only carries out predetermined communication and does not respond to unplanned requests from stakeholders.

29. The project manager who has been managing a large, multi-year network infrastructure project recently left the company, and you were assigned as a project manager to continue with the project. There are more than five different vendors, fifteen team members, and several key stakeholders involved in this very important project. While trying to identify stakeholder communication requirements, format, method, time frame, and frequency for the distribution of required information, which of the following will you be referring to?

A. Communications Management Plan

B. The information Distribution Plan

C. Project Management Plan

D. Stakeholder Management Strategy

30. A Project Management Information System (PMIS) is used as a tool & technique in many of the forty-nine processes. Which statement describes a PMIS BEST?

A. A PMI certification for project management focused on information systems.
B. A necessary log for timekeeping.
C. A repository for project information used for future reference.
D. An automated system to support the project by optimizing the schedule and helping collect and distribute information.

31. A stakeholder is complaining that she has no clue what is going with the project as she is not receiving any kind of communications from you. You are sure that you identified this specific stakeholder and analyzed her communication need and preferred communication method in the initiation phase of the project. You went through a specific document and realized that the stakeholder asked for a monthly status report that should be posted in your partners' portal. Where did you find this information?
A. Communication Management Plan
B. Resource Management Plan
C. Stakeholder Engagement Assessment Matrix
D. Responsibility Assignment Matrix (RAM)

32. You are managing a very complex artificial intelligence project to develop a human-like robot. Since you couldn't find all the experts in US, you decided to add special expertise and competency to the project team from outside of the project's geographic area. Now, you have a virtual team comprised of team members from different countries including Switzerland, Ireland, India, Scotland, Canada, and the USA. You realized that you need to set clear expectations, develop protocols for conflict resolution, set up a robust decision-making procedure, and set up a proper recognition and reward system to make this virtual team successful. Which of the following will be the best tool that you can use to be successful?
A. Video conferencing capabilities
B. Organizational Breakdown Structure (OBS)
C. Team Performance Assessment
D. Interpersonal skills

PROJECT COMMUNICATIONS MANAGEMENT ANSWERS

1. D: Communications Requirements Analysis determines the information type, format, value, and needs of the stakeholders and identifies information that is most critical to success or where a lack of communication can lead to failure.

2. C: Monitor Communications is the process of ensuring that the information needs of the project stakeholders are met by monitoring and controlling communication throughout the project life cycle. The focus of this process is to ensure efficient information flow to all stakeholders at any moment in time within the project.

3. D: About 55 percent of all communications are nonverbal (e.g., based on physical mannerisms such as facial expressions, hand gestures, and body language).

4. A: Communication Requirements Analysis is a tool & technique in the Plan Communications Management process. Project reporting and Information Management Systems are tools & techniques within the Manage Communications process. Interpersonal skills are associated with the Manage Stakeholder Engagement process (stakeholder management).

5. B: The project manager should have an informal verbal discussion with the team member about the lack of dedication and poor performance. The goal is to address the concern of the project manager and to identify areas for improvement as well as any training needs for the team member. If this method is not effective, then the project manager should consider a formal written approach as the next step.

6. A: Even though no complaints have been filed and the issue is relatively minor, the project manager should report this sort of finding to management and take action as per management's recommendation.

7. B: Communication Change Control and Report Performances are not valid processes. Communications planning involves identifying the information and communication needs of the people involved in a project by determining what needs to be communicated, when, to whom, with what method, in which format, and how frequently. Manage Communications is the execution of your Communications Management Plan, which covers a broad range of topics such as what, how, when, and how frequently information will be communicated and requires an ample amount of communication ability and skills.

8. D: Since the stakeholder is receiving the status reports, there is no issue with the information distribution process. You should revisit your Communications Management Plan first to understand the information need, communications requirements, format, method, time frame, and frequency for the distribution of required information for this specific stakeholder. You may want to have an urgent meeting with the stakeholder once you have the details.

9. C: Pull communication utilizes intranet sites, e-learning, knowledge repositories, and other types of accessible databases for a large volume of information or for a large audience who will be accessing the contents at their own discretion. Expert judgment generally refers to the input from subject matter experts. Interactive communication is between two or more parties performing a multidirectional exchange of information; in push communication, information is distributed, but it is not certified that the information reached its intended audience or was understood.

10. D: Earned Value Management (EMV) terms such as Actual Cost (AC), Earned Value (EV), Planned Value (PV), Estimate at Completion (EAC), Estimate to Complete (ETC), Variance at Completion (VAC), and Budget at Completion (BAC) can be used for all kind of performance reports such as, status, trend, and progress reports.

11. D: Prominent records such as complex problems, the Project Management Plan, the Project Charter, important project communications, contracts, legal notices, and other items use the formal written method.

12. C: Both verbal and written communications should be used in solving complex problems. But in a written communication, your words will be documented and presented in the same form to everyone. In the case of the other methods listed, the same message will not be received by everyone; thus, they will not be as helpful as a written method.

13. B: Push communication is a way of sending information to specific recipients who need to know it. This ensures that the information is distributed, but it is not concerned with whether it reached or was understood by the intended audience.

14. B: Manage Communications is the process of making relevant information available to the project stakeholders in a timely manner as planned by creating, collecting, storing, retrieving, and distributing project information. It is performed throughout the entire project life cycle and in all management processes.

15. B: The sender-receiver model highlights awareness about the appropriate message to be delivered, the potential barriers or noises that may be encountered, and the significance of a feedback loop to improve delivery and understanding of a message.

16. D: Project reporting, Information Management System, and Communications Methods are tools & techniques in the Manage Communications process; only project communications are the outputs.

17. B: Your team currently has eleven team members including you; thus, the number of communication channels is calculated by using the formula: # of Channels = n* (n – 1)/2 = 11 (11 – 1)/2 = 55
If you add four more resources, then you will have 11 + 4 = 15 team members. So the number of channels will be 15 (15 – 1)/2 = 105
So you will have 105 – 55 = 50 more channels after adding the new resources.

18. D: Earned Value Management provides an integrated view of project performance and compares work performed with work planned to be performed and the planned cost of work with the actual cost of work. Progress reports provide information about what has been accomplished so far; a trend report examines project results over time to see if performance is improving or deteriorating. A status report describes where the project now stands regarding performance measurement baselines in cost, schedule, scope, and quality.

19. C: The methods used to transfer information to, from, and among project stakeholders can vary significantly. Factors such as availability of technology, expected project staffing, urgency of the need for information, project environment, duration of the project, and other things may play a significant role in determining the method that may be used to transfer information among project stakeholders. Stakeholder identification will provide a list of stakeholders affected by the project and does not play much of a role in this situation.

20. C: 'A' and 'B' will not help too much in this kind of situation as there is no indication here that the right people were not invited to the meeting or the meeting was not scheduled in advance. 'D' is not a rule for a meeting. People discussing topics at random suggests that there was no set agenda for the attendees to follow. Establishing and Imposing ground rules will restrict people from talking at the same time and interrupting each other or remaining busy over the phone.

21. B: Stakeholder communications requirements are determined during communications requirements analysis. The intention is to identify information that is most valuable to stakeholders. The Stakeholder Engagement Plan is an output to Plan Stakeholder Engagement process, and it defines an approach to manage stakeholders and to increase support for and minimize negative impacts on stakeholders throughout the entire project life cycle. A trend analysis examines project results over time to see if performance is improving or deteriorating. Value analysis or value engineering is associated with product analysis, and it helps to find a less costly way to do the same work without loss of performance.

22. A: The trend report examines project results over time to see if performance is improving or deteriorating.

23. A: Accommodating to planned and ad hoc information requests is part of the Manage Communications process.

24. C: Usually the project manager reports on the progress of the project in a status meeting rather than demoing any prototype or reviewing any technical documentation.

25. B: Acknowledge means the receiver has received the message, but it does not mean that the receiver necessarily agrees with the message. Noise or communication blockers play a vital role in effective communication. 55 percent of all communication is nonverbal, and verbal communication is not more important than nonverbal communication. Encoding is translating ideas and thoughts.

26. D: Communication technology will take into account urgency of the need for information, expected project staffing, and duration of the project, but not reason for the distribution of information.

27. A. Status reports address the current condition of a project, including risks and issues. Progress reports refer to work that has been completed during a reporting period, and forecasts refer to future scheduled work. The quality report is a made-up term.

28. B: Some stakeholders will need information distributed even after the product has been accepted as they want to get information about the closure of the project and the contract. The Manage Communications is an executing process. Manage Communications carries out not only predetermined communication but also handles responses to unplanned requests from stakeholders. The listed communication methods are used in Manage Communications; thus, letter 'B' is the correct answer.

29. A: Even though the Communications Management Plan is a part of the Project Management Plan, the best option here will be the Communications Management Plan, where the purpose for communication, communication requirements, method, time frame and frequency for distribution, person responsible for communication, methods for updating the communications management plan, and other communication related items can be found.

30. D: PMIS is an automated tool used to gather, integrate, and disseminate project information.

31. A: A Communication Management Plan includes purpose of communication, information needs of each stakeholder or stakeholder group, stakeholder communication requirements, and format, method, time frame, and frequency of the distribution of required information.

32. D: There are numerous challenges associated with virtual teams, such as language barriers, less bonding, time differences, cultural differences, complex communication, and other factors. Virtual team members may also have different values and beliefs that you need to adapt to. You can use your interpersonal skills such as Communication Styles Assessment, Political Awareness, and Cultural Awareness to be very effective. You can heavily use your cultural awareness and sensitivity, which is the foundation of communication and involves the ability of becoming aware of different cultural values, beliefs, and perceptions, to be successful in this situation.

CHAPTER 11

PROJECT RISK MANAGEMENT

PROJECT RISK MANAGEMENT QUESTIONS

1. You are working on the Plan Risk Management process to decide how to approach, plan, and execute risk management activities. All of the following are inputs to the Plan Risk Management process EXCEPT:
   A. Stakeholder Register
   B. Project Charter
   C. Risk Register
   D. Project Management Plan

2. You are delivering specialized medical equipment, which is worth $600,000. You have been delivering equipment for a while without much hassle or accidents in the past. This time you estimate that there is a 5 percent probability that the equipment could be damaged or lost. While exploring the possibility of transferring this risk to an insurance company, you found out the insurance premium is $15,000. What will be your BEST course of action?
   A. You do not have much information to make a decision.
   B. Do not buy the insurance premium.
   C. Develop a contingency plan.
   D. Buy the insurance premium.

3. Which one of the following is contained in the risk management plan and describes a risk category?
   A. Risk response plan
   B. Risk Breakdown Structure (RBS)
   C. Risk register
   D. Watch list

4. The team has identified several mitigation and contingency action plans to deal with potential risks within the project. Who is responsible for implementing the actions defined by mitigation and the contingency plan in risk management?
   A. Project expeditor
   B. Risk owner
   C. Project sponsor
   D. Project manager

5. You are working on a very critical and strategic project to develop a robust dynamic website, which will be available to approximately five million users your company has around the globe. You decided to survey the experts within your organization on any foreseeable risks with the design, structure, and intent of the website with an anonymous, simple form. You later sent out subsequent anonymous surveys to a group of experts with the collected information. This is an example of:
   A. A Delphi technique
   B. Identify Risks process
   C. Nominal group technique
   D. SWOT analysis

6. You are the project manager of a data center project. You have just completed an analysis of project risks and have prioritized them using a probability and impact matrix. The approach you used to prioritize the risks is:
   A. Qualitative analysis
   B. Quantitative analysis
   C. Sensitivity analysis
   D. Earned value analysis

7. Which one of the following is a comprehensive way of ordering risks according to their source?
   A. Product description
   B. Risk categories
   C. Assumptions
   D. Constraints

8. You are overseeing a project to implement an accounting application and are currently in the Identify Risks process of identifying and documenting the project risks. All of the following are tools & techniques for the Identify Risks process EXCEPT:
   A. Data Gathering
   B. Data Analysis
   C. Prompt Lists
   D. Monte Carlo simulation

9. Your team is performing a quantitative risk analysis using the Monte Carlo simulator. Which one of the following statements is FALSE about this Monte Carlo analysis?
   A. It translates the uncertainties specified at a detailed level into their potential impact on project objectives at the level of the whole project.
   B. It is a modeling technique that computes project costs one time.
   C. It involves determining the impact of the identified risks by running simulations to identify the range of possible outcomes

for a number of scenarios.
   D. It usually expresses its results as probability distributions of possible costs.

10. One of your hardware vendors sends you an e-mail stating that due to severe weather she may not be able to deliver the networking equipment on time. Which of the following statements is TRUE?
   A. This is a residual risk.
   B. This is a risk trigger.
   C. This is a risk event.
   D. This is a secondary risk.

11. You have identified several problems along with their causes in your web-based application development project. Which one of the following have you probably used to show the problem and its causes and effects?
   A. Ishikawa diagram
   B. System flow diagram
   C. Process diagram
   D. Histogram

12. Your team is performing a risk probability and impact assessment for each risk to investigate the likelihood and potential effect on the project objectives, such as time, cost, scope, and quality. The numeric impact scale is expressed as values from 0.0 to 1.0 and can be stated in equal (linear) or unequal (nonlinear) increments. Your team is using:
   A. An ordinal scale
   B. Monte Carlo analysis
   C. Influence diagram
   D. A cardinal scale

13. Expected Monetary Value (or simply expected value) is a statistical concept that calculates the average outcome of a decision. The two dimensions of risk used to determine this expected value are:
   A. Probability and threshold
   B. Probability and tolerance
   C. Consequence and contingencies
   D. Probability and consequence

14. While overseeing a complex software project to develop a sophisticated golf simulator for a local golf club, you realize that the team is lacking the required technical expertise and experience. You also do not have the required tools and development environment for this kind of complicated software development. After discussing with the sponsor, you decide to give the design and development work to a vendor who specializes in the specific technical area. This is an example of:
   A. Passive acceptance
   B. Active acceptance
   C. Risk avoidance
   D. Risk transfer

15. Steve, a project manager, has a robust risk response plan for his ERP implementation project. The team has utilized all of the appropriate tools & techniques and has executed the predefined preventive and contingency actions to respond to identified project risks. He finds out that some of the risks have been reduced in impact but still remain as potential threats. Steve decides to develop additional contingency and fallback plans for these risks as soon as possible. These risks are called:
   A. Secondary risks
   B. Residual risks
   C. Primary risks
   D. Workarounds

16. You are in the Monitor Risks process of identifying, analyzing, and planning for newly arising risks, keeping track of identified risks, reanalyzing existing risks, monitoring trigger conditions, monitoring residual risks, and reviewing the execution and effectiveness of risk responses. Outputs from the Monitor Risks process include all of the following EXCEPT:
   A. Data Analysis
   B. Work Performance Information
   C. Change requests
   D. Project management plan updates

17. Project risk is an uncertain event or condition in the future; if it occurs, it will have a positive or negative impact on one or more project objectives including scope, schedule, cost, and quality. Project risk is typically characterized by three elements:
   A. Risk event, probability, and amount at stake
   B. Severity, duration, and cost of impact
   C. Source, probability, and frequency of risk
   D. Timing, frequency, and cost of risk

18. Designing redundancy in the system, taking early action, adopting less complex processes, conducting more tests, and developing

prototypes are all examples of:
- A. Risk avoidance
- B. Risk transfer
- C. Risk mitigation
- D. Risk acceptance

19. You are the project manager assigned to a critical project that requires you to handle project risk intentionally and methodically, so you have assembled only the project team. The team has identified thirty-two potential project risks, determined what would trigger the risks, and have rated and ranked each risk using a risk rating matrix. You have also reviewed and verified all documented assumptions from the project team and verified the sources of data used in the process of identifying and rating the risks. You are continuing to move through the risk management process. Which one of the following important steps have you missed?
- A. Engage other stakeholders.
- B. Conduct a Monte Carlo simulation.
- C. Determine which risks are transferable.
- D. Determine the overall riskiness of the project.

20. You are managing the construction of a disaster center for a financial institute. After the preliminary survey, you found out that the location that was selected for the disaster center was highly prone to earthquakes. You raised your concern to management, but due to a specific strategic reason you were told that changing the location would not be an option. In order to deal with this situation, you have selected a specific architectural design that is technologically advanced and earthquake resistant. This is an example of which of the following?
- A. Accept risk
- B. Transfer risk
- C. Avoid risk
- D. Mitigate risk

21. During the initial stage of project planning, you made a guess that all the construction materials such as sand, cement, concrete, rods, and other items would be available within a reasonable price during building construction. While identifying the risk in your project, you found out that the price for cement significantly increased due to heavy demand and less supply. You decided to add this as a new risk in your project. This is an example of:
- A. Assumptions analysis
- B. Diagramming techniques
- C. SWOT analysis
- D. Expert judgment

22. Steve, an IT project manager, is overseeing a project to develop a new wireless media streaming device. He is using various techniques such as Root Cause Analysis, SWOT Analysis, and Assumption and Constraint Analysis to determine what could cause potential risks to his project. Which one of the following Risk Management Processes is he in now?
- A. Plan Risk Management
- B. Identify Risks
- C. Perform Qualitative Risk Analysis
- D. Monitor Risks

23. You have been working on the Plan Risk Management process of establishing the basis to approach, plan, and execute risk management activities and have developed a risk management plan. Which one of the following will NOT be included in your risk management plan?
- A. Methodology: Defines approaches, tools, and data sources for risk management.
- B. Roles and Responsibilities: Defines the roles and responsibilities and sometimes includes non-team members who may have certain roles in risk management.
- C. Identified Risks: A list of identified risks in the project.
- D. Risk Categories: A group of potential causes for risk that can be grouped into categories, such as technical, political, external, project, environmental, and others.

24. Which one of the following will NOT be considered a valid way of reducing risks in your project?
- A. Plan to mitigate the risk.
- B. Develop a workaround.
- C. Select a specific contract type to distribute risk between the buyer and the seller.
- D. Purchase insurance against the risk.

25. You are in the Plan Risk Responses process of developing options and actions to reduce threats and enhance opportunities to your project objectives. The tools & techniques of the Plan Risk Responses process include:
- A. Audits
- B. Escalate, avoid, transfer, mitigate, and accept
- C. Data Analysis
- D. Meetings

26. You planned a trip to a destination four hundred miles away from home. You found out that there is a long stretch of construction on one of the major highways that you are planning to use. You decide to use another highway for that stretch of driving so that you do not have to wait too long in traffic. This is an example of:
    A. Avoiding risk
    B. Creating contingency reserves
    C. Creating a workaround
    D. Creating a fallback plan

27. You will be overseeing a project to develop a smartphone application. While analyzing your project, you identify that there is a 55 percent probability of making $120,000 a 45 percent probability of losing $55,000. What does $41,250 represent in this case?
    A. Net Present Value (NPV)
    B. Return on Investment (ROI)
    C. Economic Value Added (EVA)
    D. Expected Monetary Value (EMV)

28. Your team has identified several risks in the project as well as their probability, impact, and priorities. The team is now exploring the response strategies to risks if they occur. The team identified that a couple of the programmers on the team might leave, which would significantly impact the project, but they decided to deal with it if and when it occurs. Which one of the following statements is true?
    A. This is passive acceptance.
    B. This is active acceptance.
    C. This is risk avoidance.
    D. This is risk mitigation.

29. You are overseeing a project to implement a smartphone application and are currently in the Identify Risks process of identifying and documenting the project risks. While exploring the elements of the enterprise environmental factors as inputs to the Identify Risks process, your team will be exploring all of the following elements EXCEPT:
    A. Organizational risk attitudes
    B. Commercial databases
    C. Assumption and Constraint Analysis
    D. Published checklist

30. You have been working on the Plan Risk Management process of establishing the basis to approach, plan, and execute risk management activities and have developed a risk management plan. Each of the following statements is true regarding the Plan Risk Management process EXCEPT:
    A. The risk management plan, which is a part of the overall project management plan, is an input to all other risk processes.
    B. The risk management plan includes a description of the responses to risks and triggers.
    C. The risk management plan is an output of the Plan Risk Management process.
    D. The risk management plan includes methodology, roles and responsibilities, budget, risk categories, definition of risk probability and impact, revised stakeholder tolerances, reporting formats, and other items.

31. Your company, ITPro Consultancy, has assigned you as the project manager to upgrade the call center in your organization. The number of calls the customer support agents have to answer each month has increased drastically in the last five months, and the phone system is approaching the maximum load limit. You worked with the team and identified several risk items in your project in the Identify Risk process. In which of the following process will you be identifying more risk items?
    A. Plan Risk Responses
    B. Implement Risk Responses
    C. Monitor Risks
    D. Perform Qualitative Risk Analysis

32. A project manager working on implementing WIMAX connectivity in a rural area has to deploy several network devices and set up POPs to house those devices. The project manager just completed the Plan Risk Response process and developed options and action items to enhance opportunities and reduce threats to her project. Which of the follow item should the project manager be working on next?
    A. Update Work Breakdown Structure (WBS) with additional work packages
    B. Numerically analyze the effect of identified risks
    C. Review the execution and effectiveness of risk responses
    D. Prioritize risks by assessing and combining their probability of occurrence and impact

PROJECT RISK MANAGEMENT ANSWERS

1. C: The risk register is an output of the Identify Risks process.

2. D: The cost of probable loss or damage is $600,000 times 5 percent, which equals $30,000. The cost of the insurance premium is $15,000; therefore, you should purchase the insurance premium.

3. B: Risk categories are a group of potential causes for risk and can be grouped into categories, such as technical, political, external, project, and environmental. In order to systematically identify risks to a consistent level of detail, we can use the form of a simple list of categories or a Risk Breakdown Structure (RBS). It's a comprehensive way of ordering risks according to their source.

4. B: The risk owner for a particular risk is responsible for implementing the actions defined by mitigation and the contingency plan in risk management.

5. A: The Delphi technique is mainly focused on preventing group thinking and finding out the true opinions of the participants. This is done by sending a request for information to experts who are participating anonymously, compiling their responses, and sending the results back to them for further review until a consensus is reached.

6. A: Perform Qualitative Risk Analysis is the process of prioritizing risks by assessing and combining their probability of occurrence and impact to the project if they occur. This fast, relatively easy to perform, and cost effective process ensures that the right emphasis is on the right risk areas as per their ranking and priority and helps to allocate adequate time and resources for them. This process utilizes the experience of subject matter experts, functional managers, best practices, and previous project records. Even though numbers are used for the rating in Perform Qualitative Risk Analysis, it is a subjective evaluation and should be performed throughout the project.

7. B: Risk categories are a group of potential causes for risks that can be grouped into categories, such as technical, political, external, project, and environmental. In order to systematically identify risks to a consistent level of detail, we can use the form of a simple list of categories or a Risk Breakdown Structure (RBS). Assumptions are information not generally considered to be based on factual data items and should be verified. Constraints are limitations that should be considered when developing project plans. The product description provides details about the complexity of the product to be delivered.

8. D: Monte Carlo simulation is associated with the Perform Quantitative Risk Analysis process and determines the impact of identified risks by running simulations to identify the range of possible outcomes for a number of scenarios.

9. B: Monte Carlo simulation generates information through iterations. Project information at the activity level is chosen at random during the process and produces data that illustrates the likelihood of achieving specific cost or schedule targets.

10. B: Risk triggers are symptoms or warning signs that a potential risk is about to occur within the project. For instance, a key team member searching for a better job opportunity is a warning sign that the person may be leaving the team soon, causing schedule delay, increased cost, and other issues. Risk events are actual occurrences of an identified risk event. Residual risks are the remaining risks after the execution of risk response planning and for which contingency and fallback plans can be created. Secondary risks are new risks created by implementing the selected risk response strategies.

11. A: The Ishikawa diagram, also called a cause and effect flow chart or a fishbone diagram, shows the relationship between the causes and effects of problems.

12. D: Ordinal scales utilize a narrative description and assign values as high, medium, low, or a combination of these. This numeric scale, also called a cardinal scale, is expressed as values from 0.0 to 1.0 and can be stated in equal (linear) or unequal (nonlinear) increments.

13. D: Risk ratings are determined by the product of probability and impact or consequences when using qualitative analysis and to determine Expected Monetary Value (EMV) when utilizing a decision tree (quantitative analysis). EMV is the product of the probability and consequences of an event or task.

14. D: Transferring is shifting the negative impact of a threat, along with the ownership of the response, to a third party to make it their responsibility. It only gives another party responsibility for its management but does not eliminate the risk. It nearly always involves payment to the third party for taking on the risk. Risk mitigation simply means a reduction in the probability and/or impact of an adverse risk event to an acceptable threshold. Since it is seldom possible to eliminate all risks and also since the cost or impact of avoid, transfer, and mitigate is too high, acceptance can be the preferred strategy. It indicates that the project team is simply accepting the risk and will continue with the project. Passive acceptance requires no action. The active acceptance strategy aims to establish contingency reserves to handle threats. Avoid indicates that you are eliminating the threat by eliminating the root cause of the threat.

15. B: Residual risks are the risks that remain after the execution of risk response planning and for which contingency and fallback plans can be created. Their probability and impact have been reduced through mitigation. These risks are included in the outputs of the Plan Risk Responses process and are expected to remain as threats. Primary risks included in the initial risk identification process are generally most obvious. Secondary risks are new risks that are created due to the implementation of selected risk response strategies. Workarounds are unplanned responses developed to deal with the occurrence of unanticipated risk events.

16. A: Data Analysis such as Technical Performance Analysis and Reserve Analysis are tools & techniques used in the Monitor Risks process.

17. A: A risk event is the actual occurrence of the risk, such as an equipment failure. Risk probability is the likelihood that a risk event may occur. The amount at stake refers to the impact or consequence of the risk on one or more project objectives including scope, schedule, cost, and quality.

18. C: These are all examples of risk mitigation. Risk mitigation simply means a reduction in the probability and/or impact of an adverse risk event to an acceptable threshold. Transferring is shifting the negative impact of a threat, along with the ownership of the response, to a third party to make it their responsibility. An example of this would be insurance bonds, warranties, guarantees, and contracts. Avoidance is eliminating the threat by eliminating the cause or changing the project management plan. An example of this would be using a slower but reliable technology instead of a cutting-edge one to avoid associated risk. Since it is seldom possible to eliminate all risks and also since the cost or impact of avoid, transfer, and mitigate is too high, acceptance can be the preferred strategy. It indicates that the project team is simply accepting the risk and will continue with the project.

19. A: Stakeholders may be great contributors for identifying potential risks in the project. You should have involved other stakeholders instead of only working with the team members on risk management activities.

20. D: Since you are taking action to lower the probability and impact of the risk, you are mitigating the risk.

21. A: This is an example of assumptions analysis. This is an analysis of the validity of assumptions, hypotheses, and scenarios developed in project initiation to identify risks from inaccuracies, incompleteness, and inconsistencies of assumptions. The assumptions that turn out to be invalid should be evaluated, qualitatively and quantitatively analyzed, and planned for just like other risks.

22. B: The Data Analysis Technique, such as Root Cause Analysis, Assumption and Constraint Analysis, and SWOT analysis, are used as tools & techniques in the Identify Risks process.

23. C: A list of identified risks will be included in the risk register, not in your Risk Management Plan.

24. B: Workarounds, unplanned responses developed to deal with the occurrence of unanticipated risk events, are not valid ways of reducing risks in a project.

25. B: Audits and Data Analysis Techniques such as Technical Performance Analysis and Reserve Analysis are tools & techniques used in the Monitor Risks process. Strategies for negative risks or threats such as escalate, avoid, transfer, mitigate, and avoid are used as tools & techniques in the Plan Risk Responses process.

26. A: Risk avoidance is the elimination of the threat by eliminating the cause or changing the project management plan. This is an example of avoidance since you are changing your travel plan to eliminate the threat of traffic delay.

27. D: The expected monetary value is calculated by multiplying the probability with the impact.

The EMV for the opportunity is 55 percent * $120,000 = $66,000 and for the threat is 45 percent * $55,000 = $24,750. The total EMV in this case is $66,000 – $24,750 = $41,250 profit.

28. A: Since it is seldom possible to eliminate all risks and also since the cost or impact of avoid, transfer, and mitigate is too high, acceptance can be the preferred strategy. It indicates that the project team is simply accepting the risk and will continue with the project. The team has decided to go for passive acceptance, which requires no action.

29. C: Assumption and Constraint Analysis is a Data Analysis Technique that is not used as an input but as a tool & technique in the Identify Risks process.

30. B: The Plan Risk Management process establishes the basis to approach, plan, and execute risk management activities throughout the life of the project and develops the risk management plan. The risk management plan does not include a description of the responses to risks or triggers. Responses to risks are documented in the risk register as part of the Plan Risk Responses process.

31. C: Risk items will be identified throughout the project life cycle. The team will identify most of the project risk items in the Identify Risk process and newly emerging risks will be identified in the Monitor Risk process.

32. A: The project manager is currently in the Planning Process Group which needs to be completed prior to moving to the Executing Process Group. Prioritizing risks by assessing and combining their probability of occurrence and impact is carried out in the Perform Qualitative Risk Analysis process. Numerically analyzing the effect of identified risks is carried out in the Perform Quantitative Risk Analysis process. Both of these risk analysis processes are done prior to the Plan Risk Response process. Reviewing the execution and effectiveness of risk responses is carried out in the Monitor Risks process in Monitor and Control Process Group. Adding work packages that are part of the newly planned risk responses should be the next item in the planning.

CHAPTER 12

PROJECT PROCUREMENT MANAGEMENT

PROJECT PROCUREMENT MANAGEMENT QUESTIONS

1. Your management asked you to finalize a contract for an online gaming portal with one of the vendors. You want to make sure that through negotiation you are clarifying and reaching mutual agreement on the structure and details of the contract prior to signing. You also want to make sure while negotiating that you cover major negotiation items, such as authority, responsibilities, price and payment, financing, management approach, and applicable laws. You estimate that it will take another ten days to complete the negotiation and finalize the contract, but the project manager needs to initiate work on several items right away in order to avoid drastic schedule problems in the future. What will be the BEST course of action in this situation?
    A. Verbally asked the vendor to start working while the negotiation is ongoing.
    B. Send the Statement of Work (SOW) to the vendor.
    C. Issue a letter of intent or letter contract.
    D. Inform the project manager that work cannot start prior to signing the final contract.

2. Which one of the following is NOT true about a cost reimbursable contract?
    A. The buyer bears the most risk as total cost is unknown until the project is finished.
    B. It requires auditing sellers' invoices.
    C. Buyers usually write a detailed Statement of Work (SOW).
    D. The seller has only a moderate incentive to control cost.

3. In a Cost Plus Incentive Fee (CPIF) contract, the target cost is estimated at $250,000 and the fee at $35,000. The actual cost came to be $210,000. Since there was a cost savings, the seller shares the savings at a 70/30 ratio (70 percent to the buyer and 30 percent to the seller). What are the final fee and final price?
    A. $47,000 and $257,000
    B. $47,000 and $210,000
    C. $35,000 and $257,000
    D. $35,000 and $210,000

4. You are working on a construction project and successfully completed all the work. Your stakeholders were very pleased and recently communicated their final acceptance of the project. You are now meeting with your team to update the organizational process assets with a record of knowledge gained about the project to help future project managers with their projects. Once the lessons learned are completed, what should you do NEXT?
    A. Release the team
    B. Close the contract
    C. Get formal acceptance
    D. Write lessons learned

5. You are in charge of the bidding process for a government railway project. You are trying to come up with a set of minimum criteria sellers must meet to be considered. Which of the following are you working on?
    A. Screening system
    B. Proposal evaluation technique
    C. A weighting system
    D. An independent or in-house estimate

6. Your company is working on a government railway infrastructure upgrade project. You have signed a Fixed Price (FP) contract and will be paid a fee of $380,000 to complete the work. It's now six months into the project, and your costs have just exceeded $340,000. As per the contract, your company is now responsible for any cost overrun from this point forward, and the buyer will not share any of it. This situation is BEST described as:
    A. The project manager spent too much money on the project.
    B. The project has reached the Point of Total Assumption (PTA).
    C. The buyer is cheating the seller.
    D. The project budget was miscalculated initially.

7. You are working on a software development project to automate an accounting process. You, your team, and your senior manager all feel that the work is complete. However, one of your important clients disagrees and feels that one of the deliverables is not acceptable, as it does not meet the requirements specification. What is the BEST way to handle this conflict?
    A. Issue a change order.
    B. Renegotiate the contract.
    C. File a lawsuit to force the stakeholder to accept the deliverable.
    D. Meet with the responsible team member to review the WBS dictionary.

8. While in the Control Procurements process, you are meeting with your seller to check on the product itself and its conformance to specification. Which one of the following are you performing?
    A. Performance reporting
    B. Procurement performance reviews

C. Inspections and audits

D. Claims administration

9. Which of the following is NOT true about the Close Project or Phase process and the Control Procurements process?

    A. Project closure happens at the end of the project or project phases, whereas there may be many procurement closures as there may be several procurements in a project.

    B. It is not required to close all procurements prior to final project closure.

    C. Project closure may happen at the end of each phase and at the very end of the entire project.

    D. Upon completion of the contract for each of the procurements, a procurement audit should be carried out to close the procurement.

10. You found your vendor's subcontractor to be much more professional and easy to work with and started directly contacting them for project updates and other concerns. You are informed by the vendor that, as per the contractual relationship, this is not an ideal situation since you are only supposed to contact the vendor and not the vendor's subcontractor. The legal contractual relationship that exists between a buyer and a seller after the contract is signed that the vendor is referring to is known as:

    A. Bilateral agreement

    B. Legally bonded relationship

    C. Obligation

    D. Privity

11. The risk associated with performance specifications is usually the responsibility of the:

    A. Project manager

    B. Buyer

    C. Project sponsor

    D. Seller

12. You requested your experts to prepare an independent estimate, or in-house estimate, for your contract to help judge whether the Statement of Work (SOW) was adequate in its description or that the seller understood or responded fully to it. You also want to check the reasonableness of the seller's response and proposed pricing. Which of the following BEST describes what you are doing?

    A. Plan Procurement Management

    B. Conduct Procurements

    C. Control Procurements

    D. Close Procurements

13. You are asked by management to select a contract type that will obligate the seller to accept all liability for poor workmanship, engineering errors, and consequential damages in the project. Which of the following contract types will you select?

    A. Fixed price

    B. Time & material

    C. Cost plus incentive fee

    D. Purchase order

14. You have tried to close most of the concerns and areas of disagreement with the vendor while negotiating prior to signing the final contract. You still do not rule out the possibility of misunderstanding and situations that may adversely affect your project. As an alternative, cheaper method to court for dispute resolution, you have assigned a neutral, private, third party to resolve the disputes. What is this referred to in contract terms and conditions?

    A. Force majeure

    B. Indemnification

    C. Arbitration

    D. Fait accompli

15. You were asked by your management to investigate the cause of severe cost overrun in one of the projects that was completed last year. You found out that a certain contract was used in the project that is considered to be very risky for the buyer, as it does not encourage the seller to control costs; rather, it incentivizes the seller to be inefficient. What sort of contract was used in the project?

    A. Cost Plus Percentage of Cost (CPPC)

    B. Cost Plus Award Fee (CPAF)

    C. Cost Plus Incentive Fee (CPIF)

    D. Fixed Price Economic Price Adjustment (FPEPA)

16. After reviewing your project schedule and resource calendars, you realize that your resources are 100 percent occupied and will have no time to work on a new component. So, you decide to outsource the component and start negotiating with a couple of potential vendors. While outsourcing, which of the following should you be MOST concerned about?

    A. The technical background of the vendor

    B. The financial capability of the vendor

    C. The relevant experience of the vendor

    D. Proprietary data of your organization

17. Sabrina, a project manager for ITPro Consultancy, LLC, is overseeing the design and development of an indoor room temperature and humidity controlling device. While working on the procurement plan, she compared the cost of an off-the-shelf product to the cost of her programmers' design to develop the custom device. Sabrina is engaged in which of the following?
   A. Using expert judgment
   B. Coming up with source selection criteria
   C. Performing a Make-or-buy analysis
   D. Working on the procurement statement of work

18. While working on a data mining project, you realize that you need a data validation tool that was never thought of earlier. After reviewing your project schedule and resource calendars, you realize that your resources are 100 percent occupied and will have no time to work on this new component. So, you decide to outsource the component and start negotiating with a couple of potential vendors. You quickly realize that you do not have a clear definition of the scope, but the vendor agrees with you that the project will be relatively small and you have an urgent need. Which contract type is MOST appropriate in this kind of situation?
   A. Cost Plus Fixed Fee (CPFF)
   B. Cost Plus Award Fee (CPAF)
   C. Fixed Price Economic Price Adjustment (FPEPA)
   D. Time and Materials (T & M)

19. You are in the Control Procurements process and are ensuring that the seller's performance meets contractual requirements by monitoring contract performance and making appropriate changes and corrections. Which of the following will you most likely NOT use as an input in this process?
   A. Procurement documents
   B. Work performance information
   C. Contract
   D. Seller proposals

20. You are the project manager of a data center construction project. Your company made it mandatory to solicit quotes from three separate vendors before submitting the purchase request to the finance department for buying switches, routers, firewalls, PCs, servers, etc., for the data center. What type of input is this policy to the procurement process?
   A. Make-or-buy decision
   B. Procurement document
   C. Source selection criteria
   D. Organizational process assets

21. You are managing a software development project to automate an accounting process. In this Cost Plus Incentive Fee Contract, you have negotiated the following:
Target cost: $120,000 and target fee: $8,000 Max fee: $12,000 and min fee: $4,000 Sharing ratio: 80/20 (buyer/seller)
The actual cost was $145,000. What is the total price the buyer will pay?
   A. $148,000
   B. $149,000
   C. $144,000
   D. $153,000

22. Which of the following is the process of documenting project purchasing decisions, specifying the approach, defining selection criteria to identify potential sellers, and putting together a Procurement Management Plan?
   A. Conduct Procurements process
   B. Plan Procurement Management process
   C. Close Procurements process
   D. Control Procurements process

23. Steve is a program manager overseeing an ERP implementation project where the team has already completed the finance, sales, and admin modules out of seven total modules. Steve was informed that the client has terminated the project as they found a cheaper and faster off-the-shelf solution for their need and no longer want the project to continue. Which of the following is TRUE?
   A. The team must keep working on the project to give senior management time to discuss with the client.
   B. Steve must stop all work and release the team immediately.
   C. Steve must work with the team to document the lessons learned.
   D. Steve must close the contract.

24. You are in the Control Procurements process and want to document the procurement lessons learned from everyone involved in your project to help improve how your organization will handle procurements in the future. Lessons learned Register is created as a result of the procurement audit and include all of the following EXCEPT:
   A. Things that went right or wrong
   B. Successes and failures that should be recognized
   C. Using the payment system to process considerations as per the terms of the contract
   D. Process improvement recommendations and what will be done differently next time

25. In which procurement management process will you ensure that the seller's performance meets contractual requirements, that both the buyer and seller meet their contractual obligations, and that the legal rights of both the buyer and seller are protected?
    A. Procurement performance reviews
    B. Inspections and audits
    C. Performance reporting
    D. Control Procurements

26. You are in charge of the bidding process for a government solar power plant project. You are trying to make sure that no seller receives preferential treatment and that all sellers have a clear, common understanding of the procurement (technical requirements, contractual requirements, etc.). Your key objective is to provide all potential contractors with the information they need to determine if they would like to continue with the contracting process. Which one of the following will assist you with your goal?
    A. Source selection criteria
    B. Bidder conference
    C. Independent estimate
    D. Procurement negotiation

27. Lars is a project manager overseeing an online age verification application for one of the very important clients for his organization. Three months in the project, Lars got a call from the client who informed him that they would end the contract due to a change in business direction. The client also discussed the compensation that the seller's organization is offering to Lars's organization for the work completed so far. This is an example of which one of the following?
    A. Letter of intent
    B. Breach of contract
    C. Material breach
    D. Termination for convenience

28. During the Plan Procurement Management process, your team developed the procurement document to solicit proposals from prospective sellers and to easily compare their responses. All of the following statements are true about the procurement document EXCEPT:
    A. It may include the procurement statement of work and evaluation criteria.
    B. It should not be too rigorous to allow any flexibility for the sellers to be innovative.
    C. It contains clear, complete, and concise descriptions of performance, design, functionality, reporting, format, and support requirements.
    D. It may contain a Request For Proposal (RFP), a Request For Bid (RFB), and a Request For Quotation (RFQ).

29. Sandi is working as a project manager in a drug manufacturing company, Ultra Medicine, LLC. Ultra-Medicine is very excited to introduce a new drug in the market that will stop the human aging process and drastically improve the quality of health. Sandi initiated a conversation with one of the foreign vendors about outsourcing the production of this new drug. The vendor is also very enthusiastic about the potential of the new drug and has requested a copy of the Statement of Work (SOW) so that they can start learning about it. Which one of the following is FALSE about the SOW?
    A. The SOW should contain the details of the new drug.
    B. The SOW should have the details as required but not so much as to give out all the sensitive information and trade secrets of Ultra Medicine.
    C. The SOW should have enough detail for the vendor to figure out if they are capable and qualified to manufacture the drug.
    D. Ultra-Medicine must write the SOW with the necessary detail.

30. While managing a nanotechnology project to build an elevator/tunnel from the ground to the space station, you need to procure a new material called carbon nanotube, which is extremely strong and resistant to heavy air pressure. Due to patent constraints, there is only one supplier in a different state who can provide you with this material. You checked the supplier's website and realized that the price listed for the material on the site would be within your approved limit. What should you do in this situation?
    A. Consider purchasing the material from the source even though it is a sole source.
    B. Keep exploring the option to use some other material to build the tunnel.
    C. Notify management that there is only one source; thus, you cannot purchase the material from the single source.
    D. Ask the procurement department to take care of this situation.

31. As a buyer's project manager, you always try to bring the seller's objectives in line with those of yours. You also understand that for the sellers, the focus is on the profit. Your project has an emergency and needs contracted work to be completed as soon as possible. Which one of the following would be most helpful to add to the contract under this crucial situation?
    A. A Time is of the Essence clause
    B. A robust procurement statement of work
    C. A retainage clause
    D. Incentives

32. Lars is a project manager overseeing an online age verification application for one of the very important clients for his organization. Three months into the project, Lars got a call from the client who informed him that they would not be able to make the partial payment

for the design work due to a financial crisis. The client mentioned that they were very unsatisfied with the quality of the requirement document that the seller submitted. The client's organization also thinks that the contract is no longer valid and needs to be terminated. Lars realizes that once signed, a contract is legally binding unless:

    A. The contract is in violation of applicable laws.
    B. The buyer's legal counsel considers the contract to be null and void.
    C. The seller fails to perform.
    D. The buyer fails to pay for the work.

33. As a buyer's project manager, what is the BEST way for you to ensure that the seller is not making extra profits in a Cost Plus Fixed Fee (CPFF) contract?

    A. You only pay the fee when the project is completed.
    B. You do not authorize any unexpected cost overrun.
    C. You audit all invoices and make sure that you are not charged for items not chargeable to the project.
    D. You ensure that the sellers are not cutting scope.

34. While working on a data mining project, you realize that negotiation is essential to develop a good understanding and relationship with the seller as well as to obtain a fair and reasonable price for the product, service, and result. During which procurement process will procurement negotiation occur the MOST?

    A. Conduct Procurements
    B. Plan Procurement Management
    C. Control Procurements
    D. Close Procurements

PROJECT PROCUREMENT MANAGEMENT ANSWERS

1. C: A letter of intent is a letter expressing the intention of the buyer to hire the seller. It is not a contract; thus, it does not have any legal binding. Usually, the buyer gives a letter of intent to the seller when completion of contract negotiation and finalization will take a significant amount of time but the project needs to be initiated as soon as possible.

2. C: In a cost reimbursable contract, sellers usually write a detailed statement of work. Buyers mostly use this sort of contract in research and development or in information technology projects where the scope is unknown.

3. A:

Target Cost	$250,000
Target Fee	$35,000
Target Price	$285,000
Actual Cost	$210,000
Sharing Ratio	70/30

Final Fee
Total savings is $250,000 – $210,000 = $40,000
Seller portion is $40,000 * 30 percent = $12,000
So, the final fee will be $35,000 + $ 12,000 = $ 47,000
Final Price = $ 210,000 + $47,000 = $257,000

4. A: You should release the team once the lessons learned are documented and added to the organizational process assets. Most contracts have payment terms that allow for some period of time before full payment is required; thus, the last thing you do on the project is close the contract.
The order should be: get formal acceptance, write lessons learned, release the team, and close the contract.

5. A: A screening system is a set of minimum criteria a seller must meet to be considered, such as proficiency with certain products or techniques, safety record, number of years of relevant experience, etc. Prior to reviewing the detailed proposals, a buyer may review the qualifications of sellers who have indicated an interest to bid. A weighting system is generally utilized to score qualified sellers after proposals have been submitted. The procuring organization can prepare its own independent estimate to judge whether the statement of work was adequate in its description or that the seller fully understood or responded fully to the statement of work. This estimate also helps the organization check the reasonableness of the seller's response and proposed pricing.

6. B: The Point of Total Assumption (PTA) is the cost point in the contract where the seller assumes responsibility for all cost overruns as costs beyond this point are considered to be due to mismanagement.

7. D: The very first thing we should do is to find out the details of the issue by reviewing the requirements and meeting with the responsible team member to review the WBS dictionary. We need to find out if there is something wrong in the details of the work package or in how the team member completed the work. If needed, we can then issue a change order. When there's a dispute between a buyer and a seller, it's called a claim. Most contracts have some language that explains exactly how claims should be resolved—and since it's in the contract, it's legally binding, and both the buyer and seller need to follow it. Usually it's not an option to renegotiate a contract, especially at the end of the project after the work is completed. Lawsuits should only be filed if there are absolutely, positively no other options.

8. C: Inspections and audits are activities mainly focused on the product itself and its conformance to specification. Performance reporting is an excellent tool that provides management with information about how effectively the seller is meeting contractual objectives. This report can produce earned values, schedule and cost performance index, trend analysis, etc. Procurement performance review is a structured review that consists of seller-prepared documentation, buyer inspection, and a quality audit of the seller's progress to deliver project scope and quality within cost and on schedule as compared to the contract. The objective is to identify performance progress or failures, non-compliances, and areas where performance is a problem. Claims handling is one of the most frequent activities in the Control Procurements process. Claims, disputes, or appeals are requested when the buyer and seller disagree on scope, the impact of changes, or the interpretation of some terms and conditions in the contract.

9. B: Control Procurements occurs before Close Project or Phase. We should close all procurements prior to final project closure.

10. D: Privity is the contractual relationship that both buyer and seller have to realize and maintain. A bilateral agreement is a binding contract between the two parties that have agreed to mutually acceptable terms.

11. D: Function specifications and performance specifications are the responsibility of the seller, whereas design specifications are usually provided by the buyer; also, risks associated with design are the responsibility of the buyer.

12.   B: We use a Procurement Document such as Independent Cost Estimates as an input in the Conduct Procurements process.

13. A: The fixed price or lump sum contract, which usually pays a lump sum amount for all the work, places the risk on the seller. The seller may include a contingency in the contract to assist in minimizing the risk of reduced profits.

14. C: Arbitration is an alternative, cheaper method to the court system for dispute resolution. A neutral, private, third party is assigned to resolve the dispute. Indemnification identifies parties liable for accidents, personal injury, or damages in a project. Fait accompli is a negotiation tactic of using rules/laws, decisions already made, etc., as mandatory to avoid any further discussion. Force majeure is the allowable excuse for either party for not meeting contractual obligations in the event that something is considered to be an act of God, such as fire, earthquake, flood, freak electrical storm, etc. Since the event is considered to be neither party's fault, usually the seller receives a time extension, and risk of loss is borne by the seller, which is usually covered by insurance.

15. A: In a Cost Plus Percentage of Cost (CPPC) contract, the buyer pays actual cost plus a percentage of cost as a fee. So, the more cost the seller shows, the more money the seller makes. Sellers have no incentive to control cost; rather, they get awarded for being inefficient. This type of contract is illegal in the United States.

16. D: The technical background, financial capability, and relevant experience of the vendor are all very important factors while outsourcing, but we should be very concerned about the sensitive and confidential proprietary data of our organization that we may need to turn over to the vendor.

17. C: Make-or-buy analysis is concerned with determining whether a product can be cost effectively produced in-house or whether it should be purchased, leased, or rented. While performing this analysis, we must consider indirect as well as direct costs, availability in addition to related risk, schedule, etc. Source selection criteria is developed and used to provide sellers with an understanding of the buyer's need and also to help them in deciding whether to bid or make a proposal on the project. Later on, it also helps to evaluate sellers by rating or scoring them. The procurement Statement of Work (SOW) describes the subject item in sufficient detail to allow prospective sellers to determine offerings (bids, proposals, etc.). It documents details of the work to be performed by the seller under a contract.

18. D: This time-based fee plus cost of materials contract is used for smaller amounts and shorter times and requires little or no defined scope of work. In a T & M contract, the seller pays a rate for each of the people working on the team plus their material costs. The "time" part means that the buyer pays a fixed rate for labor, usually a certain number of dollars per hour. And the "materials" part means that the buyer also pays for materials, equipment, office space, administrative overhead costs, and anything else that has to be paid for.

19. D: Seller proposals are inputs to the Conduct Procurements process for obtaining seller responses, selecting a seller, and awarding the procurement, usually in the form of a contract. This is an official response to the buyer's procurement document, including the details the buyer is looking for, how the work will be performed, and pricing. Procurement documents, work performance information, and contracts all are used as inputs for administering procurements in the monitoring & controlling process group.

20. D: Any type of corporate policy or formal and official procurement procedure is an organizational process asset.

21. B: There is a cost overrun of $145,000 - $120,000 = $25,000.
Seller's fee will be decreased by $25,000 * 20% = $5,000.
Thus, seller final fee will be $8,000 - $5,000 = $3,000.
The minimum fee was set to $4,000. So, in this case, the final fee will $4,000, not $3,000.
Buyer's total price will be $145,000 + $4,000 = $149,000.

22. B: Plan Procurement Management is the process of documenting project purchasing decisions, specifying the approach, defining selection criteria to identify potential sellers, and putting together a Procurement Management Plan.

23. C: A project can be terminated any time for a certain cause or simply for convenience of the buyer. If a project is terminated before the work is completed, you still need to document the lessons learned and add them to the organizational process assets. There are always important lessons that you can learn when a project goes seriously wrong even when you did nothing to contribute to the disaster.

24. C: Unless there was a problem processing or making payment, the payment system will not be a part of the procurement audit. The other remaining choices will be included in the procurement audit and captured in the Lessons Learned Register.

25. D: Control Procurements is the process of ensuring the seller's performance meets contractual requirements, ensuring that both seller and buyer meet their contractual obligations, and ensuring that legal rights of both seller and buyer are protected. The focus here is to manage the relationship between buyer and seller, monitor contract performance, and make appropriate changes and corrections. Procurement performance reviews, inspections and audits, and performance reporting are tools & techniques used in the Control Procurements process.

26. B: A bidder conference is intended to assure that no seller receives preferential treatment and that all sellers have a clear, common understanding of the procurement (technical requirements, contractual requirements, etc.). The goal of the bidder conference is to make sure that all questions are submitted in writing and issued to sellers as an addendum to the procurement document so that all sellers respond to the same scope of work, there is no collusion among sellers and/or buying agents, and sellers do not save questions for later private meetings in order to gain competitive advantage. Independent estimates are often prepared by the procuring organization to judge whether the statement of work was adequate in its description or that the seller fully understood or responded fully to the statement of work; these estimates also help the organization check the reasonableness of the seller's response or cost proposal and

proposed pricing. The goal of procurement negotiation is to achieve clarification and agreement on the structure and requirements of the contract prior to signing.

27. D: Termination for convenience is a contract clause that permits the buyer to terminate a contract at any time for a cause or convenience. Usually, there will be specific conditions associated with the execution of this clause. A letter of intent is a letter expressing the intention of the buyer to hire the seller. It is not a contract; thus, it does not have any legal binding. Most of the time, the buyer gives a letter of intent to the seller in the following circumstances:
   - Completion of contract negotiation and finalization will take significant amount of time, but the project needs to be initiated as soon as possible.
   - The seller has no option but to hire people and order equipment in order to meet contractual requirements before the contract is signed.
A breach/default is not meeting contractual obligation by the seller or the buyer. A material breach is so severe that it is not possible to continue work under the contract.

28. C: Usually a Statement of Work (SOW) document contains a clear, complete, and concise description of performance, design, functional, reporting, format and support requirements, not a procurement document. Well- designed procurement documents help in easier comparison of seller responses, more complete proposals, more accurate pricing, and decrease in the amount of changes in the project. Procurement documents may contain all the work that is to be completed, as well as terms, conditions, and evaluation criteria. You want the seller to be as innovative as possible when they come up with the design and methods for completing your project. It may contain request for proposal (RFP), invitation for bid (IFB, or request for bid, RFB), and request for quotation (RFQ).

29. D: It is not mandatory for the buyer to come up with the SOW all the time. The seller can come up with the SOW through requirements collection tools & techniques. Also, seller can update the buyer's SOW and get it reviewed and approved.

30. A: In noncompetitive forms of procurement, usually a seller is selected from a list of qualified sellers interested in and capable of doing the job. Even though competition can result in the selection of a better seller and decreased price, there is no reason for going through the entire procurement process unless law requires it. Two types of noncompetitive forms of procurement are described below:
Single source (preferred seller): In this case the buyer has worked with the seller before, and due to good experience and other convenience with the seller, the buyer does not want to look for another seller.
Sole source (only seller): In this case the seller may be the only one in the market or may have a patent, thus limiting the option of selecting other sellers.

31. D: Under normal circumstances, if you follow the proper project management processes, you should have good definition of scope. In this situation, you should have a quality procurement statement of work. You need good scope definition as well as incentives as you need the seller to share your need for speed. A quality procurement document alone will not ensure speed. Incentives will bring the seller's objectives in line with the buyer's and would be most useful in this case. The "Time is of the Essence" clause states that any delay will be considered as a material breach as delivery dates are extremely important. The "Retainage" clause states that in order to ensure full completion, an amount of money, usually 5 to 10 percent, is withheld from each payment and paid in full once the final work is completed. These two clauses may help but would not be as effective as incentives.

32. A: It is important to understand that once signed, a contract is legally binding unless it is in violation of any applicable law. The failure to perform or make payment usually does not alter the fact that the contract is binding. The contract will remain in binding if only one party considers that the contract is no longer valid. However, if both parties negotiate and agree to terminate the contract, the contract should move into the Control Procurements process.

33. C: In a Cost Plus Fixed Fee (CPFF) contract, the fee is usually paid on a continuous basis during the life of the project. It is unreasonable and unrealistic not to authorize any unexpected cost overrun. Cutting scope would not be a way for sellers to make additional profits as it decreases the profit for this type of contract. The best way is to audit all invoices and make sure that you are not charged for items not chargeable to the project.

34. A: During Conduct Procurements, negotiation occurs to finalize the terms and conditions of the contract. In this process, a contract or agreement is created that is approved by both parties through much negotiation. In order to settle any pending disputes or concerns, negotiation will also be used in the Control Procurements process.

CHAPTER 13

PROJECT STAKEHOLDER MANAGEMENT

PROJECT STAKEHOLDER MANAGEMENT QUESTIONS

1. You are efficaciously managing a business automation project, and most of the deliverables were delivered on time by the team members. This project is extremely critical as it will drastically cut down the time and cost of regular business activities for several departments. Stakeholders and customers have articulated their satisfaction with the project, but you were also criticized for the number of changes made in the project. Which of the following is the MOST likely cause of the project problem?

    A. You failed to identify some of the key stakeholders in your project.
    B. You should have more project management training and experience.
    C. Change Control Board (CCB) members approved almost all of the change requests.
    D. The project should have had a better change control system.

2. You are in the Monitor Stakeholder Engagement process of evaluating and monitoring overall stakeholder relationships and ensuring stakeholders' appropriate engagement in the project by adjusting plans and strategies as required. Which one of the following is an important input to the Monitor Stakeholder Engagement process?

    A. Agreements
    B. Project Charter
    C. Change log
    D. Project Document - Issue log

3. You are performing stakeholder analysis and utilizing different models to identify the interests, expectations, and influence of the stakeholders to classify them. The model that helps to analyze a stakeholder's power or ability to impose his or her will, urgency, or need for immediate attention from the project team along with the legitimacy of his or her involvement is the:

    A. Power/interest grid
    B. Salience model
    C. Power/influence grid
    D. Influence/impact grid

4. You are in the Plan Stakeholder Engagement process of defining an approach to manage stakeholders throughout the entire project life cycle as per their interest, impact, importance, and influence over the project. Which of the following is an input to this Plan Stakeholder Engagement process?

    A. Impact/power grid
    B. Stakeholder Register
    C. Stakeholder Engagement Assessment Matrix
    D. Stakeholder Cube

5. You are in the Manage Stakeholder Engagement process and are focused on meeting and exceeding the stakeholders' expectations by continuously communicating with them, clarifying and resolving their issues, addressing their concerns, and improving project performance by implementing their change requests. Which of the following is a tool & technique used in this process?

    A. Interpersonal and Team Skills
    B. Change log
    C. Issue log
    D. Project Charter

6. You are assigned as a project manager for one of the most imperative and strategic projects in your organization. As the stakeholders will play a vital role in the success of your project, you are trying to identify all your internal and external stakeholders. In which project management process group will you identify stakeholders in your project?

    A. Initiating
    B. Initiating and planning
    C. All process groups
    D. Planning and monitoring & controlling

7. You have been managing a government railway project and dealing with several stakeholders. You have spent a considerable amount of time identifying all your internal and external stakeholders and their interest, influence level in your project, and their key expectations. Managing stakeholder expectations is the responsibility of which party?

    A. Since the project manager alone cannot manage all the stakeholders on a complex, large project, the project manager and project team together are responsible for managing stakeholders' expectations.
    B. Project sponsor, as this individual funds the project and has greater control over the stakeholders.
    C. Stakeholders should make sure that their expectations are managed appropriately and that they receive the required information on the project as needed.
    D. This is the responsibility of the project manager alone.

8. You have thirteen stakeholders in the construction project that you are overseeing. Your initial study about these stakeholders tells you that most of them will actively support your project to be successful, but you have a couple of stakeholders who may deleteriously impact your project. There is one specific stakeholder you are particularly concerned about as he is known to be exceptionally critical

about the way the project managers in the organization manage projects. He also has the reputation for requesting many changes in projects and antagonistically pursuing his demands. You realized that you need to be meticulous in dealing with this stakeholder and plan to take which of the following approaches:

    A. Carefully eradicate the need of this stakeholder and remove him from the stakeholder list.

    B. Have a discussion with the stakeholder's boss and find a way to make the stakeholder support the project positively by not being too critical and aggressive.

    C. Simply deal with the stakeholder and refuse his requests for changes.

    D. Involve this stakeholder in the project as early as possible and work closely with him throughout the project.

9. A trustworthy, senior team member informs you that two of the stakeholders are very apprehensive about the ERP project you are overseeing. The first stakeholder is very panicky that once the ERP is implemented in his department a lot of people will lose their jobs. The second stakeholder is skeptical about the capability of the team to implement such large, multifaceted project. As the project manager, what should you do in this kind of situation?

    A. Set up a meeting with these two stakeholders and discuss their concerns.

    B. Report to the sponsor about these two stakeholders.

    C. Set up a question-and-answer session about the project and invite all the stakeholders.

    D. You should send an official e-mail to the stakeholders asking them to direct any queries about the project in writing to you.

10. You have several stakeholders in the shopping mall construction project that you are overseeing. You know that actively engaging the stakeholders throughout the project and getting their support is key for project success. In which of the following areas will the external stakeholders be able to assist you the MOST?

    A. Project Charter, assumptions, and Project Management Plan

    B. Activity resource constraints and needs

    C. Requirements, deliverables, and schedule

    D. Product deliverables and project constraints

11. You have thirteen stakeholders in the construction project that you are overseeing. Your initial study about these stakeholders tells you that most of them will actively support your project to be successful, but you have couple of stakeholders who may adversely impact your project. When do you think these stakeholders will have the MOST influence on your project?

    A. Throughout the project life cycle

    B. At the completion of the project

    C. At the beginning of the project

    D. During Executing and Monitoring & Controlling Process Groups

12. What is the best way to manage stakeholders who are high on power but low on interest?

    A. Monitor

    B. Keep informed

    C. Keep satisfied

    D. Manage closely

13. While analyzing stakeholders in your project, you identified one stakeholder who is so formidable and influential that he forced the team to implement many of his last-minute change requests in one of the previous projects. There is also a common understanding that he used his influence to dismiss a very important project during executing in the past. What will be your BEST course of action with such a persuasive stakeholder?

    A. Involve this stakeholder as little as possible in the project.

    B. Involve this stakeholder from the very beginning and closely manage him.

    C. Give highest priority to his expectations, concerns, and issues.

    D. Get approval from the sponsor to remove this stakeholder from the project.

14. You are assigned as a project manager to implement an ERP solution for one of the retailers in your area. Currently, you are working on identifying stakeholders and their level of involvement, roles, and responsibilities. Who will be able to help the team the MOST to identify what roles the stakeholders will play and how and what they will contribute to the project?

    A. The sponsor

    B. Senior Management

    C. Functional managers

    D. Stakeholders

15. Due to time and budget constraints, senior management decided not to include the requirements of several stakeholders in a project. The project manager finalized the project management plan but encountered significant challenges in receiving formal acceptance. The stakeholders were extremely upset and tried every possible way to include their requirements in the project as it would take several years for the organization to initiate another project to implement their desired functionalities. After several attempts, the project was finally approved and initiated a couple of months ago. Which of the following preventive actions should the project manager NOT consider in this case?

    A. Make sure that the stakeholders will not use the change control process as a mean to add their requirements.

    B. Document what is out of scope and in scope in the project.

C. Review and confirm the requirements that will be out of scope in the project with the stakeholders.

D. Develop a stakeholder register and stakeholder management strategy.

16. Steve is trying to figure out whether a stakeholder is at an "unaware" state or not so that he can identify required actions and communication needed to minimize the gap between the desired and actual level of engagement of this stakeholder. Which of the following is a tool to assess the current and desired state of engagement of a stakeholder on the project?

 A. Stakeholder Engagement Assessment Matrix

 B. Issue Log

 C. Stakeholder Register

 D. Stakeholder Engagement Plan

17. You are reviewing the Stakeholder Engagement Plan and Communications Management Plan and focusing on meeting and exceeding the stakeholders' expectations by continuously communicating with them, elucidating and resolving their issues, addressing their apprehensions, and improving project performance by implementing their change requests. Which stakeholder management process are you in at this time?

 A. Monitor Stakeholder Engagement

 B. Manage Stakeholder Engagement

 C. Plan Stakeholder Engagement

 D. Identify Stakeholders

18. You are overseeing a web-based application project to automate the business process of one of your clients. You are working on identifying all the internal and external stakeholders who have interest in your project and can positively or negatively impact your project. While identifying the stakeholders, you realize that stakeholder identification is:

 A. To be focused only on stakeholders who will contribute positively to your project:

 B. To be completed in the initial stage of the project life cycle

 C. A responsibility of the project sponsor

 D. To be carried out throughout the project life cycle

19. Stakeholder management necessitates all of the following EXCEPT:

 A. Giving stakeholder extras if needed to meet and exceed their expectations

 B. Identifying both internal and external stakeholders

 C. Assessing stakeholders' skills, knowledge and expertise

 D. Identifying stakeholders' influence-controlling strategies

20. You are overseeing a project to build a plant for a semiconductor company. You have completed your internal and external stakeholder identification and have come up with a list of thirteen stakeholders for the project. You expect that most of the stakeholders will play an affirmative role in the project and will contribute significantly. While working on your Project Management Plan, you were notified by one of the team members that a stakeholder from the automation department is missing in the published stakeholder list. What will be your best course of action in this situation?

 A. Add the stakeholder in your stakeholder list immediately and update everyone.

 B. It is too late to add any more stakeholders and consider their requirements, so ignore the stakeholder.

 C. Validate the information received from the team member.

 D. Set up a meeting with the stakeholder and the team member.

21. You have been managing a government railway project and dealing with several stakeholders. You have spent a considerable amount of time identifying all your internal and external stakeholders and their interest, influence level in your project, and their key expectations. As part of your analysis of the level of engagement of stakeholders in your project, you have classified them as:

 Unaware: Stakeholders are ignorant about the project and apparent impacts.

 Neutral: Stakeholders are aware of the project and apparent impacts but neither accommodating nor resistant.

 Resistant: Stakeholders are aware of the project and apparent impacts and opposed to changes.

 Supportive: Stakeholders are aware of the project and apparent impacts and accommodating to changes.

 Leading: Stakeholders are aware of the project and apparent impacts and enthusiastically involved in making certain the project is a success.

What sort of techniques are you using in this case?

 A. Information gathering techniques

 B. Stakeholder Analysis

 C. Delphi technique

 D. Data Representation – Stakeholder Engagement Assessment Matrix

22. You identified all people who would be impacted by the project and documented relevant information regarding their interests, expectations, involvement, and influence on the project success in a stakeholder register. The stakeholder register will NOT be used as an input to which of the following processes?

 A. Collect Requirements and Identify Risks

 B. Plan Risk Management and Plan Resource Management

 C. Plan Quality Management and Plan Communications Management

D. Develop Project Charter and Perform Integrated Change Control

23. Your company, ITPro Consultancy, has assigned you as the project manager to upgrade the call center in your organization. The number of calls the customer support agents have to answer each month has increased drastically in the last five months, and the phone system is approaching the maximum load limit. While identifying the stakeholders, you realize that there are more than 180 potential stakeholders, 19 team members, and 6 different vendors that you will need to deal with. What will be your BEST course of action?
   A. Have an urgent meeting with the sponsor and request him not to include some of the stakeholders.
   B. Identify an effective approach to determine the needs of all stakeholders.
   C. Identify the key stakeholders and concentrate only on their needs.
   D. Report to the management that the project is too large to manage by one person.

24. Project Stakeholder Management consists of processes to identify the internal and external stakeholders, determine their expectations and influence over the project, develop strategies to manage them, and effectively engage them in project execution and decision. Which one of the following is the key objective of the Stakeholder Management?
   A. Keeping the stakeholders happy and satisfied
   B. Maintaining a robust communication with all stakeholders
   C. Keeping a positive relationship with all stakeholders
   D. Establishing a good coordination among stakeholders

25. You are in the process of evaluating and monitoring overall stakeholder relationships and ensuring stakeholders' appropriate engagement in the project by adjusting plans and strategies as required. The Work Performance Data that is an input to this Monitor Stakeholder Engagement process usually comes from:
   A. Validate Scope
   B. Perform Integrated Change Control
   C. Monitor and Control Project Work
   D. Direct and Manage Project Work

26. A stakeholder register includes all of the following items EXCEPT:
   A. **Stakeholder classification:** Internal/external, neutral/resistor/supporter, and others.
   B. **Identification information:** Name, title, location, organization, role in the project, position, and contact information.
   C. **Assessment information:** Key requirements and expectations, potential impact, importance, and influence on the project.
   D. **Strategies:** The strategies to interact with stakeholders, increase their positive influence, and control their negative influence.

27. One of your primary goals in your project is to have more interaction and build a positive relationship with your stakeholders. You are particularly interested about 4 stakeholders and trying to figure out which one you should make it a priority to get to know. The first one is an employee from the Sales Department who thinks that the product of the project will drastically improve productivity. The second one is Chief Information Officer (CIO) who has been very helpful to all your projects. The third one is a programmer from IT department who is the Subject Matter Expert (SME) but has no interest in introducing the product in his department. And the last one is the Engineering Department Head who will be using your product but known to be very resistant to changes. You should be giving the highest priority to:
   A. The employee from the Sales Department.
   B. The Chief Information Officer (CIO)
   C. The programmer from IT department
   D. The Engineering Department Head

PROJECT STAKEHOLDER MANAGEMENT ANSWERS

1. A: The root cause of the significant number of changes in the project is that some of the key stakeholders were not identified and their requirements were not captured. These missing stakeholders have submitted several change requests to accommodate their needs. Nothing in this scenario advocates that the project manager does not have the required project management training and experience. A vigorous change control board will be efficiently evaluating the change requests to approve or reject them, but they cannot really help with the number of changes a project will have.

2. D: The Issue Log is an important input to the Manage Stakeholder Engagement process. An issue is an obstacle that threatens project progress and can block the team from achieving its goals. An Issue Log is a written log document to record issues that require a solution.

3. B: The salience model addresses stakeholder power or ability to impose their will, urgency, or need for immediate attention from the team and legitimize their involvement (whether their involvement is appropriate) in a project. Power/interest grid is based on the level of authority or power and level of concern or interest a stakeholder has regarding the project outcome. Power/influence grid is based on the level of authority or power and active involvement or influence a stakeholder has. Influence/impact grid groups stakeholders based on their involvement or influence and their ability to affect changes to planning or execution(impact).

4. B: The Stakeholder Register is an input to the Plan Stakeholder Engagement process. Impact/power grid, Stakeholder Engagement Assessment Matrix, and Stakeholder Cube are tools and techniques used in different Stakeholder Management Processes.

5. A: Interpersonal skills, such as conflict management, cultural awareness, negotiation, observation/conversation, and political awareness, are crucial tools & techniques used in the Manage Stakeholder Engagement process. Issue Log and Change Log are never tools & techniques as they are always inputs or outputs. A Project Charter is also not a tool and technique.

6. C: Stakeholders can be identified throughout the project management process groups of initiating, planning, executing, monitoring & controlling, and closing. In order to determine the requirements and expectations of the stakeholders, they should be identified and should be involved at the beginning of the project as much as possible. If all the stakeholders' needs and requirements are not taken into consideration prior to plan finalization, the results may be very expensive changes or dissatisfaction later in the project.

7. D: The project manager is responsible for managing stakeholder expectations.

8. D: The project manager simply cannot remove the stakeholder from the stakeholder list since he has a stake in the project. It will be best to involve this stakeholder in the project as early as possible and work closely with him throughout the project to understand his requirements and expectations and gain his constructive support.

9. A: An informal verbal communication by setting up a meeting with these two stakeholders and discussing their concerns should be the best approach here. Reporting to the sponsor without much detail about these two stakeholders will not solve any real problem. Since not all stakeholders have concerns, setting up a question-and-answer session about the project with all the stakeholders will not be appropriate. Sending an official e-mail to the stakeholders asking them to direct any query on the project in writing to the project manager will most probably estrange them.

10. D: The project manager creates the Project Management Plan, schedule, and activity resource needs with input from the team members. The project sponsor will approve the project charter. External stakeholders may help the team in determining product deliverables and project constraints.

11. C: Stakeholder influence is highest at the start and diminishes as the project proceeds.

12. C: The strategy for stakeholders who are high on the power but low on the interest is "keep satisfied."

13. B: The project manager simply cannot remove the stakeholder from the stakeholder list since he has a stake in the project. It will be best to involve this stakeholder in the project as early as possible and work closely with him throughout the project to understand his requirements and gain his constructive support.

14. D: Stakeholders will be able to help the project manager and team members the most in identifying what roles they will play in the project. The project manager will decide how and what kind of contributions stakeholders will make in the project by discussing with team members, the sponsor, and stakeholders. The project manager should evaluate the knowledge and skill sets of stakeholders in order to identify stakeholders' roles and have a discussion with them to make sure that they approve the roles.

15. C: As the project was approved and work was begun, the issue should not be a concern anymore. Having further meetings with the stakeholders will be excessive and will not add any real value.

16. A: A Stakeholder Engagement Assessment Matrix is a tool to assess the engagement levels of the stakeholders on a project. The matrix can be utilized to compare the actual engagement levels to the planned levels. Any discrepancies can be examined, and communication to adjust the engagement levels can then be implemented.

17. B: All these activities typically belong to the Manage Stakeholder Engagement process.

18. D: Stakeholder identification will persist throughout the project life cycle. As the project proceeds through each phase, additional

stakeholders may become involved while others will be released from the project. Some stakeholders will be identified during the initiating phase in the project charter, while other stakeholders may only be interested in the end product and will be involved only at the closing phase.

19. A: Giving stakeholder extras or gold plating should always be avoided. Gold plating is not the preferred way of meeting and exceeding stakeholder expectations.

20. C: Before you take any other step, you should validate the information received from the team member.

21. D: A Data Representation technique such as Stakeholder Engagement Assessment Matrix is used to classify stakeholders as per their level of engagement in the project during the Plan Stakeholder Engagement process.

22. D: The Stakeholder Register will be used as an input to the Collect Requirements, Plan Resource Management, Plan Risk Management, Identify Risks, Plan Quality Management, and Plan Communications Management processes. It is not an input to the Develop Project Charter and Perform Integrated Change Control processes. The Develop Project Charter process is executed prior to the Identify Stakeholder process where the Stakeholder Register will be developed.

23. B: In order to minimize numerous changes later in the project, you need to identify all stakeholders and their needs as early as possible. Stakeholder analysis will be a more complicated task if there are numerous stakeholders and an effective way to determine their needs must be identified.

24. A: Keeping stakeholders happy and satisfied is the main objective of the stakeholder management. Maintaining a robust communication, keeping a positive relationship, and establishing a good coordination will collectively contribute to achieve stakeholder satisfaction.

25. D: All Work Performance Data comes from executing process group. In this case, Work Performance Data comes as an output of the Direct and Manage Project Work, an executing process.

26. D: The strategies to interact with the stakeholders are included in the Stakeholder Management Plan, not in the Stakeholder Register.

27. D: As the Engineering Department Head this person may have significant influence on other stakeholders in his department. You need to reassure this key stakeholder about your product since he is not open to changes or he will use his influence to disrupt your project.

CHAPTER 14

CODE OF ETHICS

AND
PROFESSIONAL
CONDUCT

PROJECT CODE OF ETHICS AND PROFESSIONAL CONDUCT QUESTIONS

1. You are accountable for a large data center project and have requested proposals from several vendors. You will be purchasing $1.2 million worth of networking equipment, a software application, and an ERP solution for the project. Once informed about your upcoming family vacation on an island, one of the vendors offered you to stay in his summer cabin on forty acres land he happens to have on that island. What should you do in this situation?

    A. Decline the offer as it will be considered an integrity issue on the part of the vendor.
    B. Decline the offer as it is an integrity issue and will be considered as your personal gain.
    C. Accept the offer and also inform the project sponsor about it.
    D. Accept the offer as you do not see any integrity issue or conflict of interest.

2. While discussing the project schedule with the sponsor, both of you recognize that the project is behind schedule and that there is no way to meet the deadline that was committed. The sponsor asked you not to reveal this fact to the customer in the impending status meeting later on that day. What will be your BEST course of action?

    A. Have a quick chat with the customer and explain your situation.
    B. Request the sponsor to have a conversation with the customer.
    C. Postpone the status meeting.
    D. Explain to the sponsor that it is not ethical to knowingly report an incorrect project status to anyone in the project.

3. Your project to build a water park in one of the east side subdivisions has been going pretty well. Recently you noticed that two of the team members are unremittingly arguing about project priorities, work assignments, and technical options. This is having an adverse impact on the overall project, and other team members have also complained to you about this concern. What will be your BEST course of action?

    A. Have a discussion with the concerned functional manager.
    B. Remove those two team members from the team.
    C. Have a meeting with these two team members to discuss and understand their concerns and points of view.
    D. Issue a warning letter to both of the team members.

4. You are working for a consultancy firm that provides PMP training and consultancy. You notice that the firm is encouraging the candidates to be untruthful about their required project management experience and training hours to be eligible to take the test. What will be your MOST appropriate course of action?

    A. Since you are not involved in the registration process, simply ignore what is going on in the organization.
    B. Ask the manager responsible to stop any such unethical practice.
    C. Contact PMI and explain the situation.
    D. Quit your job.

5. You are a senior project manager, and recently you were asked to manage a project to build a brick manufacturing plant. While the team was conducting the feasibility study, you learned that the plant could severely contaminate the air and water in the neighborhood. You became apprehensive that this catastrophic impact could be long lasting. You discussed your concern with the sponsor and recommended to implement robust waste management procedures that will add cost to the project. The sponsor contended that the project should be completed as soon as possible with the defined scope and no extra cost. What will be your BEST course of action in this situation?

    A. Politely refuse to take charge of the project.
    B. Take charge of the project and inform the local residents about the potential negative impact of the manufacturing plant.
    C. Agree with the sponsor.
    D. Take charge of the project and do not disclose any information about the negative impact of the manufacturing plant to the local residents.

6. You have been assigned as a project manager for a project in a country where employees take long lunches and nap breaks, enjoy six weeks of paid vacation each year, and observe several supplementary holidays that are not offered in your home country. You have been asked by your local team members to authorize the same kind of vacation time and holidays to maintain team equality. What will be your BEST course of action?

    A. Inform the foreign team that they must follow the vacation and holiday guidelines of the head office.
    B. Be fair and allow the local team to enjoy the same kind of relaxed lifestyle.
    C. Treat all the extra vacation days and holidays as schedule constraints in your project.
    D. Explore the option of outsourcing this part of the project to some other geographic location.

7. The software project to build a new office application is in progress. While reviewing one of the components, you discover that it does not meet the quality standards of your company. Upon further investigation, you realize that the component does not necessarily need to meet the specified quality standards as it will function just fine as is. The team member responsible for the component also mentioned to you that meeting the specified quality standards will be time consuming and pricey. What should be your BEST course of action as a project manager?

    A. Accept this particular component, but make sure that the remaining components meet the specified quality standards.
    B. Report the concern about the level of quality and seek a solution.
    C. Modify the specified quality standards to match the level achieved.
    D. Report the component as satisfactory.

8. While managing a web-based application project to automate the accounting process, one of your valuable clients requested you to bypass developing a quality policy for the project to save time. There is no existing organizational or industrial quality policy that you can use in the project. You have expressed your strong disagreement with the customer, but they were pretty unwavering about their approach. What will be your BEST course of action?
    A. Contact PMI immediately and report the situation.
    B. Request the sponsor to have a discussion with the customer on the necessity of the quality policy.
    C. Follow the customer's wishes as the customer is always right.
    D. Ignore the customer's request and create the quality policy for your project.

9. There are several potential projects in your organization, but the organization needs to select the best project to work on due to limited resources, cash flow, and different strategic objectives and priorities. Higher management asked you to compare these potential projects and find out the best one with the most value based on the project triggers and benefit measurement methods. You are a project manager with several years of experience in implementing IT projects, but you are not conversant with project selection methods. What should you do in this situation?
    A. Inform higher management that you are lacking experience and expertise in project selection methods.
    B. Do your best and select the project that you think will bring the most value.
    C. Politely inform management that you are unable to take the assignment at this time.
    D. Seek expert opinion to select the best project.

10. You are substituting a project manager who just left the organization. While reviewing the deliverables and their status, you notice that several deliverables that were reported as completed are still in development. Additionally, management is under the impression that the project is on track when, in fact, it is behind schedule and over budget. What will be your BEST course of action?
    A. Politely refuse the project assignment.
    B. Revise the status and notify management.
    C. Have an urgent meeting with the key stakeholders and ask for suggestions on what to do.
    D. Explore crashing the project to bring it back on track.

11. While finalizing the biweekly project status and progress reports, you observe that a few deliverables that are reported as completed are not actually done and that the team members also did not report the days spent on the activities correctly. Your project statistics and updates become very unrealistic with these wrong estimates given by the team members. What should you do in this kind of situation?
    A. Report the information as is.
    B. Provide accurate and truthful project information in a timely manner.
    C. Inform the functional managers about the actions of the team members.
    D. Replace the team members who are providing wrong estimates

12. One of your best friends in charge of maintaining customers' finances and investments is working in the same financial institution with you. She shared a secret with you and asked you not to divulge the secret to anyone. She told you that she has been using clients' money to invest in the stock market and has made a substantial amount of money doing so. She also asked you to join with her so that both of you can make a fortune. What should you do in this kind of situation?
    A. Report your friend to the appropriate authority.
    B. Explore different stock options and find out the best way to make a large amount of money.
    C. Find out if what your friend is doing is really illegal or not.
    D. Ask your friend to stop the illegal activity, but do not mention it to anyone else.

13. You did not utilize all the tools & techniques of risk identification and disregarded a potential risk. The risk shows up during the project planning phase and surprises the team. What kind of response is expected from you as a project manager?
    A. Have a discussion with the sponsor and seek guidance.
    B. Develop the risk response plan and determine preventive and corrective actions.
    C. Take responsibility and evaluate the impact of the risk item.
    D. Immediately inform the customers about the risk event.

14. You recently found out that one of your best friends has been pretending to be a PMP. She thinks that the certification is helping her immensely, but she never thought of pursuing it in real life due to the difficulty of the exam. What will be your BEST course of action?
    A. Report to your friend's boss.
    B. Hand your friend over to the police immediately.
    C. Encourage your friend to get the real certification.
    D. Contact PMI and report the situation.

15. Higher management is exploring the option to open a branch office in a foreign county to outsource backup, storage, and support activities. While conducting the feasibility study, you found out that women are not allowed to work in several sectors, and the country's law also postulates that the salary of a woman should be 60 percent of that of a man's for the same job. The country is very welcoming to your business, and the process of opening a new business is simple and fast. Experts with required expertise are easily available, and your company will also save a substantial amount of money in labor, equipment, raw materials, and low taxes. What should be your recommendation?
    A. Ignore the law and compensate the women you will be hiring equally.
    B. Consider not hiring any women to avoid conflicts.

C. Negotiate with the official and ask to be excused from laws discriminating women.

D. Consider not opening the branch office in this country.

16. Your company has been working with numerous financial institutions for several years and has built spectacular relationships with them. Recently you submitted a proposal in response to a bid for a data and disaster center project for one of these financial institutions in which your company has no previous experience and lacks required expertise. Which of the following is TRUE regarding this situation?

A. It is a common practice to exaggerate expertise and experience when submitting a proposal for a bid.

B. You have not violated the PMI code of ethics and professional conduct, but you have violated the procurement code.

C. There is no violation in this situation.

D. You have violated the PMI code of ethics and professional conduct.

17. You are one of the members of the proposal evaluation team responsible for evaluating and awarding contracts to eligible vendors. While reviewing the list of potential vendors, you notice that one of your good friends is a participant in the bidding process. You know that your friend is an expert in his domain and the project will be greatly benefited if he is awarded the contract. What will be the BEST course of action in this situation?

A. Keep silent and continue with the procurement process.

B. Convince the proposal evaluation team to award your friend the contract.

C. Inform the sponsor and the evaluation team about your relationship.

D. Offer your friend some good tips to increase his chance of winning the bid.

18. As a project manager, you are assigned to oversee a network infrastructure project in a foreign country for six months. At the end of the first introductory meeting, all six participants from your team were given exclusive gifts. When you were reluctant to accept your gift, you were told that it is a custom in their country to give this kind of gift to business partners. What will be your BEST course of action?

A. Decline the gift as accepting it will be considered personal gain in your country.

B. Decline the gift as accepting it will be considered conflict of interest in your country.

C. Accept the gift and inform your management so that your integrity will not be questioned later on.

D. Accept the gift as you do not consider it to be a conflict of interest or integrity issue.

19. You are implementing a WIMAX network for one of your clients in a rural area. You recently implemented a similar network for another client and installed several towers and POPs for them throughout the same region. The current client can save a considerable amount of time and money if they can rent the existing infrastructure instead of setting up their own towers and POPs. You have a nondisclosure agreement with the previous client, and you are not supposed to disclose any information on their infrastructure or network architecture. What will be your BEST course of action?

A. Ignore the nondisclosure agreement as it is not legally enforceable and share the network architecture and infrastructure from the previous project.

B. Install new towers and POPs for the existing customer and ignore the fact that the existing infrastructure can be used for the benefit of both organizations.

C. Seek guidance from your Project Management Office (PMO).

D. Have a discussion with your previous client and seek permission to share the information on the existing infrastructure.

20. You are participating in a bid in a foreign country for a company that wants to procure several expensive pieces of hospital equipment. You are told by the procuring organization that you need to obtain a trade license from the local authority and that the entire process will take approximately four weeks. There is only one week left for the bidding, and you cannot really wait four weeks for the trade license. While discussing it with one of the local officials, you discover that you can fast-track the process and obtain the trade license in three days if you pay an "urgent fee" of $750. Which of the following should you consider if the fee is within the approved limit in the budget?

A. Wait four weeks if needed, but do not pay the additional fee under any circumstance.

B. Pay the urgent fee and obtain the license in three days.

C. Negotiate the urgent fee and try to lower it as much as possible.

D. Participate in the bidding without the local trade license.

21. Your company just assigned you as a project manager for a large data center project. You were asked by the sponsor to complete the project in six months and within $120,000. You soon realize that both the time and cost estimation from higher management is impractical. Your estimation shows that the project could take as long as ten months and that the cost will be at least 20 percent more than the initial estimation. The sponsor tells you that she is considering another project manager to take care of the project in case you do not agree with her time and cost estimations. What will be your BEST course of action?

A. Excuse yourself from the project.

B. Document the time and cost constraints and carry on with the project as instructed.

C. Submit your detailed time and cost estimations and justification to the sponsor.

D. Have an urgent meeting with the client and explain the situation.

22. You are in charge of a very important, big-budget video game project. You have thirteen identified stakeholders and ten team members in the project. You notice that one of the team members who has a major role in the project has been meeting with an anonymous stakeholder to discuss the project details. What should you do in this situation?

A. Have a discussion with the team member and express your concern.

B. Report it to the functional manager.

C. Have a meeting with the team member and the unidentified stakeholder.

D. Make sure you continue to keep an eye on the team member.

23. You are overseeing a software project to develop a challenging and innovative video game. One of your friends, who is a connoisseur in this field and has several of his very popular games in the market, has requested you to give him a copy of the game prior to its release so that he can check it out and provide his feedback. You know his feedback will be valuable to find any defects and improve the game. What should you do in this situation?

A. Ask your friend to sign a nondisclosure agreement prior to giving him a copy.

B. Give him a copy of the game since he is an expert and may provide valuable feedback about the game.

C. Make sure that your friend will provide you with the required feedback and suggestions prior to giving him a copy of the game.

D. Decline the request as the game is the intellectual property of your company.

24. Your company just initiated a project to install a Wi-Fi network in one of the Asian countries. One of the clients offers gifts to all your team members and requests you to give his office a dedicated connection with the max bandwidth possible. What should you do in this situation?

A. Reject the gifts and never communicate with that client again.

B. Accept the gifts but refuse to give the dedicated connection.

C. Reject the gifts as accepting gifts is a violation of the code of ethics and professional conduct.

D. Accept the gifts and agree to give the dedicated connection as it will not cost any extra to the project.

25. You are participating in a bid in a foreign country for a company that wants to procure several expensive pieces of hospital equipment. You have meticulously followed the bidding procedure and are expecting to be the most qualified and lowest bidder. One of the representatives of the procuring company contacted you and asked for 10 percent commission on the total price or they would award the deal to some other vendor. What will be your BEST course of action?

A. Contact PMI immediately and report the situation.

B. Negotiate the commission and try to bring it down as much as possible.

C. Deny the offer and notify your management.

D. Agree to give 10 percent to secure the deal.

PROJECT CODE OF ETHICS AND PROFESSIONAL CONDUCT ANSWERS

1. B: You should decline the offer based on the fact that it will be considered as personal gain on your part and your integrity will be questioned. Option A will not be the correct answer because you are not responsible for the integrity of others.

2. D: The best course of action will be to explain to the sponsor that under all circumstances you are obligated to conduct yourself in a truthful manner and report the truth regarding project status. You are also obligated not to deceive others and not to make false or half-true statements. It is not ethical to knowingly report an incorrect project status to anyone in the project.

3. C: One of the mandatory standards in the PMI code of ethics and professional conduct is respect. It involves the way we conduct ourselves in a professional manner and listen to other viewpoints. As a project manager, you should approach those two team members directly to understand their concerns. If this problem persists, you should have a discussion with the concerned functional manager, issue a warning letter, or remove them from the team (in an extreme situation).

4. C: You are obligated to report any violation of the PMI code of ethics and professional conduct to PMI.

5. A: One of the mandatory standards in the PMI code of ethics and professional conduct is responsibility. Responsibility is the act of making and taking ownership of our decisions, admitting our mistakes, and being responsible e for our decisions and actions. As a project manager, you must make decisions based on the best interests of society, public safety, and the environment. It is not advisable to undertake a project that will work against the interests of the public.

6. C: One of the mandatory standards in the PMI code of ethics and professional conduct is respect. As a project manager, you should respect personal, ethnic, and cultural differences and avoid engaging in behaviors might be considered disrespectful. The only valid action will be to treat all extra vacation days and holidays as schedule constraints in your project.

7. B: You should report the concern with the level of quality so that the experts can find an appropriate resolution. It would be unethical to modify the specific quality standards and report the component as satisfactory. Making sure that the remaining components will meet the quality standards will not really solve the existing problem.

8. B: In a difficult situation that is beyond the control of the project manager, the sponsor may get involved and act as a liaison to the customer. When there is a dispute, we should always try to resolve it in favor of the customer, but as a project manager, you should also remember that the customer is not always right. You must create a quality policy for your project in case there is no existing organizational or industrial policy document that you can use.

9. A: One of the mandatory standards in the PMI code of ethics and professional conduct is honesty. Honesty i s the act of communicating and conducting ourselves in a truthful manner, reporting the truth regarding project status, not deceiving others, not making false or half-true statements, and being honest about our own experience and expertise. In this particular scenario, you should honestly report your lack of experience and expertise in project selection methods to higher management. Also, as per the PMI code of ethics, you should accept only those assignments that are consistent with your background, experience, skills, and qualifications. Higher management may help you in various ways, including suggesting you seek expert opinion for selecting the project once they are informed about your lack of experience. So refusing the assignment will not be an appropriate action in this situation.

10. B: Since there are changes in project cost and schedule, you should revise the status and update management accordingly before you take any other action. Crashing the project usually adds cost to the project, so it will make things even worse. You cannot simply refuse to manage a project because it is behind schedule and over budget. As a project manager, you should be directing the project instead of asking the stakeholders to do so.

11. B: One of the mandatory standards in the PMI code of ethics and professional conduct is honesty. Honesty is the act of communicating and conducting ourselves in a truthful manner, reporting the truth regarding project status, not deceiving others, and not making false or half-true statements. As a project manager, you should always provide accurate and truthful information in a timely manner. It would be unethical to report the wrong project status to anyone in the project. You should have a discussion with the team members about the negative impact of their actions. If needed, you may need to inform functional managers about the actions of the team members.

12. A: You are obligated to report any illegal activity to the appropriate authority.

13. C: One of the mandatory standards in the PMI code of ethics and professional conduct is responsibility. Responsibility is the act of making and taking ownership of our decisions, admitting our mistakes, and being responsible for our decisions and actions. As a project manager, you must take responsibility for the failure in identifying the risk and evaluate the impact to develop the risk response plan. Once you have the detail on the risk item, you can have a discussion with the customer. Also, you may escalate the risk to the sponsor if the risk is beyond your control.

14. D: You are obligated to report any PMI code of ethics and professional conduct violation to PMI.

15. D: One of the mandatory standards in the PMI code of ethics and professional conduct is fairness. Fairness includes making decisions

impartially and objectively and avoiding favoritism and discrimination against others. As a project manager you need to make sure that there will be no discrimination against others based on, but not limited to, gender, race, age, disability, nationality, or sexual orientation. You also need to make opportunities equally available to all qualified candidates. Your best course of action will be to recommend not opening the branch office in this country.

16. D: You have violated the PMI code of ethics and professional conduct. As a project manager, you should be honest about the experience and expertise of your organization.

17. C: Since there is a potential conflict of interest, you should discuss the relationship with the sponsor and evaluation team. It will be up to the evaluation team and sponsor to decide whether you should disassociate yourself from the bidding process or not.

18. C: You should accept the gift because if you decline and reciprocate the gesture, it can severely affect your relationship with the customer. You should also immediately inform your management so that your integrity will not be questioned later on.

19. D: You need to work in the best interest of your client and try to save money and time for them if possible by exploring the option of using the existing infrastructure rather than installing new towers and POPs. Even if the nondisclosure agreement is not legally enforceable, you are ethically bound to comply with it. The best course of action will be to have a discussion with the previous client and seek permission to share the information on the existing infrastructure. Seeking guidance from the PMO will not be essential since approval from the PMO to share the information will not make it acceptable.

20. B: In this case, the fee has a valid purpose and should not be considered a bribe. You should pay the urgent fee of $750 and obtain the trade license.

21. C: You cannot simply refuse to manage the project because you do not agree with the time and cost estimations of the sponsor. As a project manager, you are expected to present truthful and accurate information regarding time, cost, and other project objectives. So you should submit your detailed time and cost estimations and justification for the longer duration and additional budget. If your justification is reasonable, the sponsor should agree with your argument. Continuing with the project with unrealistic time and cost expectations will be a recipe for failure. Having an urgent meeting with the client will not be appropriate in this situation.

22. A: At first you should have a discussion with the team member to find out why she is meeting with the unidentified stakeholder. Reporting the incident to the functional manager will not be appropriate until you identify any problem.

23. D: You should decline the request as the video game is the intellectual property of your organization.

24. C: The client is making a request by offering gifts; thus, you should reject the gifts as it is a violation of the PMI code of ethics and professional conduct. A project manager is expected to be honest and should not engage in dishonest behavior with the intention of personal gain or at the expense of others. If it is customary in that country to offer gifts, you may accept the gift without agreeing to the client's request of dedicated connection. Not communicating with the specific client may impact the project.

25. C: You should never bribe even though it may help you win a project. Your best course of action will be to deny the offer and disclose the incident to higher management.

FINAL EXAM

FINAL EXAM QUESTIONS

1. A project manager managing a video simulator project was informed by one of the team members about a complex problem that can have a drastic negative impact on the project. The project manager immediately defined the cause of the problem by analyzing the problem using a fishbone diagram, identified a solution, and implemented the solution. The project manager recently received a call from the same team member and was informed that the same problem had resurfaced. What did the project manager most likely forget to do?
   A. Validate the solution with the sponsors.
   B. Confirm that the solution actually solved the problem.
   C. Use a Pareto chart.
   D. Identify why the problem occurred.

2. You are overseeing the implementation of a new computer structure at the local hospital. You are currently working on identifying all the internal and external stakeholders who have an interest in your project and can positively or negatively impact your project. While identifying the stakeholders, you realize that stakeholder identification is:
   A. The responsibility of the project sponsor.
   B. To be carried out throughout the project life cycle.
   C. To be completed in the initial stage of the project life cycle.
   D. To be focused only on stakeholders who will contribute positively to your project.

3. Company ABC invested $400,000 in a project with expected cash inflows of $40,000 per quarter for the first two years and $80,000 per quarter from third year. Another project has a payback period of 2.5 years for the same amount of investment. Which project should you select?
   A. The first project
   B. The second project
   C. Cannot be determined
   D. Both projects

4. Which of the following is NOT true about the fundamental functionality of the Control Quality process?
   A. Implement approved changes to the Quality Baseline.
   B. Recommend changes, corrective and preventive actions, and defect repairs to Integrated Change Control in order to eliminate noncompliance in the project deliverables.
   C. Ensure that the deliverables of the project comply with relevant quality standards.
   D. Ensure project work is directed toward the completion of the defined scope.

5. You are an IT project manager working on several networking and software development projects. It is becoming increasingly difficult for you to keep track of the latest trends in your field as technology is continuously changing. You would love to try out the latest technology and tools available, however your organization has advised you to play it safe. In the last three years, the organization has not invested in new technology and won't adapt to anything that is not well tested and used by others in the industry. In terms of risk attitude, your organization could best be described as:
   A. Risk Seeker
   B. Risk Neutral
   C. Risk Averse
   D. Risk Lover

6. You have been assigned as a project manager to implement a new office automation application. Management asks you to make sure that the new application will work on the existing infrastructure and can easily be integrated with other major applications currently running in the organization. This is an example of which one of the following?
   A. Assumptions
   B. Project Scope
   C. Constraints
   D. Expectations

7. Which one of the following techniques translates project objectives into tangible deliverables and requirements by improving the project team's understanding of the product?
   A. Product Analysis
   B. Alternative Analysis
   C. Inspection
   D. Decomposition

8. Claims Administration is used as a tool & technique in which of the following procurement management processes?
   A. Plan Procurement Management
   B. Conduct Procurements
   C. Control Procurements
   D. Close Procurements

9. You are working for a healthcare facility and are overseeing the implementation of a new computer infrastructure and office automation project at the local hospital. You made all the efforts to ensure that a rigorous test was done and scope was validated prior to any major release in the project. Recently, you made the final delivery to the customer and communicated the successful news to all the relevant members of the project. You were surprised when the customer called to inform you that he was not very happy with the release as it did not support one of his key functionalities and demanded that the feature be added as soon as possible. What should you do first in this kind of situation?

    A. Estimate the time, cost, and resources required to add the feature as specified by the customer.
    B. Have an urgent meeting with the sponsor to discuss the customer's concern.
    C. Inform the customer that the project is delivered and closed and any addition must be handled as a new project.
    D. Find out the lacks in scope validation and in-house testing procedures to identify the root cause.

10. A software company created a base package that must be implemented for each customer. Which one of the following will be used to ensure that the new base functionality does not break existing custom features and that these changes are evaluated across all relevant versions of the product?

    A. Configuration Management System
    B. Process Improvement Plan
    C. Perform Integrated Change Control
    D. Work Authorization System

11. Draw a network diagram based on the following criteria and answer the question below:
   – Activity A can start immediately and has an estimated duration of 3 weeks.
   – Activity B can also start immediately and has an estimated duration of 9 weeks.
   – Activity C can start after activity A is completed and has an estimated duration of 5 weeks.
   – Activity D can start after activity B is completed and has an estimated duration of 4 weeks.
   – Activity E can start after both activities C and D are completed and has an estimated duration of 7 weeks.
   – Activity F can start after activity D is completed and has an estimated duration of 4 weeks.

A new activity G is added to the project which will take 10 weeks to complete and must be completed before activity F and after activity D. You are worried that the addition of the new activity will add an additional 8 weeks to the project, so you calculate how much it will actually delay the project. What amount of time will be added to your project in this case?

    A. 7 weeks
    B. 6 weeks
    C. 8 weeks
    D. 28 weeks

12. Which of the following theories demonstrates that employees who believe their efforts will lead to effective performance and expect to be rewarded for their accomplishments remain productive as rewards meet their expectations?

    A. Abraham Maslow's Hierarchy of Needs
    B. Alderfer's Existence, Relatedness, Growth (ERG) needs
    C. McClelland's Achievement Motivation theory
    D. Victor Vroom's Expectancy theory

13. You have recently been assigned as a project manager for a new and highly complex project to send a satellite into space. There are several stakeholders in the project, and you are working on a communications plan to identify the information and communication needs of the people involved. You do this by determining what needs to be communicated, when, to whom, with what method, in which format, and how frequently. It is extremely important that you develop your communications plan:

    A. Evenly throughout the project life cycle
    B. At the earliest stages of the project
    C. Upon completion of the project plan
    D. During execution

14. Which one of the following statements is NOT true about a watch list?

    A. It consists of risks that do not have a high enough probability or impact to make it into the risk register, but that still need to be monitored.
    B. It documents low probability and low impact risks for historical use only.
    C. It is an output of the Perform Qualitative Risk Analysis process.
    D. Noncritical risks on the watch list need to be reviewed at intervals during the project to ensure they have not become critical.

15. Which of the following statements is FALSE concerning a Project Management Office (PMO)?

    A. It can be responsible for the direct management of projects and programs.
    B. It is an organizational body responsible for establishing and maintaining templates, policies, procedures, best practices, and standards for project management methodologies.
    C. In order to be managed together, the various projects supported by a PMO should be related.
    D. It conducts periodic project audits to monitor compliance with project management standards.

16. You are managing a large IT project when a severe cost overrun causes a major concern to the key stakeholders and the sponsor.

You schedule an urgent meeting to discuss the root cause of the concern and illustrate the corrective and preventive actions you are planning to take. You are also planning to inform the audience in the meeting that the project is ahead of schedule and that most of the major deliverables are already completed and accepted by the stakeholders. What kind of communication does this meeting represent?

- A. Informal verbal
- B. Formal written
- C. Informal written
- D. Formal verbal

17. Which of the following is NOT true about Herzberg's Motivator-Hygiene theory?
- A. Hygiene factors are not sufficient to motivate people, and motivating agents provide the best positive reinforcement.
- B. Hygiene factors can destroy motivation, but improving them under most circumstances will not improve motivation.
- C. Motivating people is best done by rewarding people and letting them grow.
- D. Improving hygiene factors will certainly improve motivation.

18. Ashley, a senior project manager, recently took over a project to produce a safe and effective drug from another project manager who just left the company. Ashley was surprised to find out that there was no Change Control Board (CCB) or change control process established for the project. Why is it important to have a robust change control process for any project to be successful?
- A. It will ensure that only stakeholders with significant authority can submit the change requests.
- B. It will minimize the number of changes in the project.
- C. It will ensure that only necessary changes are considered and implemented.
- D. It will maintain the record of all changes for budget tracking purposes.

19. Your sponsor mentioned that the project must be completed within six months and should not exceed $50,000. You should consider this a:
- A. Project assumption
- B. Project constraint
- C. Stakeholder expectation
- D. Project boundary

20. You were given a budget of $3,000, and you spent $2,000. However you only completed $1,200 worth of work. What do you currently expect the TOTAL project to cost considering your situation?
- A. Not possible to estimate.
- B. $5,000
- C. $6,000
- D. $6,200

21. You are performing a quantitative risk analysis and modeling technique that helps to determine which risks have the most potential impact on a project. Your goal is to find whether the occurrence of a particular threat would be merely an inconvenience or would ruin the project. Which of the following tools will be most appropriate for your analysis?
- A. Tornado Diagram
- B. SWOT Analysis
- C. Expected Monetary Value
- D. Reserve Analysis

22. You have received many complaints from your customers indicating that the screens of laptops manufactured at your plant are getting black spots and marks after six months of use. Which of the following tools should your team members use to identify potential causes of this problem?
- A. Flowchart
- B. Statistical Sampling
- C. Design of Experiments
- D. Ishikawa Diagram

23. While reviewing your project schedule, you realize that you have two pending activities that you need to complete as soon as possible. The plan would be for you to set up the development server in the lab and then start coding. But upon further investigation, you find out that you must run the server for 3 days, without failure, before the coding starts. This is an example of:
- A. Lead
- B. Crash
- C. Critical chain
- D. Lag

24. You are utilizing a technique of reconciling the expenditure of funds with the funding limits set for the project. As per the variance between the expenditure of funds and planned limit, you are trying to reschedule activities to level out the rates of

expenditures. This technique is known as:
- A. Funding Limit Reconciliation
- B. Cost Aggregation
- C. Reserve Analysis
- D. Forecasting

25. You are overseeing a project to implement an online travel package reservation system that has 6 sponsors and 13 stakeholders. You want to make sure that your project stakeholders will receive the correct version of the product. Which of the following plans will you use to specify how versioning information will be tracked?
- A. Quality Management Plan
- B. Scope Management Plan
- C. Change Management Plan
- D. Configuration Management Plan

26. Senior management has asked you to shorten your project schedule by 2 months by any means. In order to achieve the target, you added a couple of additional resources to the team and also approved unlimited overtime for the team members. You realize that you are taking the risk of potential conflicts, additional management time, and cost to the project. The technique you are using is:
- A. Crashing
- B. Critical Chain
- C. Critical Path
- D. Fast Tracking

27. You are overseeing a custom software development project to implement an accounting and financial system for one of your clients. Currently, you are in the process of obtaining the formal acceptance of the completed project scope and associated deliverables from the sponsor, customers, and other stakeholders. This process is closely related to which one of the following?
- A. Control Quality
- B. Manage Stakeholder Engagement
- C. Manage Quality
- D. Monitor Risks

28. During the executing stage of a project to develop a cashiering application for a retail customer, a senior stakeholder requested that you slightly modify the project scope to incorporate an additional feature. What will be your first course of action?
- A. Submit the change request to the Change Control Board (CCB) for their approval or rejection.
- B. Document the change request as per the Project Scope Management Plan.
- C. Perform an impact analysis on all project objectives such as scope, time, cost, quality, risk, resource, and others.
- D. Deny the request since it is too late in the project life cycle to incorporate any new change.

29. Which one of the following statements is NOT true about project life cycle?
- A. An iterative life cycle builds the concept in successive levels of details in order to create the end result.
- B. An incremental life cycle delivers a complete, usable portion of the product in each iteration.
- C. An adaptive life cycle defines the fixed scope, schedule, and cost with the clear understanding that it will be refined and adjusted as the project progresses.
- D. Iterative, incremental, and adaptive are different types of a plan-driven project lifecycle.

30. You are trying to address the limitations associated with a network diagram and are utilizing a modified network diagram that will allow feedback loops and conditional branches. Which method are you using?
- A. PERT
- B. GERT
- C. Precedence Diagram
- D. Arrow Diagram

31. A project manager is in the Sequence Activities process of identifying and documenting relationships among defined activities and arranging them in the order they must be performed. While in this process, the project manager decides to utilize a Precedence Diagramming Method (PDM) for sequencing the activities. All of the following are true about a precedence diagramming method EXCEPT:
- A. This method creates a schematic display of the sequential and logical relationships of project activities.
- B. It usually shows dependencies and the order in which activities in a project must be performed.
- C. It uses four types of dependency relationships, including finish-to-start.
- D. This diagramming method uses Activity-on-Arrow (AOA) convention, as arrows are used to represent activities and circles show dependencies.

32. You are overseeing a project to build a robot, which will operate on electricity as well as solar power. The robot should have face and voice recognition capability. It should help the owner with daily household activities and keep him or her company. The robot

should be able to learn from various experiences, develop its memory, and gradually make more complex decisions on its own. This information should be captured in which of the following documents?
- A. Project Scope
- B. Scope Baseline
- C. Product Scope
- D. Requirements Traceability Matrix

33. One of your stakeholders is very disheartened about the fact that three of her key recommendations were not implemented in the project. She sends you an e-mail stating that she will not be able to review and approve the user test case document that you sent her as she thinks her feedback really does not matter much. What is your best course of action?
- A. Immediately implement her recommendations.
- B. Remove the stakeholder from the stakeholder register and avoid further communication.
- C. After investigating why her recommendations were excluded, schedule a meeting with the stakeholder to discuss.
- D. Have an urgent meeting with the sponsor to discuss the next strategy.

34. You are managing a software application project to develop an online PMP exam simulator to assist students to practice exam questions in a similar real-life environment. The team has completed design work, received approval from the technical review team, and initiated coding work. When your management asked what you currently expect the TOTAL project to cost, you assured that the current variances are atypical and similar variance will not occur in the future; thus, the rest of the job will be done as per budget. Which one of the following formulas will you use to get the most accurate Estimate at Completion (EAC)?
- A. EAC = AC + (BAC – EV)
- B. EAC = AC + Bottom-up ETC
- C. EAC = (BAC – EV) / CPI * SPI
- D. EAC = BAC/CPI

35. A new stakeholder has recently been identified for your project. He will be helping team members with data validation and other testing. The stakeholder asks the project manager about the scheduling methodology and tools that will be used in the schedule development. He would also like to know about schedule change control procedures, reporting formats, and frequencies. Which one of the following documents may the project manager refer him to?
- A. Project Charter
- B. Stakeholder Register
- C. Schedule Management Plan
- D. Schedule Baseline

36. Your team is working on the installation and configuration of a database server. A project manager from another project called to inform you that he is waiting for the completion of the server set up as his team will also be using the server for their testing. You were not aware of this and inform the project manager that the server installation and configuration will be delayed by a few days. What kind of dependency does the other project have on your project?
- A. Discretionary dependency
- B. Mandatory dependency
- C. Internal dependency
- D. External dependency

37. Data Analysis Techniques such as Reserve Analysis and Alternative Analysis are used as a tool & technique in which Cost Management Process?
- A. Plan Cost Management
- B. Estimate Costs
- C. Determine Budget
- D. Control Costs

38. A project manager is in the Direct and Manage Project Work process and making sure that team is completing the work defined in the Project Management Plan to satisfy the project specifications and objectives. All of the following are executed in this process EXCEPT:
- A. Implementing changes that have been approved by the Change Control Board (CCB)
- B. Setting up a change control system
- C. Managing team members and keeping them involved in the project
- D. Identifying required changes in the project

39. Your management asked you to negotiate with the vendor to implement an extremely important component as soon as possible in order to avoid losing a significant market share. What advice should you give to your management to include in the contract in this

situation?
- A. A force majeure clause
- B. A time is of the essence clause
- C. A retainage clause
- D. Incentives

40. As a project manager, you and your team are mainly focused on finding a less costly way to do the same work and on achieving more out of the project in every possible way to increase the bottom line, decrease costs, improve quality, and optimize the schedule without reducing or impacting the scope. You are most likely using which of the following techniques?
- A. Benchmarking
- B. Value Analysis
- C. Life Cycle Costing
- D. Reserve Analysis

41. To calculate the project cost, the project manager utilizes the cost aggregation method by which activity costs are rolled up to the work packages costs; the work packages costs are then rolled up to the "control account" or "cost account" costs and finally to the project cost. At this moment the project manager is in the final stages of determining the cost baseline for the project and funding requirements. Which process is the project manager working on now?
- A. Plan Cost Management
- B. Estimate Costs
- C. Determine Budget
- D. Control Costs

42. A project manager working for an electric utility company has been assigned to create a new substation that will supply power to a newly developed subdivision. While performing the forecasting analysis, the project manager found that the EAC = $159,000 and became worried to discover that the SPI = 0.74 and the CPI = 0.86. What is the possible reason for this occurrence?
- A. One of the subcontractors needed to be replaced due to poor performance.
- B. An activity with no buffer unexpectedly took longer and required additional manpower to be completed.
- C. The team had to purchase an expensive piece of safety equipment that was not originally planned.
- D. The client made several scope changes.

43. You have been managing a top-secret government project, which has been progressing as planned up until last night. Suddenly, one of your team members called and informed you that an unexpected major problem occurred that was not included in the Risk Register. The problem will now cost the project an additional amount. What should be your first course of action?
- A. Accept the risk.
- B. Update the Risk Management Plan.
- C. Use the management reserves.
- D. Have an urgent meeting with the stakeholders and find out the problem details.

44. A project manager working on implementing WIMAX connectivity in a rural area has to deploy several network devices and set up POPs to house those devices. She performed a cost-benefit analysis and was concerned about the high cost of nonconformance as a result of not following the proper quality procedures in the project. What should the project manager do?
- A. Look for benchmarks.
- B. Allocate additional budget to deal with the situation.
- C. Utilize the existing reserve money to deal with the situation.
- D. Perform an audit.

45. While supervising a construction project, a project manager noticed that for a construction process, standard deviation associated with the product variation was 0.7 inches and with the measurement variation was 0.5 inches. What is the total standard deviation here?
- A. 1.2
- B. 0.86
- C. 0.49
- D. 0.25

46. While working in quality management, you have identified the point where the benefits or revenue from improving quality equals the incremental cost to achieve that quality. You have performed which one of the following analyses?
- A. Marginal Analysis
- B. Root Cause Analysis
- C. Benchmarking
- D. Quality Control Analysis

47. A project manager is trying to identify the specific training, coaching, mentoring, assistance, or changes required to improve the team's performance and effectiveness by making formal or informal assessments of the project team's effectiveness. Which of the

following is the project manager performing?
- A. Team Performance Assessment
- B. Project Performance Appraisal
- C. Observations and Conversations
- D. Team-building Activities

48. A project manager overseeing a WIMAX deployment project just completed negotiation for three additional resources from different functional areas as well as extra reserve money for her project. During the negotiation, two of the functional managers were very skeptical about the request for additional resources and were reluctant to assign their resources to her project. She attempted to influence the functional managers by using her association with a high- level executive for leverage. Which of the following forms of power is she using in this situation?
- A. Referent
- B. Coercive
- C. Expert
- D. Reward

49. A project manager overseeing a construction project negotiated a deal with a tools and equipment rental company for ten different tools needed for his project. As part of the deal, the rental company will supply all ten pieces of equipment for a total price of $3,000/month for the duration of the project. This is an example of which of the following costs?
- A. Indirect Cost
- B. Sunk Cost
- C. Opportunity Cost
- D. Fixed Cost

50. A project manager is in the Acquire Resources process and is trying to secure the best possible resources to build a project team for carrying out the project activities efficiently. What will be the output of this process?
- A. Resource Management Plan
- B. Physical Resource Assignments
- C. Team Performance Assessments
- D. Resource Requirements

51. A contract is an entire formal agreement between two parties and it is the principle endeavor of procurement management. Which of the following is NOT true about contracts?
- A. Contracts are legally binding and backed by the court system in most countries.
- B. A contract cannot be terminated at any time by the buyer for a cause or convenience.
- C. A contract should help reduce project risks.
- D. A contract is legally binding unless it is in violation of applicable law.

52. Which one of the following is NOT true about issues in a project?
- A. An issue log is a document to record issues that require a solution.
- B. It helps monitor who is responsible for resolving specific problems by a target date.
- C. There should be one owner assigned for each issue reported in the project.
- D. Issues and risks refer to the same thing.

53. In Abraham Maslow's Hierarchy of Needs, accomplishment, respect, attention, and appreciation are categorized as:
- A. Physiological
- B. Self-actualization
- C. Esteem
- D. Social

54. You presented your project cost estimates to the sponsor, and she is upset about the inaccuracy of the estimates and demands that the estimates be as accurate as possible. Which of the following techniques will help you most in this situation?
- A. An order of magnitude estimate
- B. A heuristic estimate
- C. A bottom-up estimate
- D. A top-down estimate

55. Steve is a systems engineer who is extremely dedicated and hardworking. His deliverables are always on time, accurate, and of desired quality. He also has a reputation of being a "nice guy" and being liked by everyone in the organization. Considering all these factors, senior management has decided to assign Steve as a project manager in a new critical engineering project. This is an example of which of the following?
- A. Rewarding good behavior
- B. The Halo effect
- C. Victor Vroom's Expectancy theory
- D. Perquisites

56. A project manager utilizes different conflict resolution techniques to resolve conflicts in his project. He created an open

environment so that his team members feel free to discuss their concerns and issues. He is also focused on resolving issues rather than fixing the personalities of his team members, and he pays more attention to the present than the past. Which of the following conflict resolution techniques will lead to the LEAST sustaining positive result?

A. Withdrawing or avoiding
B. Forcing
C. Confronting or problem solving
D. Compromising

57. This tool & technique is a graphical representation of a process to help analyze how problems occur and also identifies potential process improvement opportunities:

A. Benchmarking
B. Root Cause Analysis
C. Flowchart
D. Design of Experiments (DOE)

58. A Communications Management Plan is a subsidiary of the Project Management Plan that can be formal or informal, highly detailed or broadly framed, and is based on the needs of the project. It should include all of the following EXCEPT:

A. Project communications
B. Stakeholder communication requirements
C. Method, time frame, and frequency for the distribution of required information
D. Glossary of common terms

59. You are responsible for making all kinds of arrangements for your company's annual picnic. You have taken all the necessary actions and have reserved an outdoor park on a particular day. You are now only three days away from the big event, and the weather forecast suggests a light rain shower on the day of the picnic. You bought umbrellas and rented tents just in case you need them. Which of the following risk response strategies are you using in this case?

A. Passive acceptance
B. Contingency planning
C. Avoidance
D. Transference

60. In the communication process, a basic model of communication that exhibits how information is sent from the sender and how it is received by the receiver has all of the following components EXCEPT:

A. Sender
B. Message and feedback message
C. Urgency
D. Noise

61. Steve is a project manager for a power company and is currently supervising a solar panel installation project for a local real estate builder. The project has around fifteen team members and eighteen internal and external stakeholders. One of the team leads sent Steve a status report on his team's deliverables where he indicated that a major component was completed. Steve is convinced that the team lead was not fully honest in his communication, and the major component is far from being completed. Steve is about to have a meeting with the key stakeholders on the project status. What is the best course of action for Steve in this kind of situation?

A. Ask the team under the team lead to explain the cause of the discrepancy.
B. Challenge the team lead about the validity of the report.
C. Attend the status meeting with the stakeholders and do not mention anything about the major component.
D. Inform the stakeholder that you need a little more time to verify the information about the major component and will follow up with him/her shortly.

62. While overseeing a software engineering project, you find that one of the subcontractors failed to deliver on the last three projects. Upon further investigation, you learn that there are several complaints filed against this subcontractor, and that they have a very bad reputation in the market. Realizing that it is too big of a risk, you terminate the contract with the subcontractor and instead hire a couple of individuals to work on the components. Which risk response strategy did you use in this situation?

A. Accept
B. Transfer
C. Mitigate
D. Avoid

63. Your management asked you to study the work method to determine a faster, less costly, and more efficient method to complete the project. This is an example of which one of the following?

A. Value Engineering
B. Resource Leveling
C. Schedule Compression
D. Learning Curve

64. You are in the Monitor Risks process of identifying, analyzing, and planning for newly arising risks, taking corrective actions, and overall reviewing the execution and effectiveness of risk responses. All of the following are tools & techniques for Monitor

Risks process EXCEPT:
- A. Data Analysis
- B. Audits
- C. Meetings
- D. Enhance

65. Why is it essential to document assumptions from the point of initiation in your project?
- A. Failure to validate assumptions may result in significant risk events.
- B. Assumptions are absolute and nonnegotiable.
- C. Assumptions allow for baseline adjustments in case of project crisis.
- D. Assumptions limit the project team's options for decision making.

66. Which of the following is NOT a tool & technique of the Perform Qualitative Risk Analysis process?
- A. Risk Probability and Impact Assessment
- B. Probability and Impact Matrix
- C. Expected Monetary Value Analysis
- D. Risk Data Quality Assessment

67. You are overseeing a large construction project to build a power plant. Your company has purchased a big piece of land close to a mountain and far away from the city for the plant. One of your team members reported to you that while digging the ground they found some artifacts. Upon initial assessment, you realize that these artifacts have some archaeological significance. What should you do in this situation?
- A. Ask the team members to keep it a secret and collect all the artifacts for the benefit of the project.
- B. This kind of finding is a norm in construction projects; thus, ignore the finding and proceed with the project as per the plan.
- C. Proceed with the project as planned, but inform higher management about the finding.
- D. Stop digging and call the archaeological department to quickly research the findings.

68. An important stakeholder identified a problem with one of the features of a software application your team is working on and submitted a change request. Even though it was out of the project's scope, the Change Control Board has approved the change. What is the BEST action to take next?
- A. Add the risk to the Risk Register and gather information about its probability and impact.
- B. Disregard any risk at this stage of the project life cycle.
- C. Have a meeting with the stakeholder to discuss the risk.
- D. Identify what went wrong in the Identify Risks process.

69. Your team is trying to determine which risks have the most potential impact on the project, in other words, whether the occurrence of a particular threat would merely be an inconvenience or whether it would ruin the project. The team is using a diagram to display this sensitivity analysis data by examining all the uncertain elements at their baseline values. Which one of the following diagrams is the team using in this case?
- A. Influence Diagram
- B. Cause and Effect Diagram
- C. Scatter Diagram
- D. Tornado Diagram

70. While working on a construction project, you need to find out if any of your team members are available to work during the upcoming weekend. Which one of the following documents will help you the MOST in this situation?
- A. Project Team Directory
- B. Responsibility Assignment Matrix (RAM) chart
- C. Resource Breakdown Structure (RBS)
- D. Resource Calendar

71. You will be making $10,000 in a two year project. The cost of capital is 10 percent and the initial investment is $6,000. You have another project that has a net present value of $9500. If you compare the net present values, which project should you select?
- A. The first project
- B. The second project
- C. Neither one
- D. Cannot be determined

72. Company ABC invested $210,000 in a project, and that project returned a net profit of $14,000 in the first year of operation. The organization could have invested that same $210,000 and earned a 4 percent return. What is the Economic Value Added (EVA) in this case?

A. $5,600
B. $196,000
C. $224,000
D. –$5,600

73. While reviewing the status of your project you found out the following EV, AC, and PV. Find out the cumulative CPI and cumulative SPI for month 4.

Month	PV	EV	AC
Month 1	$30,000	$27,000	$25,000
Month 2	$35,000	$40,000	$45,000
Month 3	$90,000	$80,000	$70,000
Month 4	$150,000	$125,000	$89,000

A. 1.18 and 0.891
B. 0.891 and 1.18
C. 1.40 and 0.833
D. 0.833 and 1.40

74. Your team members have created a requirement document, a Project Scope Statement, and a Work Breakdown Structure. They have identified twenty work packages and completed the WBS Dictionary. Some of these team members were also involved in creating the Business Case and conducting the Feasibility Study at the early stage of this project. Which one of the following items will the team members work on now?
A. Help the project manager to develop the schedule.
B. Create the detailed activity list.
C. Create the network diagram.
D. Identify the sequence of the activities.

75. Your twenty mile railway construction project is not going well. You were supposed to complete the project today, exactly forty weeks from the start of the project. You found out that only 75 percent of the work is completed. Based on this status, approximately when would you expect the project to be completed?
A. 13.3 weeks
B. 10 weeks
C. 15 weeks
D. 5 weeks

76. You created a Change Control Board (CCB) for your project since there is no centralized one in your organization. You also want to follow a robust Integrated Change Control process in your project. Which of the following is not a primary goal for performing the Integrated Change Control process?
A. Prevent unnecessary changes in your project.
B. Denying changes whenever possible.
C. Evaluate the possible impacts of the changes in your project.
D. Managing changes as they occur.

77. One of your hardware vendors sends you an e-mail stating that due to severe weather she will not be able to deliver the networking equipment on time. You decide to respond to this risk by leasing the required equipment from a local company until yours arrives. Which of the following statements is TRUE?
A. This is risk avoidance.
B. This is risk mitigation.
C. This is risk acceptance.
D. This is risk exploitation.

78. You are trying to measure how diverse the population is in your data set. First you find the mean by taking the average of all data points, and then calculate the average of how far each individual point is from that mean. You are using:
A. Standard deviation
B. Statistical sampling
C. Mutual exclusivity
D. Normal distribution

79. You are overseeing a twenty mile railway construction project. You were supposed to spend $10,000 per mile of railway construction and complete the project today, exactly forty weeks from the start of the project. You found out that only 75 percent of the work has been completed. What is your Budget at Completion (BAC)?

A. $200,000

B. $150,000

C. $300,000

D. $400,000

80. Your organization is having a severe cash flow problem and you were asked to minimize the cost in your small project as much as possible. Which of the following processes may you consider eliminating in such a scenario?

    A.   Perform Quantitative Risk Analysis

    B.   Monitor Risks

    C.   Identify Risks

    D.   Plan Risk Management

81. Which of the following is TRUE about Request for Bid (RFB) or Invitation for Bid(IFB)?

    A.   Buyer's request to all potential sellers for the details of how work will be performed.

    B.   Buyer's request to all potential sellers to submit a total price bid for work to be performed.

    C.   Buyer's request to all potential sellers to submit a price quote per item, hour, foot, or other unit of measure.

    D.   Buyer's request to all potential sellers to submit a detailed statement of work from the buyer.

82. According to Herzberg's Motivator-Hygiene theory, which of the following is NOT a hygiene factor?

    A.   Variety of work

    B.   Compensation

    C.   Personal life

    D.   Working conditions

83. You decide to use a combination of tools and techniques to identify risks in your data center project. Which one of the following tools is NOT used for risk identification?

    A.   SWOT Analysis

    B.   Assumption and constraint Analysis

    C.   Brainstorming

    D.   RACI Chart

84. Which one of the following processes documents configuration management activities in a project?

    A.   Collect Requirements

    B.   Define Scope

    C.   Plan Scope Management

    D.   Validate Scope

85. While overseeing a construction project, you are informed by the site supervisor that the painting team showed up even though the dry wall team is not even half done. The painting team lead is not sure when his team is supposed to start the work. Which one of the following is contributing MOST to this issue?

    A.   This is due to poor team cohesiveness.

    B.   Lack of Communication Management Plan.

    C.   A proper Work Authorization System was not established in the project.

    D.   The site supervisor is lacking experience.

86. You remind your manager about your great contribution in a couple of projects and ask him to recommend you for a 10 percent salary increase. The manager mentions that management decided to give all the employees performing above average a 5 percent salary increase; thus, there is no need to discuss this topic any further. This is an example of which of thefollowing?

    A.   Good guy/bad guy

    B.   Personal insult

    C.   Fait accompli

    D.   Missing man

87. You are managing a software application project to develop an online PMP exam simulator budgeted for $90,000 to assist students to practice exam questions in similar real life environment. The team has completed design work, received approval from technical review team, and initiated coding work. When asked by management what you currently expect the project to cost, you think that the costs you have incurred till now are typical for the rest of the project. While reviewing at the current status of the project, you found that AC = $30,000 and EV = $ 35,000. What is your Estimate at Completion (EAC)?

    A. $85,000

    B. $77,586

    C. $90,000

    D. $60,000

88. While in the Control Procurements process, you are meeting with your seller to inspect the seller's progress to deliver project scope and quality within cost and schedule as compared to the contract. Your objective is to identify performance progress or failures, non-compliances, and areas where performance is a problem. Which one of the following are you performing?

A. Audit
B. Performance Reviews
C. Inspections
D. Payment Systems

89. You are working for a cruise company as a project manager. Your company offers luxury tours to couples at a reasonable price. Currently, the company is considering adding more tours to a few other popular destinations during the holiday season in order to increase traffic and profitability. Which risk response strategy is in use?
A. Share
B. Exploit
C. Accept
D. Enhance

90. Your organization has outsourced a large portion of the activities of an ERP implementation project to a vendor. According to the contract, the vendor is supposed to review the design and code of any major component with the Technical Review Group (TRG) of your organization. So far, the vendor has completed and deployed three major components without the approval of the TRG team. As a project manager, what should you do in this situation?
A. Terminate the contract immediately as the vendor has breached the contract.
B. Stop payment for the components that were deployed without approval.
C. Do not worry too much as the approval of the TRG is not that important.
D. Issue a default letter to the vendor.

91. Which of the following are the outputs of the Plan Scope Management process?
A. Scope Management Plan and Requirements Management Plan
B. Requirements Document and Requirements Traceability Matrix
C. Project Scope statement and Scope Baseline
D. WBS and WBS Dictionary

92. Which of the following analyses integrates scope, cost, and schedule measures to assess project performance?
A. Trend Analysis
B. Project presentations and review
C. Earned Value Analysis
D. Variance Analysis

93. You are having an issue with one of the manufacturing processes used to create the required parts for routers and switches that your company produces. Due to this major quality problem, only 15 percent of the parts manufactured have been within the control limits set by the Quality Assurance team. Higher management asks you to review the process activities to determine where the process went wrong. Which type of diagram should you use to gather this information?
A. Control Chart
B. Pareto Chart
C. Scatter Diagram
D. Flowchart

94. As an employee, working conditions, salary, status, and job security matter a lot to you, just like your other coworkers. However, you always feel that you will be more motivated and will contribute more if you are rewarded for your contribution to a project and given the opportunity to grow professionally. Which motivational theory are you referring to?
A. McGregor's Theory X and Theory Y
B. Maslow's Hierarchy of Need
C. Herzberg's Motivation-Hygiene Theory
D. Dr. William Ouchi's Theory Z

95. While determining the funds needed for your project, you obtained historical information from previous projects as the basis to determine the price per square foot of carpeting. You used this information to calculate the cost of 20,000 square feet of carpeting that is required for the project. Which technique did you use to create the estimate?
A. Analogous Estimating
B. Three-point Estimating
C. Heuristic Estimating
D. Parametric Estimating

96. The flexibility or total float in a schedule is measured by subtracting the early dates from the late dates. Which one of the following will help you to identify the flexibility in your schedule?
A. Precedence Diagramming Method

B. Resource Leveling
C. Critical Path Method (CPM)
D. Fast Tracking

97. You recently completed the SOW detailing the specifications and other requirements for an expensive item you would like to purchase for one of your projects. While working on the SOW, you identified some of the source selection criteria, terms and conditions, and the contract type that you want to use. Also, you put together some documents to solicit proposals from your potential vendors. What tools and techniques will you use in the next process?
   A. Market research, make-or-buy analysis, and expert judgment.
   B. Bidder conference, proposal evaluation techniques, and independent estimates.
   C. Procurement audits, procurement negotiations, and records management system.
   D. Contract change control system, procurement performance reviews, and claim administration.

98. An independent team from your organization has identified wasted steps that are not necessary for creating the product for your project. They have recommended a few actions for process improvement and have requested that some of the process documents be updated. Which of the following best describes what is being performed?
   A. They are performing quality management activity.
   B. They are performing quality control activity.
   C. They are monitoring and controlling quality activities.
   D. They are directing and managing project work.

99. A project manager is in the Plan Communications Management process of identifying the information and communication needs of the people involved in a project by determining what needs to be communicated, when, to whom, with what method, in which format, and how frequently. Which of the following is NOT a tool & technique in this process?
   A. Project Reporting
   B. Communication Requirements Analysis
   C. Communication Methods
   D. Communication Technology

100. Which of the following is NOT an output for the Conduct Procurements process?
   A. Agreements
   B. Selected Sellers
   C. Source Selection Criteria
   D. Project Management Plan Updates

101. While overseeing a new wireless media streaming device development project, you notice that your team members are having significant difficulties resolving an issue that they have discovered during unit testing. After working on the issue for a week, the team members identify a number of possible causes for the issue and narrowed it down to two main causes. You asked the team members to determine if there is any interdependency between these two causes that would necessitate further action. Which one of the following tools would be the BEST to use in this situation?
   A. Histogram
   B. Flowchart
   C. Scatter Diagram
   D. SWOT Analysis

102. ITPro Consultancy, LLC, an Internet Service Provider (ISP), is planning to establish its own network infrastructure. It figured out that it would cost around $180,000 to establish its own network by in-house resources. Once the network is established, there will be a recursive cost of $4,000/month for operational and maintenance activities. An experienced vendor has offered ITPro to set up the infrastructure based on a license fee of ten dollars per user per month. ITPro will have two thousand users using the network per month. It will also need to pay a junior accountant $2,000/month to manage the billing. How many more months will ITPro have to use the infrastructure after establishing the network by the in-house resources rather than hiring the vendor?
   A. Ten months
   B. Nine months
   C. Twenty months
   D. Fifteen months

103. You are overseeing a construction project to build twenty identical custom houses. Your initial estimate suggests that each of the houses will take approximately two months to complete at a cost of $50,000. The sponsor strongly disagrees with your estimate due to which of the following?
   A. You have not considered the law of diminishing return.
   B. You have not considered the learning curve.
   C. You cannot estimate the time and cost until you complete one house.
   D. The estimates are way too high.

104. You have been managing a software application project to automate the accounting system for your client. Your team has completed work as specified in the contract statement of work. You get a call from the buyer and are told that he is disappointed with

the result, even though he admits that the project team has met the terms and conditions of the contract. In this situation the contract is considered to be:

- A. Complete
- B. Waived
- C. Closed
- D. Null and Void

105. You have just finished negotiation on all terms and conditions of the contract with a selected vendor. As both parties are fully satisfied with the outcome of the negotiation, you started working on a draft official letter of notification of the contract award. Which one of the following processes are you in at this time?

- A. Plan Procurement Management
- B. Procurement Negotiations
- C. Control Procurements
- D. Conduct Procurements

106. Steve, the project manager for an ERP implementation project, was asked by the client via a change request to delay the implementation of one of the modules by one week. What should Steve do first in this situation?

- A. Instruct the team member responsible for the module to delay the implementation as per the client's request.
- B. Deny the request as it will delay the entire project.
- C. Inform the sponsor about the change request.
- D. Evaluate the impact of the requested change.

107. The Cost Baseline is displayed as an S-curve because of the way project spending occurs. This S-curve indicates that:

- A. The bulk of the project cost is spent during the initiating and the closing phases.
- B. The cost starts off low, accelerates throughout the later phases of the project, and gradually slows down during the closing.
- C. The project cost is directly proportional to the size of the project.
- D. Projects run in a cycle.

108. Your company worked on a new video console game for several months and invested a large amount of money in the development of the game. Unfortunately, the game was a flop, as one of the competitors also launched a similar but more sophisticated and higher quality game at the same time your company launched its game. The cost for research and development, patents, manpower, equipment, and intellectual property that your company spent in the development of the game is referred to as:

- A. Sunk Costs
- B. Opportunity Cost
- C. Depreciation
- D. Law of Diminishing Returns

109. Which of the following can be used to manage and store all documents, correspondence, and communication relevant to a contract?

- A. Lessons Learned Register
- B. Records Management System
- C. Audit Reports
- D. Procurement Documents

110. You are conducting a procurement performance review of the seller's progress to deliver the project. It is a structured review consisting of seller-prepared documentation, buyer inspection, and a quality audit of the seller's progress to deliver project scope and quality within cost and on schedule as compared to the contract. Your objective is to identify performance progress or failure, noncompliance, and areas where performance is a problem. You are working on which of the following processes at this time?

- A. Plan Procurement Management
- B. Conduct Procurements
- C. Control Procurements
- D. Close Procurements

111. You strongly disagree with the customer's interpretation of a clause in the contract. The customer submitted a change request and demanded that two new deliverables be implemented as per the contract immediately. You think that the customer is just being unreasonable and that her demand is simply unrealistic. What will be the best course of action to resolve the situation?

- A. Have an urgent meeting with the customer and explain the implications of accepting such a request on schedule and cost.
- B. Ignore the customer's request and continue with your project work as planned.
- C. Document the dispute and refer to claims administration.
- D. Accept the customer's demand as the customer is always right.

112. You have a signed contract in place with one of your major vendors. The vendor recently informed you that they can no longer deliver equipment on the agreed due date. This will cause a major disaster in your project since the vendor will have to wait at least

three months before they can deliver the equipment. You know that there is another vendor who can deliver the equipment for a small increase in costs. What will be your best course of action?
- A. Sue the vendor.
- B. Terminate the contract stating that it is for convenience.
- C. Terminate the contract with the vendor for defaulting.
- D. Give the vendor a time extension.

113. According to McClelland's Achievement Motivation theory, individuals who work best when cooperating with others and working in a team, seek to maintain good relationships and approval rather than recognition, and perform well in a customer-facing team position have which of the following needs?
- A. Need for power
- B. Need for affiliation or association
- C. Need for achievement
- D. Need for nothing

114. A Stakeholder Register contains stakeholder classification, identification, and assessment information. It also points out challenges related to working with the stakeholders as well as the project manager's impression of their knowledge, skills, capabilities, and attitude. Which of the following is TRUE regarding the Stakeholder Register?
- A. It should be accessible to all the team members and stakeholders.
- B. It should be accessible only to the sponsor.
- C. A project manager may publish it with other project documentation or keep it in reserve for personal use only.
- D. It should be accessible only by the PMO.

115. While reviewing the Stakeholder Engagement Assessment Matrix, you notice that one of the important stakeholders is at an "unaware" state at the moment and has no clue about what is happening in your project. As this stakeholder can contribute significantly to your project success, you decide to bring him to a "supportive" or "leading" state. Which of the following will help you to achieve your goal with this stakeholder?
- A. Send him regular reports on the project and its benefits.
- B. Offer him a paid vacation in Hawaii in exchange for his support.
- C. Assign top priorities to his expectations, concerns, and issues.
- D. Involve him in some project activities.

116. The higher management in your organization is very averse to risk. While planning the procurement strategy, you would like to make sure that you select the contract type that will have the least risk for the organization. Which of the following contract options will be best in this scenario?
- A. Cost reimbursable
- B. Fixed price economic price adjustment
- C. Fixed price
- D. Time & material

117. You are responsible for delivering a couple of very expensive pieces of equipment to a hospital in a foreign country. As per the agreement, your company is responsible for coordinating moving the equipment all the way to the nineteenth floor of the client's premises. Your local contact informs you that you need to pay a certain fee to the liftman for coordinating the movement of the equipment through the elevator to the specific floor at nighttime. What should you do in this situation?
- A. Pay the fee.
- B. Have a discussion with the customer and express your concern about the bribe.
- C. Consider the fee a bribe and refuse to pay it.
- D. Hire a local subcontractor to arrange the delivery.

118. You are currently working in the Direct and Manage Project Work process to complete the work defined in the Project Management Plan to satisfy the project specifications and objectives. All of the following are outputs from the Direct and Manage Project Work process EXCEPT?
- A. Deliverables
- B. Final products, service, or result transition
- C. Change requests
- D. Work Performance Data

119. Your management has asked you to lead a team to negotiate and finalize a deal with one of the vendors. While negotiating you will mainly be focused on all of the following EXCEPT:
- A. Developing a good understanding and relationship with the seller
- B. Obtaining a fair and reasonable price for the product, service, or result
- C. Obtaining the lowest possible price and commitment for the shortest project duration from the vendor
- D. Discovering and dealing with disputes as much as possible prior to contract signing

120. You are overseeing a large data center project and have requested bids from several vendors to procure numerous networking devices such as routers, switches, firewalls, PCs, and servers. You decide to go for the lowest bidder since all the bidders are offering

the devices from the same manufacturer. Senior management suggests that you conduct a bidder conference prior to selecting a specific seller. A bidder conference will satisfy which of the following mandatory standards in the PMI code of ethics and professional conduct?

- A. Respect
- B. Honesty
- C. Fairness
- D. Responsibility

121. While reviewing a deliverable due today to the customer, you noticed a technical defect in the deliverable. Upon further inspection, you realize that even though the deliverable fails to meet the project quality standards, it fully satisfies the contractual requirements. You are aware that the customer does not have the domain knowledge and technical expertise to notice the defect. The team member responsible for this deliverable tells you that fixing the defect will be time consuming and superfluous. What is your best course of action?

- A. Contact the customer and inform that the deliverable will be late due to some unavoidable consequences.
- B. Make sure that the issue is captured in the lessons learned so that future projects can benefit.
- C. Have a discussion with the customer about the issue with the deliverable.
- D. Do not mention anything and get formal acceptance from the customer.

122. You are overseeing a project to implement a new computer infrastructure at the local hospital. While evaluating the exact cost impact of some risks identified in the project, you found it extremely incomprehensible to estimate the value of the impact. In this kind of situation, you should consider evaluating on a:

- A. Numerical basis
- B. Quantitative basis
- C. Qualitative basis
- D. Forecast basis

123. You have been managing a top-secret government project, which has been progressing as planned up until last night. Suddenly, one of your team members called and informed you that an unexpected major problem occurred that was not included in the Risk Register. What should be your first course of action?

- A. Take corrective and preventive actions.
- B. Update the Risk Management Plan.
- C. Create a workaround.
- D. Create a fallback plan.

124. While overseeing a web-based application project, you notice that one of the team members is extremely dedicated to the project and a consistent overachiever. In order to appreciate her spectacular work and great contribution to the project, you offer her a nice corner office where she can concentrate on her work without much interruption. This kind of reward is regarded as:

- A. Perquisite
- B. Fringe benefit
- C. Special achievement award
- D. Bribe

125. It is important to realize that stakeholders play a major role in project success. In order to ensure that stakeholders' expectations are managed properly, the project manager needs to do all of the following EXCEPT:

- A. Build trust with the stakeholders.
- B. Resolve conflicts among the stakeholders.
- C. Actively listen to the stakeholders' concerns.
- D. Convey ground rules to the stakeholders.

126. One of the team members informed you that she had identified a design defect that will delay the project by two weeks. You check the Risk Register and realize that no response plan for this situation has been documented. What action should you take FIRST?

- A. Replace the team member who made the mistake in design.
- B. Call the customer immediately and inform them about the situation.
- C. Contact the sponsor for advice.
- D. Evaluate the impact and brainstorm options with the team members.

127. Which one of the following would most likely result in a change request?

- A. An overall SV of 230.
- B. An overall CV of 50.
- C. A short delay of a critical path activity.
- D. A major delay of a non-critical path activity.

128. You recently awarded a contract to one of the vendors after rigorous negotiations. You realize that you have missed out on a couple of very important clauses that you wanted to include in the contract. You decide to modify the contract and include 'time is of the essence' and "retainage" clauses. How should you proceed in this case?

A. You should proceed with a contract change control system at your end.
B. You should inform the seller about the change through a formal written communication.
C. You should have an urgent meeting with the seller to discuss the change.
D. It is too late to make any changes in the contract as it is legally binding and cannot be modified once signed.

129. You are managing a project to build a new plant for a semiconductor company. You just found out that the entire site was badly affected by a severe tornado and your newly developed structures were destroyed. Your client demands that you continue work despite the disaster and refuses to take any responsibility for the damage or allow you a time extension. Which clause in the contract may state that you are not responsible for any more work?
A. An indemnification clause
B. A mitigation clause
C. An arbitration clause
D. A force majeure clause

130. You are approaching the end of your project and were asked to release the resources so that they can be assigned to other projects. Before releasing the resources you want to make sure that you have completed the necessary actions. Which of the following is the correct order of actions that you take during the Closing processes?
A. Get formal acceptances, write lessons learned, release the team, and close the contract.
B. Get formal acceptances, release the team, write lessons learned, and close the contract.
C. Write lessons learned, release the team, get formal acceptances, and close the contract.
D. Release the team, get formal acceptances, close the contract, and write lessons learned.

131. Your team members have sent you their weekly updates on the deliverables they are working on. While reviewing and scrutinizing updates from the team members, you find out that the CPI = 1.1 and SPI = 1. What should you do next with the results of your analysis?
A. Distribute the results to project stakeholders as per your Communications Management Plan.
B. Since the project is on track, you do not have to do anything at this time.
C. Find out where you can spend the money that was saved.
D. Instruct the team members to improve their timing.

132. A project manager overseeing an age verification online tool is in the Control Procurements process of ensuring the seller's performance meets contractual requirements, ensuring that both seller and buyer meet their contractual obligations, and ensuring that the legal rights of both the buyer and seller are protected. Which of the following tools & techniques is NOT used in this process?
A. Claims Administration
B. Performance review
C. Inspections
D. Negotiations

133. Which one of the following Integration Management processes is responsible for implementing process improvement activities?
A. Direct and Manage Project Work
B. Monitor and Control Project Work
C. Develop Project Charter
D. Perform Integrated Change Control

134. You have been assigned to create a diagram that will demonstrate the logical relationships that exist between activities. You are also asked to display how long the project activities will take. Which of the following methods will you utilize to achieve this goal?
A. Pareto Chart
B. Critical Path Method (CPM)
C. Check Sheet
D. Precedence Diagramming Method (PDM)

135. You recently took over a project from a senior project manager who just left the company. You found out that several of your team members are lacking critical skills to carry out the project activities. The previous project manager also mentioned that many of the team members will need specialized training. Which of the following actions should you take next to identify the appropriate training for the team members?
A. Refer to the PMBOK® guide.
B. Review the WBS and WBS dictionary
C. Analyze the Responsibility Assignment Matrix
D. Refer to the Resource Management Plan

136. During which specific process does the project manager prevent scope changes from overwhelming the project?
A. Define Scope
B. Validate Scope
C. Control Scope

D. Perform Integrated Change Control

137. A Cost Plus Incentive Fee (CPIF) contract has an estimated cost of $250,000 with a predetermined fee of $15,000. If the seller can save the buyer any money, the sharing ratio will be 75/25 (buyer/seller). The maximum fee is $24,000, and the minimum fee is $8,000. The actual cost of the project is $225,000. What will be the final fee for the seller and the total savings for the buyer?

A. $21,250, $18,750
B. $15,000, $25,000
C. $25,000, $20,000
D. None of the above

138. As a project manager, you have managed several projects in your organization. You notice that not all the projects are given the proper support and importance from higher management. You also notice that projects get terminated while in progress due to other higher-priority projects in the organization. You will be managing an IT project soon and want to make sure that your project will get the required support from the performing organization. What will be your best course of action?

A. Make sure that the project meets the personal objectives of the sponsor.
B. Communicate the project details and benefits with higher management on a regular basis.
C. Correlate the need for the project to the organizational strategic objective and goal.
D. Justify that your project should be the highest-priority project in the organization.

139. While managing an ERP project, you realize the targeted project end date will be delayed by several days. Upon further investigation, you identify some activities that can be performed in parallel. You also realize that you have not fully utilized some of your resources in the project. What will be the BEST course of action in this situation?

A. Apply leads and lags.
B. Apply resource leveling.
C. Apply fast tracking and crashing.
D. Develop a new project schedule.

140. Which one of the following is NOT true about the goal and objective of a bidding conference?

A. All questions are submitted in writing and issued to sellers as an addendum to the procurement document so that all sellers respond to the same scope of work.
B. There is no collusion among sellers and/or buying agents.
C. Sellers do not save questions for later private meetings in order to gain a competitive advantage.
D. Select the seller who is best capable of performing the project work.

141. In a negotiated Cost Plus Incentive Fee (CPIF) contract, the following figures were finalized:
A target cost of $355,000, a target fee of $45,000, and a sharing ratio of 75/25. If the actual cost of the project is $390,000, what will be the final fee to the seller?

A. $36,250
B. $8,750
C. $35,000
D. $45,000

142. In the data center project that you are managing, you identified several internal and external restrictions or limitations that will affect the performance of a process within the project. Which of the following BEST identifies these issues?

A. Project assumptions
B. Project scope
C. Project requirements
D. Project constraints

143. You have been assigned to identify the key stakeholders for an internal project that has recently been formally approved. Which of the following is your starting point?

A. Project Charter
B. Business Case
C. Statement of Work
D. Bid Document

144. You are currently in the Monitoring and Controlling Project Work process of a networking project that you are overseeing to implement a WIFI network in a rural community. Which of the following tasks will you perform as a part of this process?

A. Manage the project's vendors closely.
B. Compare the plan to the actual performance.
C. Collect requirements from the stakeholders.
D. Produce the deliverables of the project.

145. Your team has estimated that there is a 40 percent probability of a delay in the receipt of required parts with an additional cost of $15,000 to the project. This delay will cost the company $20,000 in lost business. Upon further investigation, you identified that if an existing component could be adapted it would save the project $10,500 in engineering costs. There is a 30 percent probability

that the team can take advantage of that opportunity. What is the total Expected Monetary Value (EMV) of these two events?
- A. $10,950
- B. –$10,850
- C. $14,000
- D. $3,150

146. You are overseeing a project to implement a payroll application and are currently in the Identify Risks process of identifying and documenting the project risks. All of the following Data Gathering techniques are used in the Identify Risks process EXCEPT:
- A. Checklists
- B. Prompt Lists
- C. Interviews
- D. Brainstorming

147. Which of the following is TRUE about stakeholders?
- A. Only the stakeholders who can positively impact the project should be listed in the Stakeholder Register.
- B. Stakeholder identification is a continuous and sometimes strenuous process.
- C. Change requests from the stakeholder with the most influence should be given the highest priority.
- D. Stakeholders should be given extras in order to meet and exceed their expectations.

148. Which process is MOST closely associated with continuous process improvement?
- A. Perform Qualitative Risk Analysis
- B. Manage Quality
- C. Control Quality
- D. Plan Quality Management

149. You are trying to identify and categorize as many potential risks as possible in the mission critical project that you are overseeing. Which of the following will NOT help you with your effort of identifying risks?
- A. Delphi Technique
- B. Brainstorming
- C. SWOT Analysis
- D. Risk Register

150. The cost of developing a product fix is related to which costs of quality category?
- A. A prevention cost
- B. An internal failure cost
- C. An appraisal cost
- D. An external failure cost

151. Which of the following statements is FALSE about qualified sellers in a project?
- A. It is a list of preapproved or prequalified prospective sellers interested in and capable of doing contract services for the organization.
- B. It is a part of the Project Management Plan.
- C. It is a list of pre-screened sellers.
- D. It is a tool in the Conduct Procurement process.

152. The Change Control Board (CCB) just approved a change request to modify one of the major deliverables. In which process will this change be implemented?
- A. Perform Integrated Change Control
- B. Monitor and Control Project Work
- C. Close Project or Phase
- D. Direct and Manage Project Work

153. You have been assigned as a project manager for a project expected to last five months. The project has a budget of $450,000 and should be implemented in three different departments in your organization. While reviewing the status of the project after two months, you find that the project is 35 percent complete. Which of the following statements is TRUE about your project?
- A. Your project is on schedule.
- B. Your project is behind schedule.
- C. Your project is ahead of schedule.
- D. You cannot determine if your project is behind or ahead of schedule from the information given.

154. Your organization has enough resources only to work on one of two potential projects and decides to use the Net Present Value (NPV) to assess and select the best project for the organization. Project Alpha has an NPV of $45,000 and Project Beta has an NPV of $60,000. Project Alpha will take 3 years to complete and Project Beta will take 4 years. What will be the opportunity cost of the

project chosen?
- A. $60,000
- B. $45,000
- C. $25,000
- D. $105,000

155. Which one of the following is NOT an input in the Conduct Procurements process?
- A. Independent Cost Estimates
- B. Make-or-Buy Analysis
- C. Source Selection Criteria
- D. Seller Proposals

156. You have been appointed as a project manager in a well-reputed hospital. While working on a project, you find that your employer is violating several codes issued by the local health department. What should be your first action in this situation?
- A. Have a discussion with your employer to find out if they are aware of the violations.
- B. Immediately resign from the company.
- C. Immediately inform the local health department
- D. about the violations.
- E. Do not worry about it since it is none of your business.

157. You are a project manager working for the healthcare system and have been tasked with overseeing the implementation of a new network infrastructure at the local hospital. A month into the project, you just finished creating the Project Charter and identifying the key stakeholders. You are about to move to the planning process group when the hospital authority requests that you provide them with the budget and cost baseline. Your best response should be:
- A. Inform them that cost is a project secret and cannot be shared.
- B. Hand over the project charter to them for the details about the budget and cost baseline.
- C. Inform them that the budget and cost baseline will be finalized during the planning process group.
- D. Inform them that there is no need to worry about the budget and cost baseline for this kind of small project.

158. Higher management has assigned you as the project manager very early in the project life cycle for a very critical project. You were asked to start working on the Project Charter immediately. You will be performing all of the following activities EXCEPT:
- A. Develop the project Scope Statement Document.
- B. Identify and document high level risks.
- C. Identify project constraints and assumptions.
- D. Perform order of magnitude estimating.

159. You are a shy project manager struggling with your communication skills. You like to keep to yourself unless you are prompted for your input. On the other hand, Steve is highly regarded by everyone and very well liked. You consider Steve to be your role model as he is capable of getting others to see his way on many issues. What type of power does Steve possess?
- A. Expert power
- B. Reward power
- C. Referent power
- D. Legitimate power

160. While managing an ERP solution implementation project, you realize that you are not utilizing your resources evenly in the project. You found out that you are using almost all of your resources in some of the work weeks and hardly using any in some other work weeks. You consider moving around some of the activities and resources so that you can utilize your resources evenly throughout the project life cycle. Which of the following techniques are you using?
- A. Fast Tracking
- B. Crashing
- C. Resource Leveling
- D. Critical Chain

161. Ashley, a senior project manager, recently took over a project to produce a safe and effective drug from another project manager who just left the company. Ashley was surprised to find out that there is no Change Control Board (CCB) to review, approve, or deny a change request for the project. Upon further investigation, she finds that there is also no organizational Change Control Board to manage changes for the entire organization. What should Ashley do in this situation?
- A. Carry on with the change request without a Change Control Board.
- B. Establish a Change Control Board (CCB) for her project.
- C. Make all the decisions about the requested changes herself with the help of the team members.
- D. Ask the sponsor to approve or deny the change requests.

162. You have collected information about Sabrina, a team member, from multiple sources including other team members and management staff. You have identified several areas for improvement for Sabrina that you want to discuss with her. You are particularly concerned that Sabrina is having many conflicts with other team members. During the one-on-one meeting, both of you agree on a training program to address the concern of conflicts with other team members. You also make sure that Sabrina understands she needs to submit her status and progress reports at the beginning of every week. Which action are you currently engaged in with Sabrina?
    A. Observation and Conversation
    B. Project Performance Appraisals
    C. Team Performance assessment
    D. Conflict Management

163. You are having an issue with one of the manufacturing processes being used to create the required parts for routers and switches that your company produces. What should you use to identify the cause of this issue, and the effect it may have on your project?
    A. Continuous improvement
    B. Histogram
    C. Ishikawa Diagram
    D. Flowchart

164. While working with clients on the final acceptance of the application, you were delighted to find out that the application exceeded the performance criteria specified in the requirement specification approved by the clients. You implemented several features that were not in the project scope to meet and exceed client's expectations. What can you conclude about the project performance?
    A. The project was a success as it provided the features beyond the customers' expectation without any cost and schedule impact.
    B. The project was a success as it exceeded the customers' specified performance criteria.
    C. The project was unsuccessful as it has been gold plated.
    D. The project was a success as it made the clients really happy.

165. You are the project manager overseeing the development of a new console video game. It has 10 components, and 5 team members are working on it. There are 15 stakeholders for this project, and one of the stakeholders is the previous owner of this company. One of the components is of major concern because it is a difficult one to implement. You found out that the soonest you can start working on that component will be early next week, and it will take 10 days to complete. You also found out that as of now the CPI=.81, and the SPI=1.2. What should be your main concern in this project at this time?
    A. The stakeholder who was the previous owner
    B. Schedule
    C. Number of stakeholders in this project
    D. Cost

166. While managing a WIFI project, you discovered that a few of your team members are not getting along. You also realized that three team members are not sure how to complete their deliverables. All of your team members are working together in the same building. You also set up regular weekly meetings with all the team members in a single meeting room. Which technique will NOT be helpful in this situation?
    A. War room
    B. Training
    C. Reward and recognition
    D. Negotiation

167. While creating the Stakeholder Register, you realize that some of the stakeholders can negatively impact your project. Which of the following elements should you NOT include in your Stakeholder Register?
    A. List of key expectations identified for each stakeholder.
    B. Contact information of the stakeholders.
    C. A rating of the stakeholder's impact and influence on the project.
    D. A plan to increase support and minimize obstruction for each stakeholder.

168. The trustworthiness of a message to its receivers may be prejudiced by their level of trust in the communicator. This is an example of which of the following?
    A. Encoding
    B. Decoding
    C. Noise
    D. Medium

169. Your sponsor is not very happy about the cost estimate you submitted for a construction project. The sponsor suggested that you come up with an exceptionally accurate cost estimate at your earliest convenience. What will be your best course of action in this situation?
    A. Use the historical information from a similar project and make adjustments for known differences.
    B. Use a rule of thumb estimate.
    C. Perform a cost aggregation for raw materials and labor for each activity in the WBS.
    D. Use the three-point estimates technique.

170. You are overseeing an ERP implementation project that will cost the company $1 million and will take three years to complete. Six months into the project, higher management decided to terminate your project as they found an off- the-shelf solution that can be implemented in three months at a fraction of the planned cost. What is the first thing you should do in this situation when your project no longer seems commercially viable for the company?
    A. Conduct scope verification.
    B. Release the team immediately.
    C. Document the lessons learned.
    D. Have an urgent meeting with the sponsor to discuss the situation.

171. You are overseeing a software project to develop a new video console game. Which of the following statements is TRUE about your project?
    A. A phase will never start until the deliverables for the previous phase have been reviewed and approved.
    B. Your internal and external stakeholders will have the same level of influence throughout your project.
    C. Any scope change during the initial phase of the project will be very time consuming and expensive.
    D. You will be acquiring several of your team members during the executing phase.

172. While overseeing a new smartphone application development project, you notice your team members are measuring the quality of an item on a pass/fail basis. Which of the following methods are the team members using?
    A. Mutual exclusivity
    B. Statistical independence
    C. Normal distribution
    D. Attribute sampling

173. You decided to use a technique called rolling wave planning in your web-based insurance and tax payment application project. Which one of the following may be your key reason for selecting this technique?
    A. To prioritize project activities.
    B. To achieve the appropriate level of detail in each work package at the right time.
    C. To sequence project activities.
    D. To estimate the duration of project activities.

174. Your PMO stipulates that plurality support is the minimum level of support for any major decision in a project. You disagree with a block of supporters on a plan to purchase a piece of expensive equipment for your project. This block is larger than any other in your team even though it is only 45 percent of the total team. What should you do in this kind of situation?
    A. Have an urgent meeting with the sponsor.
    B. Insist that any major decision should be supported by more than 50 percent of the team.
    C. Do nothing as PMO permits decisions to be made by a plurality, rather than a majority.
    D. Ask PMO to reevaluate their policy.

175. You have been assigned as a project manager for an ongoing project and asked to provide activity duration estimates as soon as possible. You were surprised to find out that there was no detailed information available on the project. You explored your organizational process assets and identified a few similar projects that had been completed in the past. Which one of the following will be the correct tool to utilize in this kind of situation?
    A. Analogous Estimate
    B. Three-point Estimate
    C. Heuristic Estimate
    D. One point Estimate

176. A control chart measures the results of processes over time, displays them in a graphical format, and measures variances to determine whether process variances are in control or out of control. The upper and lower control limits are usually set as:
    A. $+ -1$ Sigma – 68.26 percent of the occurrences will fall within 1 sigma from the mean.
    B. $+ -2$ Sigma – 95.46 percent of the occurrences will fall within 2 sigma from the mean.
    C. $+ -3$ Sigma – 99.73 percent of the occurrences will fall within 3 sigma from the mean.
    D. $+ -6$ Sigma – 99.99985 percent of the occurrences will fall within 6 sigma from the mean.

177. Five process groups are by no means completely linear, and they interact and overlap with each other. Which two process groups do not usually overlap unless a project is canceled or terminated?
   A. Planning and closing
   B. Planning and executing
   C. Initiating and closing
   D. Executing and monitoring and controlling

178. Referring to the following table, determine the cost to crash the project schedule by seven days.

Task	Duration	Predecessor	Normal Cost	Crash Cost (per day)	Max Crash Days
M	8	–	$3,000	$300	0
N	10	M	$4,000	$300	2
O	9	N	$3,000	$400	2
P	10	O	$5,000	$400	1
Q	6	O	$4,000	$600	2
R	5	P, Q	$2,000	$500	3

   A. $5,000
   B. $3,500
   C. $2,800
   D. $3,000

179. Workarounds, or unplanned responses to emerging risks that were previously unidentified or accepted, are determined during which Risk Management Process?
   A. Plan Risk Management process
   B. Monitor Risks process
   C. Plan Risk Responses process
   D. Perform Quantitative Risk Analysis process

180. You identify that there are 36 communication channels in your project. How many members do you have in your team?
   A. 9
   B. 10
   C. 36
   D. 18

181. While identifying risks in your project, your team cannot find any efficient ways to reduce the impact and probability or to insure against one of the risks. The relevant work is integral to the project; thus, you cannot simply remove the work package, and there is no suitable company to outsource the work to either. What is the best course of action in this situation?
   A. Identify ways to transfer the risk.
   B. Accept the risk and have contingency reserves.
   C. Identify ways to avoid the risk.
   D. Keep looking for ways to mitigate the probability and impact of the risk.

182. You notice that you are not utilizing your resources evenly in the project. You want to apply resource leveling by moving some of your activities from the week when you are using many resources to a week when you are hardly using any. Which of the following tools and techniques would be a good choice in this situation?
   A. Network Diagram
   B. Responsibility Assignment Matrix
   C. Organizational Breakdown Structure
   D. Resource Histogram

183. A project manager is using a chart that cross-references team members with the activities or work packages they are to accomplish. Which one of the following is an example of this kind of chart?
   A. Gantt Chart
   B. RACI Chart
   C. Milestone Chart
   D. Flowchart

184. Steve, a project manager, is overseeing a web-based accounting automation project that needs rigorous testing prior to implementation. The project is behind schedule and customers are strongly opposed to an extension of the duration since it was delayed twice in the past. Steve's manager asks Steve to skip most of the volume and stress testing and, if asked, instructs him to tell the customers that the testing was completed according to the approved specifications. What is Steve's best course of action in this situation?
  A. Skip the volume and stress testing as suggested by his manager.
  B. Only do a limited amount of volume and stress testing to make sure that the system will function correctly.
  C. Discuss the situation with the sponsor and seek advice.
  D. Politely refuse to skip the volume and stress testing.

185. What are the end results of the Plan Quality Management process?
  A. Quality Control Measurements, Validated Changes, and Change Requests
  B. Quality Management Plan, Quality Metrics, and Project Management Plan Updates
  C. Quality Management Plan, Quality Checklist, and Quality Control Measurements
  D. Work Performance Information, Quality Management Plan, and Process Improvement Plan

186. A project manager is interested to know the approximate cost of her project so that she can identify the rationality of the vendors' offered price. The best tool to use in this scenario is:
  A. Inspection and Audits
  B. Independent Estimate
  C. Screening System
  D. Weighting System

187. During a brainstorming session your team members came up with several ideas and later ranked and prioritized them using the nominal group technique. Which of the following techniques will you use to sort these ideas into groups by similarities for review and analysis?
  A. Delphi Technique
  B. Mind Mapping
  C. Decision Making Techniques
  D. Affinity Diagram

188. While planning resources for a data center project you are overseeing, you used a graphical and hierarchical structure of the identified resources arranged by resource category (such as labor, material, equipment, and supplies) and type (such as expertise level, grade, and experience). This hierarchical chart is also helpful in tracking project costs and can be aligned with the organization's accounting system. You are using a:
  A. Work Breakdown Structure (WBS)
  B. Resource Breakdown Structure (RBS)
  C. Cost Breakdown Structure
  D. Human Resource Cost Chart

189. While overseeing a new wireless media streaming device development project, you notice that your team members are having significant difficulties resolving an issue that they discovered during unit testing. Upon further investigation, you realize that the approach team members are using to resolve the issue is arbitrary and disorganized. What is the correct approach for the team members to take in this kind of situation?
  A. Use the Cause and Effect Diagram to identify the root cause of the issue.
  B. Use the Pareto Chart to identify the causes causing 80 percent of the problem.
  C. Use the Control Chart to determine where the process is going out of control.
  D. Use the Monte Carlo Analysis to do a detailed what if analysis.

190. You may have two activities to design a software component and test it. Depending on the result of the testing, you may or may not redesign the component. Which of the following network diagram techniques will you use that permits loops to represent non-sequential activities?
  A. Graphical Evaluation and Review Technique (GERT)
  B. Activity on Node (AON)
  C. Activity on Arrow (AOA)
  D. Precedence Diagramming Method (PDM)

191. A bidder conference is:
  A. An output of the Conduct Procurements process.
  B. A method for selecting the best vendor for the project.
  C. A technique to review the proposals from the vendors.
  D. A tool and technique to provide all competing vendors with the same information about the bidding process.

192. While working in a foreign country, you are asked to pay the security guard for private protection service every time there is a need to transfer expensive equipment from one warehouse to another. You know this would not be a common practice in the US as it may be considered a bribe, but it is customary in the country you are now working. What is your best course of action?
   A. Pay for the service, as it is customary in the country you are now working.
   B. Never pay for the private protection service.
   C. Ask for guidance from PMO.
   D. Ask for guidance from the sponsor.

193. You have been working with a few vendors to procure the services and goods you need for one of the critical projects you are overseeing. You sent out your RFP template to these vendors so that they can submit their proposals to you. The RFP contains a narrative description of the products and services that you need for the project. Which part of the RFP document does this BEST describe?
   A. Statement of Work (SOW)
   B. Business Case
   C. Resource Management Plan
   D. Project Charter

194. Your organization is working on several critical projects and none of them are going well. Higher management has decided to adopt the Kaizen approach to improve the performance of all the projects. You have been assigned as a project manager to apply this approach throughout the organization. What kind of service are you involved in?
   A. Plan Quality
   B. Control Quality
   C. Manage Quality
   D. Close Quality

195. You are working for a healthcare facility and overseeing the implementation of a new computer infrastructure and office automation project at the local hospital. The project is progressing well, and not many change requests have been submitted so far. Recently, you made a major release in the project and communicated the successful news to all the relevant members of the project. You were surprised when the customer called to inform you that he was not very happy with the deliverable and would be asking for a major modification soon. What should you do first in this kind of situation?
   A. Do a scope verification of this deliverable to check if it satisfies project objectives.
   B. Have an urgent meeting with the sponsor to discuss the situation.
   C. Ignore the customer's concern and concentrate on the next deliverable to complete the project on time.
   D. Assure the customer that the next deliverable will have additional features to meet and exceed his expectations.

196. One of your clients did not approve a major component that your team has just completed and requested several changes. You consider the component to be fully completed as per the specifications. It also meets all the required quality criteria. You were unable to come up with an agreement on the appropriate compensation for the changes the client was asking for. Both of you have been handling the disputes in accordance with the resolution procedures outlined in the contract. You are currently involved in:
   A. Procurement Negotiations
   B. Procurement Audits
   C. Claims Administration
   D. Procurement Performance Review

197. One of the projects that you are currently managing has recently been canceled due to a change in marketplace conditions. What is your best course of action in this situation?
   A. Renegotiate with the higher management to continue the project.
   B. Gather lesson learned.
   C. Complete the project deliverables.
   D. No action is needed since the project is canceled.

198. Your organization has recently been awarded a fixed price contract and also received an SOW. As a project manager for the project, you will expect to see all of the following components in the SOW EXCEPT:
   A. Business need
   B. Product scope description or what is to be done
   C. How the project supports the strategic plan
   D. Market conditions

199. While reviewing the status of your project, you found that for a given time period your AC is $390,000 and PV is $380,000. You have a budget of $900,000 and so far have completed 40 percent of the work. What should you report to the management about your project?
   A. The project is behind schedule and over budget.
   B. The project is behind schedule but under budget.
   C. The project is progressing according to the plan.
   D. The project is ahead of schedule and under budget.

200. A noncompetitive form of procurement can be considered in all the following situations EXCEPT:
   A. The project is under extreme time constraints and needs to be completed soon.
   B. The law requires at least three quotations or proposals.
   C. A seller has unique qualifications that no other sellershave.
   D. There is no other seller except one who can provide the goods or services.

FINAL EXAM ANSWERS

1. B: Even though the project manager spends a great deal of energy and time preventing problems, there are still problems that need to be resolved. Below is the problem-solving technique:
– Define the cause of the problem (not just the symptoms)
– Analyze the problem (cause and effect diagram)
– Identify solutions
– Implement the selected solution
– Review the solution
– Confirm that the solution solved the problem

Here the project manager probably forgot to confirm that the solution actually solved the problem.

2. B: Stakeholder identification will continue throughout the project life cycle. As the project proceeds through each phase, additional stakeholders may become involved while others will be released. Stakeholder identification is conducted primarily by the project management team, but some stakeholders may be identified in the Project Charter. Stakeholders may include people and organizations that may be affected either negatively or positively by the project outcome.

3. A: The initial investment is $400,000. There are 4 quarters(3 months in each) in a year thus Cash inflows for the first year is 4 * $40,000 = $160,000
So in two years the cash inflow will be $160,000 * 2 = $320,000
In the first quarter of the third year the cash inflow will be $80,000, thus total cash inflow by that time will be $320,000 + $80,000 = $400,000 which is equivalent to the initial investment.
The payback is 2 years and 3 months since it will take this amount of time to get the initial investment back. The second project has a longer payback period so we should go for the first project.

4. D: The Control Quality process is about monitoring specific project results to determine if they comply with relevant quality standards and identifying ways to eliminate causes of unsatisfactory results. Monitoring adherence to the project scope is addressed in the Control Scope process, not in the Control Quality process.

5. C: Risk averse is someone who does not want to take risks, and the project manager seems to be part of such an organization. Risk neutral describes a person or an organization indifferent to risk. Risk seeker suggests an aptitude to take risks with an opportunity for higher returns. Risk lover is a made-up term.

6. C: This is an example of constraints. Constraints are limitations that limit the available options for a project.

7. A: Product Analysis techniques such as product breakdown, systems analysis, system engineering, value engineering, value analysis, functional analysis, and others, may be used to perform a detailed analysis of the product, service, or result. This technique translates project objectives into tangible deliverables and requirements by improving the project team's understanding of the product.

8. C: Claimed Administration is used as a tool & technique in the Control Procurements process. The key objective of negotiated settlement in claimed administration is the settlement of all outstanding issues, claims, and disputes if possible.

9. C: Once the project scope has been completed, validated and final delivery has been made, the project is considered to be completed. Any kind of disputes should be resolved in favor of the customers as much as possible, but the project manager should also be aware that customers are not always right and should resist in this sort of situation. Once the project is completed, any addition to the project should be considered as a new project, and detailed impact analysis should be carried out.

10. A: A Configuration Management System is the subset of the Project Management Information System (PMIS) that describes the different versions and characteristics of the product, service, or result of the project and ensures accuracy and completeness of the description. It is all about managing different configurations of a product. At some point in time, a product will be base lined, and different configurations, versions, and branches are managed from that point. The process improvement plan looks at processes and outlines the activities and steps that will enhance their value. Perform Integrated Change Control is the process necessary for reviewing change requests and, approving or disapproving, and managing changes to the deliverables, project management plan and documents, and the organizational process assets. A work authorization system is a formal, documented procedure to describe how to authorize and initiate work in the correct sequence at the appropriate time.

11. A

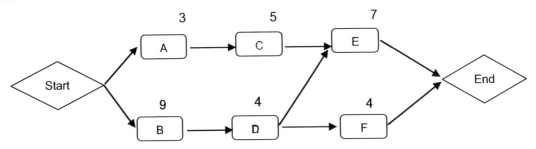

We have three paths in the network diagram as below:
Start, A, C, E, End = 15 wks.
Start, B, D, F, End = 17 wks.
Start, B, D, E, End = 20 wks.
The duration of the critical path is 20 wks.

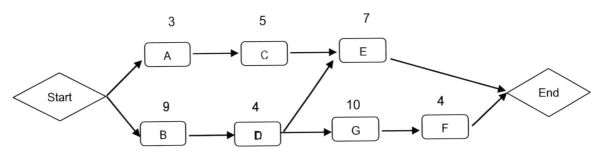

After adding the new activity G we have a new critical path – Start, B, D, G, F, End = 27 wks. The old duration of the project was 20 weeks thus additional 27 – 20 = 7 wks will be added to the project to complete the new activity G.

12. D: Victor Vroom's Expectancy theory demonstrates that employees who believe their efforts will lead to effective performance and who expect to be rewarded for their accomplishments remain productive as rewards meet their expectations.

13. B: Plan Communications is included in the planning process, which is generally completed prior to executing. Updates to the project plan, including the Communications Management Plan, will occur during the entire project life cycle.

14. B: Noncritical risks on the watch list are not only for historical use, but also need to be monitored at intervals during the project to ensure they have not become critical.

15. C: The nature and structure of a PMO depends on the needs of the organization it supports. The projects supported by a PMO may not be related other than being managed together.

16. A: The subject matter and topics discussed in the meeting may be important, but meetings are considered as informal verbal.

17. D: As per Herzberg's Motivator-Hygiene theory, hygiene factors are not sufficient to motivate people, and motivating agents provide the best positive reinforcement. Hygiene factors can destroy motivation, but improving them under most circumstances will not improve motivation.

18. C: A robust change control process will ensure that only the necessary changes are considered and implemented. A change control process cannot really help with the number of changes that will be requested in the project as the number of changes depend on how well defined the scope of the project is. Again, all stakeholders, regardless of their authority, should be able to submit change requests.

19. B: Constraints are restrictions, such as limitations on time, budget, scope, quality, schedule, resource, and technology a project faces. An imposed deadline and budget are examples of constraints.

20. B: Estimate at Completion (EAC) = BAC / CPI
Here we have BAC = $3,000, AC = $2,000 and EV = $1,200
CPI = EV / AC = 1200 / 2000 =.6
So EAC = 3000 / .6 = 5,000

21. A: A Tornado Diagram is a diagramming method to display sensitivity analysis data by examining all the uncertain elements at their baseline values. It gives a quick overview of how much the project will be impacted by various elements. The element with the greatest impact on the project appears at the top. This diagram can be used to determine sensitivity in cost, time, and quality objectives and is helpful in determining detailed response plans for elements with greater impacts.

22. D: Ishikawa Diagram is a tool used for systematically identifying and presenting all the possible causes and sub causes of a particular problem in a graphical format. It can help in quality control by identifying the causes which contributed to a quality problem.

23. D: Lag is an inserted waiting time between activities. In this case, there is a 3 day delay before we can start coding.

24. A: Funding Limit Reconciliation is a technique of reconciling the expenditure of funds with the funding limits set for the project. As per the variance between the expenditure of funds and planned limit, the activities can be rescheduled to level out the rates of expenditures.

25. D: Configuration Management Plan is a subset of the Project Management Information System (PMIS) that describes the different versions and characteristics of the product, service, or result of the project and ensures accuracy and completeness of the description.

26. A: Crashing is a technique of adding additional resources to a project activity to complete it in less time. Examples of crashing could include approving overtime, bringing in additional resources, or paying to expedite delivery to activities on the critical path. Crashing does not always produce a viable alternative and may result in increased risk, more management time, and/or cost. Increasing the number of resources may decrease time, but not in a linear amount as activities will often encounter the law of diminishing returns.

27. A: You are in the Validate Scope process, which is closely related to the Control Quality process. Both the Control Quality and Validate Scope processes can be performed simultaneously, but Control Quality is usually performed prior to Validate Scope. Control Quality verifies correctness of the work, whereas Validate Scope confirms completeness. Control Quality is focused on measuring specific project results against quality specifications and standards, whereas Validate Scope is mainly focused on obtaining acceptance of the product from the sponsor, customers, and others.

28. B: The project manager should document the change request as per the Project Scope Management Plan and then submit the change request to the Change Control Board (CCB) once the impact analysis is completed. The Change Control Board will either approve or deny the request.

29. D: Iterative, incremental, and adaptive are different types of change-driven project life cycles.

30. B: GERT is a modified network diagram drawing method that allows conditional branches and loops between activities. For example, you may have two activities to design a software component and test it. Depending on the result of the testing, you may or may not redesign the component.

31. D: The Precedence Diagramming Method (PDM) usually uses the Activity-on-Node (AON) convention where boxes/nodes are used to represent activities and arrows show dependencies.

32. C: Product scope describes the features, functions, and physical characteristics that characterize a product, service, or result. On the other hand, project scope describes the work needed to deliver a product, service, or result with the specified features and functions. Product scope may include subsidiary components, and project scope results in a single product, service, or result. Product scope completion, measured against the product requirements to determine successful fulfillment and project scope completion, is measured against the project plan, Project Scope Statement, Work Breakdown Structure (WBS), WBS Dictionary, and other elements.

33. C: You should proactively work with stakeholders to manage their expectations, address their concerns, and resolve issues. In this case, after investigating why her recommendations were excluded, schedule a meeting with the stakeholder to discuss her concerns.

34. A: You are assuming that the current variances are atypical and similar variance will not occur in the future; thus, the rest of the job will be done as per budget; all you need to do is take the remaining work (BAC – EV) and add funds spent, AC.

35. C: The Schedule Management Plan defines how the project schedule will be planned, developed, managed, executed, and controlled throughout the project life cycle. It serves as guidance for the scheduling process and defines the roles and responsibilities for stakeholders, along with scheduling methodologies, tools, schedule change control procedures, reporting formats, and frequencies.

36. D: An external dependency is related to a non-project activity and is considered outside the control of the project team. This is an example of external dependency since the other project manager does not have control over the completion of the server setup but the project has a dependency on it.

37. B: Data Analysis Techniques such as Reserve Analysis and Alternative Analysis are used in the Estimate Costs process. Reserve Analysis is used as a tool and technique in the Determine Budget process.

38. B: A Change control system is determined and set up during project planning, not during project executing.

39. D: Incentive is a bonus in addition to the agreed-upon price for exceeding time or cost objectives as specified in the contract. For the seller, the focus is on profit, and for buyers, the focus can be a combination of cost, time, and performance. Incentives help bring the seller's objectives in line with those of the buyer. With an incentive, both the buyer and seller work toward the same objective—for instance, completing the project on time. In this specific situation, an incentive will be most effective. Force majeure is an allowable excuse for either party for not meeting contractual obligations in the event of something considered to be an act of God, such as fire, storm, flood, and freak electrical storm. Since the event is considered to be neither party's fault, usually the seller receives a time extension, and risk of loss is borne by the seller, which is usually covered by insurance. Time is of the essence indicates that delivery dates are extremely important and that any delay will be considered as a material breach. With a retainage clause, in order to ensure full completion, an amount of money, usually 5 to 10 percent is withheld from each payment and paid in full once the final work is completed.

40. B: Value Analysis is also referred to as "Value Engineering" or "Value Methodology." It is the technique of finding a less costly way to do the same work and of achieving more out of the project in every possible way to increase the bottom line, decrease costs, improve quality, and optimize the schedule without reducing or impacting the scope.

41. C: The project manager is in the process of determining the project budget. The cost baseline and the project funding requirements are outputs of the Determine Budget process.

42. B: Both the SPI and CPI are less than one, which suggests that the project is behind schedule and over budget. An activity with no buffer suggests that it is on the critical path. If a critical path activity takes longer and needs more manpower to complete, then it will obviously negatively impact both time and cost. The subcontractor who was replaced may not be working on a critical path activity. Purchasing an expensive piece of equipment will definitely add additional cost, but it will not necessarily add time. The client may add or reduce the scope, so there is a possibility that it will reduce the cost and time.

43. D: Your first course of action should be to find out more information about what happened so that you can chose the correct course of action. Meeting with the stakeholders and finding out the details will assist you to address the crisis. Since the problem has occurred, the next thing you should do as a project manager is address the risk. You accept the risk when you have no other option. As a project manager, you would use your available reserves in this kind of situation. The contingency reserves are for "known unknowns;" thus, you use them to pay for risks that you've planned for. You may need to use the management reserves as they are for "unknown unknowns," or problems that you did not plan for but they showed up anyway. Once the issue is addressed, you may need to reevaluate your risk identification process, look for unexpected effects of the problem, inform management, update the risk management plan, create a fallback plan, and take corrective and preventive actions.

44. D: A quality audit is a scheduled or random structured review performed by internal or third-party auditors to determine whether quality management activities comply with organizational and project processes, policies, and procedures. It ascertains inefficient and ineffective activities and processes used in the project as well as lessons learned, such as gaps and best practices, that can improve the performance of the current project or future ones. A quality audit to correct any deficiencies in the quality processes should result in a reduced cost of quality and an increase in stakeholders' acceptance of the product.

45. B: In chapter 6, project Schedule Management, we learned the following two formulas:
Standard Deviation (SD) = (P – O) / 6
Variance = $[(P - O)/6]^2$
We can see that variance is the square of standard deviation, so if we take the square root of variance, we will also get the standard deviation. We also know that total SD cannot be calculated by adding up the SD of two processes. We need to add the variances and then take the square root of the sum to get the SD. In this case, the SD for product variation is 0.7 inches and the measurement variation is 0.5 inches.
0.7 * 0.7 = 0.49 and 0.5 * 0.5 = 0.25. So, total SD is the square root of (0.49 + 0.25) = 0.86.

46. A: A Marginal Analysis refers the point where the benefits or revenue from improving quality equals the incremental cost to achieve that quality.

47. A: The goal of Team Performance Assessments is to identify the specific training, coaching, mentoring, assistance, or changes required to improve the team's performance and effectiveness. The project management team makes formal or informal assessments of the project team's effectiveness while team development efforts, such as training, team building, and colocation are implemented. A team's performance is measured against the agreed-upon success criteria, schedule, and

budget target.

The evaluation of a team's effectiveness may include indicators such as:
- How well the team is performing, communicating, and dealing with conflicts
- Areas of improvement in skills that will help individuals perform assignments more efficiently and areas of improvement in competencies that will help the team perform better as a team
- Increased cohesiveness where team members work together to improve the overall project performance by sharing information and experiences openly and helping each other more frequently
- Reduced staff turnover rate

48. A: Referent power is based on referring to someone in a higher position to leverage some of the superior's power. Penalty (coercive/punishment) is predicated on fear and gives the project manager the ability to penalize a team member for not meeting the project goals and objectives. Expert power is based on the knowledge or skill of a project manager on a specific domain. Being the subject matter expert or project management expert will give the project manager substantial power to influence and control team members. Reward power imposes positive reinforcement, and it is the ability of giving rewards and recognition.

49. D: This is an example of fixed cost since regardless of how many times the team will use the tools they will pay $3,000/month.

50. B: Physical Resource Assignments are the output in the Acquire Resources process. The Resource Management Plan is an output of the Plan Resource Management process, Team Performance Assessments is an output of the Develop Team process, and Resource Requirements is an output of the Estimate Activity Resources process.

51. B: Termination for convenience is a contract clause that permits the buyer to terminate a contract at any time for a cause or convenience. Usually there will be specific conditions associated with the execution of this clause.

52. D: Issues and risks are not the same thing. An issue is an obstacle that threatens project progress and can block the team from achieving its goals. Risk is an uncertain event or condition that may have a positive or negative effect on the project's objective if it occurs.

53. C: In Abraham Maslow's Hierarchy of Needs, accomplishment, respect, attention, and appreciation are represented as esteem.

54. C: A bottom-up estimate is the most time-consuming and generally the most accurate estimate. In this technique, one estimate per activity is received from the team members. This estimate can be based on expert judgment, historical information, or an educated guess. A rough order of magnitude is an approximate estimate (–25 percent to 75 percent) made without detailed data. It is used during the formative stages for initial evaluation of a project's feasibility. A heuristic estimate is based on rule of thumb, such as the 80/20 rule. A top-down estimate is usually given to the project manager from management or the sponsor. This type of estimate measures the project parameters, such as budget, size, complexity, and duration based on the parameters of a previous similar project and historical information. It is usually done during an early phase of the project when not much information is available; thus, it is less accurate even though it is less costly and less time consuming.

55. B: The tendency to rate high or low on all factors due to the impression of a high or low rating on a specific factor is known as the Halo effect. This kind of action has negative impacts on the project and the performing organization.

56. A: Withdrawing or avoiding is the technique of retreating from conflict and avoiding or postponing resolution. This technique leads to the least sustaining positive results.

57. C: A Flowchart helps the project team anticipate and identify where quality problems might occur in a project, which in turn, helps the team develop alternatives when dealing with quality problems.

58. A: Project communications is an output of the Manage Communications process. All other items listed are included in the Communications Management Plan.

59. B: The contingency plan is the specific action that will be taken if opportunities or threats occur.

60. C: Urgency is not included in the basic communications model but should be considered when determining the method of communication to be used.

61. D: A project manager should always be truthful in his/her communications and should provide accurate information in a timely manner. A project manager should not deceive others or make misleading half-truths or false statements. None of the options listed in 'A,' 'B,' or 'C' will resolve this issue immediately, and Steve should inform the stakeholder that he needs a little more time to verify the information about the major component and will follow up with him/her shortly when he has an accurate update.

62. D: Avoid is the elimination of the threat by eliminating the cause or changing the project management plan. Here you utilized the avoid strategy by terminating the contract with the subcontractor to eliminate the threat to your project.

63. A. Value Engineering is mainly focused on finding a less costly way to do the same work and on achieving more out of the project in every possible way to increase the bottom line, decrease costs, improve quality, and optimize the schedule without reducing or impacting the scope.

64. D: Enhance is a strategy to deal with an opportunity. By influencing the underlying risk triggers, this strategy increases the size, probability, likelihood, and positive impact of an opportunity. Data Analysis Techniques such as Technical Performance Analysis and Reserve Analysis, meetings, and audits are used as tools and techniques in the Monitor Risks process.

65. A: Assumptions are not based on factual information, and failure to validate an assumption may result in significant risk events. Assumptions are usually documented during the project initiating and planning processes. These assumptions are not absolute and can be negotiable. Assumptions do not limit the project team's options for decision making, however constraints do. Assumptions also do not allow for baseline adjustments in case of project crisis as it's not the correct process for adjusting project baselines.

66. C: Perform Qualitative Risk Analysis is the process of prioritizing risks by assessing and combining their probability of occurrence and impact to the project if they occur. This fast, relatively easy to perform, and cost effective process ensures that the right emphasis is on the right risk areas as per their ranking and priority and helps to allocate adequate time and resources for them. Even though numbers are used for the rating in Perform Qualitative Risk Analysis, it is a subjective evaluation and should be performed throughout the project. Perform Quantitative Risk Analysis is the process of numerically analyzing the effect of overall project objectives of identified risks. It mostly performs numerical analysis using a modeling technique such as Expected Monetary Value (EMV) of the probability and impact of risks moved forward from the Perform Qualitative Risk Analysis process. Data Analysis Techniques such as Risk Probability and Impact Assessment and Risk Data Quality Assessment and a Data Representation Technique such as Probability and Impact Matrix are used as tools and techniques in the Perform Qualitative Risk Analysis process.

67. D: A project manager should understand the significance of this sort of findings and must consult the experts before proceeding further.

68. A: Any time you come across a new risk, the first thing you should do is document it in the risk register and then analyze the impact as well as the probability of that risk. You should not take any further action until you've analyzed the risk.

69. D: Sensitivity analysis helps to determine which risks have the most potential impact on a project, or in other words, whether the occurrence of a particular threat would merely be an inconvenience or whether it would ruin the project. A tornado diagram can be used to display the sensitivity analysis data by examining all the uncertain elements at their baseline values. It gives a quick overview of how much the project will be impacted by various elements, and the element with the greatest impact on the project appears at the top. This diagram can be used to determine sensitivity in cost, time, and quality objectives and will be helpful to determine a detailed response plan for the elements with greater impacts.

70. D: A resource calendar shows who is and who is not available to work during any given time period. The resource calendar may consider attributes such as experience, skill level, expertise, capabilities, and geographical locations for human resources to identify the best resources and their availability.
A project team directory includes information about the team members, such as name, contact details, role, and functional area. A Responsibility Assignment Matrix (RAM) is a chart that cross-references team members with the activities or work packages they are to accomplish. One example of a RAM is a RACI (Responsible, Accountable, Consult, and Inform) chart, which can be used to ensure clear divisions of roles and responsibilities. A Resource Breakdown Structure (RBS) is a graphical and hierarchical structure of the identified resources arranged by resource category (such as labor, material, equipment, and supplies) and type (such as expertise level, grade, and experience).

71. B: We know $PV = FV / (1 + r)^n$
Initial cost = \$6,000 and interest rate= 10 percent
So Present Value (PV) for the first project is $\$10,000 / (1 + .1)^2 = \$9,009$
The other project has a bigger NPV of \$9,500. So we should select the second project.

72. A: EVA = After Tax Profit – (Capital expenditures * Cost of Capital)
= 14,000 – (210,000 * .04) = \$5600
ABC gained \$5600 as determined by EVA.

73. A:

Month	PV	EV	AC
Month1	\$30,000	\$27,000	\$25,000
Month2	\$35,000	\$40,000	\$45,000
Month3	\$90,000	\$80,000	\$70,000

Month4	$150,000	$125,000	$89,000

The cumulative AC for all four months was $25,000 + $45,000 + $ 70,000 + $89,000 = $229,000
The cumulative PV for all four months was $30,000 + $35,000 + $90,000 + $150,000 = $305,000
The cumulative EV for all four months was $ 27,000 + $ 40,000 + $ 80,000 + $125,000 = $272,000

We know $CPI^c = EV^c/AC^c$, so CPI^c = $ 272,000 / $229,000 = 1.18
And $SPI^c = EV^c/PV^c$, so SPI^c = $ 272,000 / $305,000 = .891

74. B: Once the WBS is created with all the work packages, the team members should work on decomposing the work packages to create the detailed activity list. Network diagram and activity sequencing can be performed only after the activity list is created.

75. A: You have completed only 20 * 75 percent = 15 miles of the railway so far. 20 miles of railway project was supposed to be finished in 40 weeks so, every mile is to be completed in 2 weeks. In this case only 75% or 15 miles of railway is completed in 40 weeks, thus, every mile is completed in 40 / 15 = 2.66 weeks. At this rate, remaining 20 – 15 = 5 miles of railway will take another 5 * 2.66 = 13.3 weeks.

76. B: Some changes in the project are inevitable. A project manager should make sure that the change requests are evaluated and presented to the CCB for review. The project manager should not have the attitude to deny changes whenever possible. The focus of the project manager should be to prevent unnecessary changes, evaluate the impacts, and manage changes as necessary.

77. B: Risk mitigation simply means a reduction in the probability and/or impact of an adverse risk event to an acceptable threshold. Leasing the equipment reduces the consequence of the threat in this specific situation.

78. A: The standard deviation measures how diverse the population is in the data set. It is calculated by finding out the mean, then calculating the average of the distance of each data point from the mean.

79. A: You have 20 miles to complete at a rate of $10,000/mile. Your budget at completion is 20*10,000 = $200,000.

80. A: Perform Quantitative Risk Analysis is the process of numerically analyzing the effect of overall project objectives of identified risks. It mostly performs a numerical analysis of the probability and impact of risks moved forward from the Perform Qualitative Risk Analysis process. A small project with limited budget may consider skipping this process if management decides that quantitative statements about risk and impact are not needed.

81. B: Invitation for Bid (IFB/request for Bid (RFB): Request from a buyer for all potential sellers to submit a total price bid for work to be performed. Request for Proposal (RFP): Buyer's request to all potential sellers for the details of how work will be performed. Request for Quotation (RFQ): Buyer's request to all potential sellers for a price quote per item, hour, foot or other unit of measure.

82. A: Variety of work is a motivational agent, not a hygiene factor.

83. D: RACI is a type of Responsibility Assignment Matrix Chart which can be used to ensure clear divisions of roles and responsibilities (RACI stands for responsible, accountable, consult, and inform). SWOT Analysis, Assumption and constraint Analysis, and brainstorming – an information gathering technique are used to identify risks in the project.

84. C: How changes to the requirements will be handled and configuration management activities are documented as a part of the Requirements Management Plan which is an output of the Plan Scope Management process.

85. C: Work Authorization System is a formal, documented procedure to describe how to authorize and initiate work in the correct sequence at the appropriate time. The other options listed here could be contributory factors, but most likely a work authorization procedure was either not properly established or not properly followed.

86. C: Fait accompli is a negotiation tactic of using rules/laws, decisions already made, etc., as mandatory to avoid any further discussion. Personal insults are a negotiation tactic of attacking an individual. Good guy/bad guy is a negotiation tactic of making one person helpful to the other party while making another person very difficult to work with during negotiation. Missing man is a negotiation tactic of using a missing individual who has the power to everything.

87. B: If CPI or past results are typical or expected to continue, the correct EAC formula is EAC = BAC/CPI.
In this case, BAC = $90,000
CPI = EV / AC = $ 35,000 /$30,000 = 1.16
EAC = $90,000 / 1.16 = $77,586

88. B: Procurement Performance Review is a structured review that consists of seller-prepared documentation, buyer inspection, and a quality audit of the seller's progress to deliver project scope and quality within cost and on schedule as compared to the contract. The objective is to identify performance progress or failures, noncompliance, and areas where performance is a problem. Inspections and audits are activities mainly focused on the product itself and its conformance to specification. The payment system is usually handled by the accounts payable system of the buyer organization and helps

avoid duplicate payments, ensures invoices and payments match up, and ensures that the right amount has been invoiced for the appropriate deliverables at the right time.

89. D: The cruise company is using the enhance strategy to increase the traffic and profitability. By influencing the underlying risk triggers, this strategy increases the size, probability, likelihood, and positive impact of an opportunity.

90. D: Anytime the vendor is not following the instructions stated in the contract, the project manager should inform the vendor that they are in default. Without informing the vendor about the concern and what they are doing wrong, you cannot terminate the contract. You also cannot simply stop any payment.

91. A. The Scope Management Plan and Requirements Management Plan are the outputs of the Plan Scope Management process.

92. C: Earned Value Analysis is used to integrate scope, cost, and schedule measures to assess project performance. Trend analysis and variance analysis are included in earned value analysis. Variance analysis may include only a comparison of actual performance with one specific baseline. Presentations may be used to deliver information obtained during earned value analysis.

93. D: A Flowchart is a graphical representation of a process to help analyze how problems occur and to identify potential process improvement opportunities. There are many styles, but all flowcharts show activities, decision points, the order of processing, points of complexity, and interrelationships between elements in the process.

94. C: According to Herzberg, destroying hygiene factors such as working conditions, salary, status, and security can destroy motivation, but improving them under most circumstances will not improve motivation. The hygiene factors are not sufficient to motivate people, and motivating agents provide the best positive reinforcement. Motivating people is best done by rewarding and letting people grow.

95. D: Parametric estimating is a technique that reviews historical data for statistical correlations. Variables are then used to estimate the costs in the current project. For example, if historical information identifies that the flooring installed in a similar project cost $1.50 per square foot, then the 20,000 square feet of flooring required for the new project would cost $30,000. Typically, this technique has been known to produce a high level of accuracy, but it will be costly due to the level of sophistication that is required to implement it. In most cases, the technique is performed when the performing organization conducts many similar projects, historical information is accurate, and the model used for the estimate is scalable.

96. C: Critical Path Method (CPM) is a technique of schedule analysis that considers activity durations, logical relationships, dependencies, leads, lags, assumptions, and constraints to determine the float of each activity and the overall schedule. This method identifies the critical path with the least flexibility and the highest risk so that it can be managed appropriately.

97. B: You just finished the Plan Procurement Management process and should be moving to the next process of Conduct Procurements. In Conduct Procurement process you should be obtaining and evaluating seller responses, selecting a seller, and awarding a contract. The tools and techniques you will be using in Conduct Procurement process are bidder conference, proposal evaluation techniques, and independent estimates.

98. A: Manage Quality is a process to determine if the project activities are complying with organizational and project policies, standards, processes, and procedures. This process is primarily concerned with overall process improvement and does not deal with inspecting the product for quality or measuring defects. The primary focus is on steadily improving the processes and activities undertaken to achieve quality.

99. A: Project Reporting is a tool & technique in the Manage Communications process, not in the Plan Communications Management process. Communication Requirement Analysis, Communication methods, and Communication Technology are tools & techniques in Plan Communications Management process.

100. C: Source Selection Criteria is not an output of the Conduct Procurements process; it is an output of the Plan Procurement Management process. It is developed and used to provide sellers with an understanding of the buyer's need and also to help them in deciding whether to bid or make a proposal on the project. Later on, it also helps to evaluate sellers by rating or scoring them.

101. C: A Scatter Diagram is a tool and technique used in quality management processes to analyze two characteristics of a process and see if there is any interdependency between them. Based on the outcome of the scatter diagram, appropriate actions can be taken to improve quality.

102. A: Let n equal the number of months when both options' cost will be the same
$((2000 * 10) + 2000) n = 180,000 + 4000 n$ or $(20,000 + 2,000) n = 180,000 + 4000 n$
or $22,000 n = 180,000 + 4000 n$ or $18,000 n = 180,000$ or $n = 180,000/18,000$ or $n = 10$

103. B: According to the learning curve theory, when a large number of items are produced repetitively, productivity will

increase but at a diminishing rate. Learning curve data indicates that as work is repeated, the time required to complete the work is reduced, but the rate of improvement decreases. For instance, installing carpet in the fiftieth room in a construction project will take less time than it did in the first room due to increased efficiency as workers become more efficient with the installation procedure.

104. A: If there are no complaints or claims filed earlier, no term or condition in the contract is breached, and work is completed as per the SOW, then we will consider the contract to be complete. Note that it does not necessarily mean the contract is closed when we say that a contract is complete. The Control Procurements process must be carried on in order to close the contract.

105. D: Conduct Procurements is the process of obtaining seller responses, selecting a seller, and awarding the procurement, usually in the form of a contract. Plan Procurements is the process of documenting project purchasing decisions, specifying the approach, defining selection criteria to identify potential sellers, and putting together a Procurement Management Plan. Procurement negotiation is not a process but is a tool & technique used in the Conduct Procurements process. The Control Procurements process is mainly concerned with completing each project procurement.

106. D: The very first thing the project manager should do upon receiving a change request is to evaluate the impact to the project objectives, such as scope, time, cost, quality, risk, resources, and others. The change request then should be submitted to the change control board for approval or rejection. Instructing the team member and informing the sponsor of the requested change would not be done prior to evaluating the impact of the requested change. Also, the project manager should make every effort to prevent unnecessary changes in the project as much as possible.

107. B: The Cost Baseline is a time-phased budget used to monitor, measure, and control cost performance during the project. It is developed by summarizing costs over time and is usually displayed in the form of an S-curve. This suggests that the cost starts off low, then accelerates throughout the later phases of the project, and gradually slows down during the closing.

108. A: The Sunk Cost is a retrospective cost that is already paid for a project and often used to describe what is written off from a canceled project as unrecoverable.

109. B: A Records Management System can include indexing, archiving, and retrieval systems to capture and store all documents, correspondence, and communication relevant to a contract. For some projects, every record such as e- mails, payments, and written and verbal communication, is recorded and stored.

110. C: You are performing a procurement performance review as part of the Control Procurements process. It is a structured review of the seller's progress to deliver project scope and quality within cost and on schedule, as compared to the contract.

111. C: Claims administration or handling of claims is one of the most frequent activities in the Control Procurements process. Claims, disputes, or appeals are requested when the buyer and seller disagree on the scope, the impact of changes, or the interpretation of some terms and conditions in the contract. All these claims should be documented, processed, monitored, and managed in accordance with the contract terms throughout the contract life cycle. It is desirable to resolve the disputes through negotiation, but unresolved claims may require escalation to dispute resolution procedures, such as arbitration or litigation, established in the contract.

112. C: In this case, the seller's failure to deliver the equipment on time will drastically impact the project. So the contract can be terminated with the vendor for defaulting. But in other instances, a contract can also be terminated for a convenience by the buyer.

113. B: According to McClelland's Achievement Motivation theory, individuals who work best when cooperating with others and working in a team, seek to maintain good relationships and approval rather than recognition, and perform well in customer-facing team positions have a need for affiliation or association. People with a need for achievements should be given projects that are challenging but reachable. These people may prefer to work alone and also like recognition. People who like to organize and influence others have a need for power.

114. C: Since a Stakeholder Register contains sensitive information, a project manager may publish it with other project documentation or keep it in reserve for personal use only.

115. D: Involving the stakeholders in some project activities is a good way to bring them to a supportive or a leading state.

116. C: Fixed price contract will be the best option in this case as this type of contract will have less risk for the buyer and most risk for the seller.

117. A: You should pay the fee since the fee has a valid purpose and should not be considered a bribe.

118. B: Final product, service, or result transition is an output in the Close Project or Phase process, not in the Direct and Manage Project Work process.

119. C: You should always try to have a win-win situation. The lowest possible price and shortest possible duration will put

the vendor in an extremely difficult situation and increase the potential for failure. Your main objective of negotiation will be to build trust, obtain a fair and reasonable price that both parties are comfortable with, and uncover the points of conflict and dispute prior to final contract signing.

120. C: The bidder conference is also called the contractor conference, vendor conference, or pre-bid conference. It is intended to assure that no seller receives preferential treatment and that all sellers have a clear, common understanding of the procurement (technical requirements, contractual requirements, etc.). The key objective is to provide all potential contractors with the information they need to determine if they would like to continue with the contracting process. The bidder conference will ensure the mandatory standard of fairness in the PMI code of ethics and professional conduct by making the opportunity equally available to all qualified vendors.

121. C: You should have a discussion with the customer about any issue with the deliverable so that a mutual solution can be identified. Capturing the issue in the lessons learned will not solve the current problem. Issuing the deliverable as is and getting the formal acceptance will not serve the best interest of the customer.

122. C: If you cannot estimate the value of the impact, you can utilize qualitative estimates such as low, medium, high, and others. Qualitative Risk Analysis is the process of prioritizing risks by assessing and combining their probability of occurrence and impact to the project if they occur. This fast, relatively easy to perform, and cost effective process ensures that the right emphasis is on the right risk areas as per their ranking and priority and helps to allocate adequate time and resources for them. Even though numbers are used for the rating in the Perform Qualitative Risk Analysis process, it is a subjective evaluation and should be performed throughout the project.

123. C: Since the problem has occurred, the first thing you should do as a project manager is address the risk by creating a workaround. Once the issue is addressed, you may need to reevaluate your risk identification process, look for unexpected effects of the problem, inform management, update the risk management plan, create a fallback plan, and take corrective and preventive actions.

124. A: Giving special rewards to some employees, such as assigned parking spaces, corner offices, and executive dining, are considered perquisites. Fringe benefits are the standard benefits formally given to all employees, such as education benefits, health insurance, and profit sharing.

125. D: A project manager should actively listen to the stakeholders' concerns, resolve conflicts among the stakeholders, and build trust. The project manager should convey the ground rules to the team members, not to the stakeholders.

126. D: In this kind of situation you should always find out details of the design defect before you have a discussion about it with the sponsor or the customers. The very first thing you should do is to evaluate the impact of the design defect and have a brainstorming session with the team members on possible solutions.

127. C: A short delay of a critical path activity will result in an overall delay of the project duration so a change request should be created. A major delay of a non-critical path activity may not have any impact on the overall project duration. A project manager can use the contingency reserve to deal with the cost and schedule variances. Fast tracking and crashing methods can also be used to deal with schedule variance.

128. A: The only way to modify a contract is through a formal, written change request. This change request then follows the formal contract change control process. Contract change control system is a tool & technique in the Control Procurements process that defines the process by which procurements can be modified and includes change procedures, forms, dispute resolution processes, necessary paperwork, required authorizations, tracking systems, and other items.

129. D: Force majeure is a kind of clause that states that if a natural disaster such as fire, hurricane, freak electrical storm, tornado, etc., happens, the event will be an allowable cause for either party for not meeting contractual obligations, as the event is neither party's fault. These are considered to be acts of God, and in most cases, you should receive a time extension and the damage should be covered by insurance.

130. A: You should not release the team until the lessons learned are documented and added to the organizational process assets as you need their help with the lessons learned. Most contracts have payment terms that allow for some period of time before full payment is required thus the last thing you do on the project is close the contract.

131. A: When the project manager ascertains the current project status, it should be communicated to the project stakeholders as per the Communications Management Plan.

132. D: Negotiation is a tool & technique in the Conduct Procurements process, not in the Control Procurements process.

133. A: Process improvement activities including corrective actions, preventive actions, and defect repairs, are implemented in the Direct and Manage Project Work process.

134. B: Critical Path Method (CPM) is a technique of schedule analysis that evaluates the activities considering activity duration, logical relationship, dependency, leads, lags, assumptions, and constraints to determine the float of each activity and the overall schedule. This method identifies the critical path with the least flexibility and the highest risk so that it can

be managed appropriately. The critical path duration is the longest path in the network diagram and the shortest amount of time the project will take to complete.

135. D: To identify the appropriate training for the team members, we should refer to the resource management plan as it identifies the training needs and certification requirements of the team members.

136. C: Control Scope is the process of monitoring the status of the project and product scope, maintaining control over the project by preventing overwhelming scope change requests, and managing changes to the scope baseline. It also assures that underlying causes of all requested changes and recommended corrective actions are understood and processed through the Integrated Change Control Process.

137. A:

Target Cost	$250,000
Target Fee	$15,000
Actual Cost	$225,000
Sharing Ratio	75/25

Here target cost = $250,000, and actual cost = $225,000; thus, savings = $250,000 – $225,000 = $25,000.
Seller portion of savings is 25 percent of $25,000 = $6,250.
Buyer portion of savings is 75 percent of $25,000 = $18,750.
Final fee for seller is $15,000 + $6,250 = $21,250.
Thus, total cost for the buyer is $225,000 + 21,250 = $246,250.
Again, initial cost was $250,000 + $15,000 – $265,000.
Now the total cost is $246,250; thus, the buyer is saving $18,750.

138. C: Correlating the need for the project to the organizational strategic objective and goal is the best approach to gain support for the project from the performing organization. Organizational planning can establish the funding and support for the component projects on the basis of specific lines of business, risk categories, and other factors. An organization's strategic goals and objectives are the primary factor guiding investments. Projects, programs, or other related works that contribute the least to the portfolio's strategic objectives may lose the support of the performing organization as soon as there is a higher-priority project that is more oriented toward the strategic objective. It is a good idea to meet the personal objectives of the sponsor, but it will not confirm the support from the performing organization. Communicating the project details and benefits will not be sufficient enough to gain support from the performing organization.

139. C: Fast Tracking is a schedule compression technique of performing critical path activities in parallel when they were originally planned in series. Crashing is another schedule compression technique of adding additional resources to project critical path activities to complete them more quickly. This technique looks at cost and schedule trade-offs and resources are added either from inside or outside the organization. Since some of the activities in the project can be performed in parallel and resources have not been fully utilized, we can use fast tracking and crashing in this project.

140. D: A bidder conference is intended to assure that no seller receives preferential treatment and that all sellers have a clear, common understanding of the procurement (technical requirements, contractual requirements, etc.). The bidder conference should help sellers determine if they should participate in the bidding process and submit their proposals.

141. A:

Target Cost	$355,000
Target Fee	$45,000
Actual Cost	$390,000
Sharing Ratio	75/25

There is a cost overrun of $390,000 – $355,000 = $35,000.
Seller portion of the cost overrun is 35,000 * 25 percent = $8,750.
So the final fee will be $45,000 – $8,750 = $36,250
The cost plus incentive fee contract shares the cost savings but could also result in reduced fees to the seller if there is a cost overrun.

142. D: Project constraints specify the limitations and restrictions, such as limitations on time, budget, scope, quality, schedule, resource, and technology a project faces.

143. A: The internal project has been formally approved recently so it should have an approved project charter. The Project Charter has the list of key stakeholders and their major expectations along with other project related information, thus it should be a good starting point for identifying key stakeholders.

144. B: The Monitoring and Controlling Project Work process usually measures the work results against the plan.

145. B: The cost of the risk is $15,000 + $20,000 = $35,000, so its EMV is 40 percent * – $35,000 = –$14,000. The value

of the opportunity is $10,500 and its probability is 30 percent, so the EMV is 30 percent * $10,500 = $3,150. The total EMV for the two is –$14,000 + $3,150 = – $10,850.

146. B: A Prompt List is not a Data Gathering technique.

147. B: Stakeholder identification is a continuous and sometimes grueling process as not all stakeholders will be identified during the initiating process. Some of the stakeholders will only be interested in the end product and will get involved in the project at its closing. Stakeholders with both positive and negative influence should be listed in the stakeholder register. All of the stakeholders should be treated equally, and change requests should be prioritized according to project need. Giving stakeholders extras or gold plating is not a preferred way to meet and exceed stakeholder expectations.

148. B: Manage Quality is the process to determine if the project activities are complying with organizational and project policies, standards, processes, and procedures. This process is primarily concerned with overall process improvement and does not deal with inspecting the product for quality or measuring defects. The primary focus is on steadily improving the processes and activities undertaken to achieve quality. Below are the key functionalities in this process:
   – Identify ineffective and inefficient activities or processes used in the project.
   – Perform continuous improvement as appropriate.
   – Perform quality audit to determine if project activities comply with organization and project policies, processes, and procedures.
   – Identify required improvements, gaps, and shortcomings in the processes.
   – Identify and correct deficiencies.
   – Recommend changes and corrective actions to integrated change control.

149. D: Risk Register is an output of the Identify Risks process. SWOT analysis and information gather techniques such as brainstorming and Delphi techniques are used in the Identify Risks process in order to identify and categorize potential risks in the project.

150. B: A product fix will require rework and the cost associated with it will fall under the cost of nonconformance internal failure cost category.

151. D: A qualified sellers list is a list of preapproved or prequalified prospective sellers interested and capable of doing the contract services for the organization. Prequalified sellers for a project are entered into the procurement management plan, which is part of the project management plan, as an output of the Plan Procurement process. The qualified seller list is used as an input in the Conduct Procurement process, and not as a tool and technique.

152. D: An approved change request for corrective actions, preventive actions, and defect repairs will be implemented in the Direct and Manage Project Work process.

153. B: The project is 5 months long so every month you are scheduled to complete 20 percent of the work. We know PV = BAC * planned % complete
After two months the Planned Value (PV) should be $450,000 * 40 percent = $ 180,000
We know EV = BAC * actual % complete
After two months you completed 35 percent of the work so the Earned Value (EV) is $450,000 * 35 percent = $157,500 We know SPI = EV/PV = 157,000 / 180,000 = .872. SPI less than 1 indicates that the project is behind schedule.

154. B: We will select Project Beta since it has a larger NPV. The number of years is irrelevant here since it is already factored into the NPV. We are not selecting Project Alpha which has a NPV of $45,000. The opportunity cost for the Project Beta will be the value of the project that we did not select or the opportunity that we missed out, in this case Project Alpha.

155. B: Make-or-Buy Analysis is a tool to determine whether a product can be cost effectively produced in-house or whether it should be purchased, leased, or rented. While performing this analysis, we must consider indirect as well as direct costs, availability in addition to related risk, and schedule. Seller Proposal and Procurement Documentation such as Independent Cost Estimates and Source Selection Criteria are used as inputs in the Conduct Procurement process.

156. A: The best option is to verify your observation by having a discussion with your employer about the violations and learn about the employer's perspective.

157. C: The Project Charter may contain the high-level budget but not the detailed cost estimates. You should inform the hospital authority that they have to wait as the project budget and the cost baseline will be finalized and accepted in the planning process group.

158. A: A Project Charter identifies the high level business objectives and needs, current understanding of the stakeholders' expectations, and the new product, service, or result that the project is intended to satisfy. The project charter is developed in the initiating phase, but project scope statement document is developed in the Define Scope process in planning phase.

159. C: Referent power is based on referring to someone in a higher position to leverage some of the superior's power. This power is also based on the respect or the charismatic personality of the project manager.

160. C: Resource Leveling is used to produce a resource-limited schedule by letting the schedule slip and cost increase in order to deal with a limited amount of resources, resource availability, and other resource constraints. It can be used when shared or critically required resources are only available at certain times, in limited quantities, or when resources have been over-allocated. We may have several peaks and valleys in our resource histogram. In order to level the resources, evenly utilize them as much as possible, or to keep resource usage at a constant level, we can move some of our activities from the week when we are using many resources to a week when we are hardly using any.

161. B: A Change Control Board (CCB) consists of members including stakeholders, managers, project team members, senior management, and other people, and it is responsible for reviewing, approving, or denying change requests. Some organizations have permanent CCB staffed by full-time employees to manage changes for the entire organization, not only for the projects. The project manager should consider establishing a CCB for the project if the organization does not have one.

162. B: While performing the Project Performance Appraisals, the project management team meets with the team members and provides feedback about team members' performance and how effectively they are performing their tasks. A 360 degree feedback is used to receive feedback from all directions including peers, superiors and subordinates, and sometimes includes vendors and external contractors.

163. C: Ishikawa Diagram, or Cause and Effect Diagram, is a tool used to systematically identify and present all the possible causes and sub causes of a particular problem in a graphical format. It can help in quality control by identifying the causes that contributed to a specific quality problem. Cause and Effect Diagrams are particularly useful for identifying the causes of risks.

164. C: The project was unsuccessful as it has been gold plated. We should always focus to meet and exceed customer expectations by delivering the features and functionalities as per the requirement specification approved by the clients. Gold plating or giving extras to the clients should be avoided by all means.

165. D: Your SPI is more than 1, which indicates that you are ahead of schedule, but your CPI is less than 1, which suggests that you are over budget. Cost should be the main concern in this project at this time.

166. A: Colocation/war room is a technique of placing many or all of the most active project team members in the same physical location to enhance their ability to perform as a team. Since all the team members are in the same building and having meetings in the same meeting room most of the time already, colocation is not a technique we should be considering in this case. Other techniques listed here will be beneficial to resolve conflict and concern about deliverables.

167. D: The Stakeholder Register contains all details related to the identified stakeholders including, but not limited to:
   - Stakeholder classification: Internal/external, neutral/resistor/ supporter, and others.
   - Identification information: Name, title, location, organization, role in the project, position, and contact information.
   - Assessment information: Key requirements and expectations, potential impact, importance, and influence on the project.

Stakeholder management plan, an output of the Plan Stakeholder Management process contains stakeholder management strategy. The stakeholder management strategy defines an approach to manage stakeholders throughout the entire project life cycle. It defines the strategies to increase the support of the stakeholders who can impact the project positively and minimize the negative impacts or intentions of the stakeholders who can negatively impact the project.

168. C: Anything that interferes with the meaning of a message is considered noise or a communication blocker. Source credibility, or the credibility of a message to its receivers, may be influenced by receivers' level of trust in the communicator. This may act as a distraction in effective communication.

169. C: Cost aggregation describes the bottom-up estimate, which will provide the most accurate estimate in this case. Other estimates such as heuristic and analogous specified in other choices are very quick, but will not produce the most accurate estimate. Three-point estimate is also not the best option in this scenario.

170. A: A project can be terminated at any time due to a specific reason or convenience. The project manager should conduct a scope verification to measure the amount of completed work up to the cancellation. All other options can be done once the scope verification is completed and the project manager has the details about the current situation.

171. D: Your project can move into a subsequent phase even if the deliverables of the prior phase are not completely approved. Any scope change in the initial stage will be the least expensive and consume the least amount of time. You will mostly acquire your team members during the project executing phase.

172. D: Attribute sampling is a method of measuring quality that consists of observing the presence (or absence) of some characteristics (attributes) in each of the units under consideration to determine whether to accept a lot, reject it, or inspect another lot.

173. B: Rolling wave planning takes the progressive elaboration approach and plans in great detail current/near term work while future work is planned in a more abstract and less detailed way. During the early strategic planning phase, work packages may be decomposed into less defined milestone levels as all details are not available. At a later date, they will be decomposed into detailed activities. This kind of planning is frequently used in IT and research projects where unknowns tend to be intangibles but less so in construction projects where unknowns are generally extremely expensive and destructive.

174. C: Plurality is a group decision making technique where a decision is based on the largest block in a group even if a majority is not achieved. Since PMO permits plurality you have no option but to agree with the largest block in the group. Asking PMO to reevaluate their policy will not resolve the problem immediately.

175. A: An Analogous Estimate measures the project parameters, such as budget, size, complexity and duration based on the parameters of a previous, similar project and historical information. It is usually done during an early phase of the project when not much information is available.

176. C: Upper and lower control limits are usually set as + − 3 Sigma – 99.73 percent occurrences will fall within 3 sigma from the mean.

177. C: As a project is refined, iterative process groups might be revisited and revised several times throughout the project life cycle as more information becomes available. Some planning must take place, then some executing, then some monitoring controlling processes, followed by further planning, further executing, and so on. Initiating and closing process groups are separated by the other three groups and the only time they will overlap when a project is canceled or terminated.

178. C:

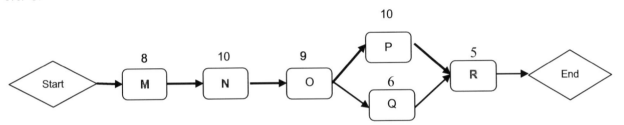

Here the critical path is Start, M, N, O, P, R, End = 42 days. So crashing the schedule by 7 days can be achieved by crashing activities N,O,P,R (2 + 2 + 1 + 2) for a cost of ((300 x 2) + (400 x 2) + (400 x 1) + (500 x 2)) = $2800.

179. B: The project must be in the Monitor Risks process if risks have occurred. Workarounds are unplanned responses developed to deal with the occurrence of unanticipated risk events that were not included in the Risk Register.

180. A: We know # of communication channels = n (n –1) / 2, where n = number of members in the team. So, 9 (9 – 1) / 2 = 72/ 2 = 36. We have 9 members in the team to have 36 communication channels.

181. B: Since the relevant work is integral to the project, you simply cannot remove the work package nor can you transfer it to a third party. The best approach will be to accept the risk and have a contingency plan to deal with it in case it happens.

182. D: A Resource Histogram is a graphic display that can be used to track resources through time when shared or critically required resources are only available at certain times, in limited quantities, or when resources have been over-allocated. We may have several peaks and valleys in our resource histogram in the stated situation. In order to level the resources, evenly utilize them as much as possible, or to keep resource usage at a constant level, we can move some of our activities from the week when we are using many resources to a week when we are hardly using any.

183. B: A Responsibility Assignment Matrix (RAM) chart cross-references team members with the activities or work packages they are to accomplish. One example of a RAM is a Responsible, Accountable, Consult, and Inform (RACI) chart, which can be used to ensure clear divisions of roles and responsibilities.

184. D: It is important to complete all aspects of the project, as agreed by the specification, even if it means the project will be delayed. The project managers should maintain their integrity and make the appropriate decision even in a situation where they have to deny their manager's request.

185. B: Plan Quality Management is the process of identifying all the relevant quality requirements, specification and standards for the project and product, and specifying how the specification will be met. Quality Management Plan, Quality Metrics, and Project Management Plan Updates are the outputs in this process.

186. B: Independent Estimates or In-House Cost Estimates are often provided by consulting services, or a procuring organization can prepare its own independent estimate. These estimates may help judge whether the statement of work was

adequate in its description, or the seller fully understood or responded fully to the statement of work as well as check reasonableness of the seller's response and proposed pricing.

187. D: Affinity Diagram is a technique in which the ideas generated from other requirements gathering techniques are sorted into groups by similarities. Each group of requirements is then given a title. This sorting makes it easier to see additional scope (or risks) that have not been identified.

188. B: A Resource Breakdown Structure (RBS) looks like a typical organizational chart, but this one is organized by types of resources. RBS can help track project cost as it ties to the organization's accounting system. For instance, you may have junior, mid-level, and senior QA testers working on your project. These testers have an average salary recorded in the organization's accounting system, which can be used to calculate the cost of these resources.

189. A: The first step to resolve an issue is to identify the root cause of the issue. Cause and Effect (Ishikawa/Fishbone) diagram is a tool used for systematically identifying and presenting all the possible causes and sub causes of a particular problem in a graphical format. It can help in quality control by identifying causes contributed to quality problems.

190. A: Graphical Evaluation and Review Technique (GERT) is a modified network diagram drawing method that allows conditional branches and loops between activities.

191. D: It is intended to assure that no seller receives preferential treatment and all sellers have a clear, common understanding of the procurement (technical requirements, contractual requirements, etc.). The key objective is to provide all potential contractors with the information they need to determine if they would like to continue with the contracting process. The bidder conference is also called a contractor conference, vendor conference, or pre-bid conference.

192. A: If it is customary in the country, you are working in to pay for the private protection service, then it will not be a bribe. As long as it is acceptable, reasonable, and legal in that country you should pay the security guard the protection fee.

193. A: In the case of an external project, the client will send out the statement of work as a part of the bidding document, such as a Request for Proposal (RFP). The SOW is a narrative description of products, results or services to be supplied by the project including the business need, product scope description or what is to be done, and how the project supports the strategic plan.

194. C: Manage Quality is a process to determine if the project activities are complying with organizational and project policies, standards, processes, and procedures. This process is primarily concerned with overall process improvement and does not deal with inspecting the product for quality or measuring defects. The primary focus is on steadily improving the processes and activities undertaken to achieve quality.

195. A: In this specific situation, the project manager should do a scope verification of the deliverables to ensure that they satisfy project objectives and were completed satisfactorily. A project manager should always get all the details first before taking any other action, such as discussing the concern with the sponsor. Gold plating or offering customers extra or additional features will not solve any real problem and should be avoided.

196. C: Claims Administration is a technique in the Control Procurements process that documents, monitors, and manages disputed changes when the buyer and seller disagree on scope, the impact of changes, or the interpretation of some terms and conditions in the contract. You would attempt to resolve the claim in this case, but if agreement cannot be reached, it should be handled in accordance with the resolution procedures outlined in the contract.

197. B: You should make sure to gather lessons learned so that future projects can benefit. There is no reason to renegotiate with the higher management at this time. The project manager should document the number of completed and pending deliverables when the project was canceled.

198. D: SOW is a narrative description of products, results or services to be supplied by the project including the business need, product scope description or what is to be done, and how the project supports the strategic plan.

199. A: We know EV = BAC * actual % complete. So EV = $900,000 * 40 percent = $360,000.
SV = EV – PV. So SV = $360,000 – $380,000 = – $20,000.
CV = EV – AC. So CV = $360,000 – $390,000 = –$30,000.
Since both CV and SV are negative, you are over budget and behind the schedule.

200. B: In noncompetitive forms of procurement, usually a seller is selected from a list of qualified sellers interested in and capable of doing the job. Even though competition can result in the selection of a better seller and decreased price, there is no reason for going through the entire procurement process unless the law requires it. If the law requires at least three proposals or quotations, then we cannot go for a single source or solesource.

Made in the USA
San Bernardino, CA
18 June 2019